"I immediately went to my nurse manager after I failed the NCLEX® and she referred me to ATI. I was able to discover the areas I was weak in, and focused on those areas in the review modules and online assessments.

I was much more prepared the second time around!"

Terim Richards
Nursing student

Danielle Platt

Nurse Manager • Children's Mercy Hospital • Kansas City, MO

"The year our hospital did not use the ATI program, we experienced a 15% decrease in the NCLEX® pass rates. We reinstated the ATI program the following year and had a 90% success rate."

"As a manager, I have witnessed graduate nurses fail the NCLEX® and the devastating effects it has on their morale. Once the nurses started using ATI, it was amazing to see the confidence they had in themselves and their ability to go forward and take the NCLEX® exam."

Mary Moss

Associate Dean of Nursing - Service and Health Division • Mid-State Technical College • Wisconsin Rapids, WI

"I like that ATI lets students know what to expect from the NCLEX®, helps them plan their study time and tells them what to do in the days and weeks before the exam. It is different from most of the NCLEX® review books on the market."

Editor

Jeanne Wissmann, PhD, RN, CNE
Director Nursing Curriculum and Educational Services
Assessment Technologies Institute®, LLC

Associate Editors

Audrey Knippa, MS, MPH, RN, CNE
Curriculum Project Coordinator

Susan Adcock, MS, RN
Consulting Associate Editor

Erika Knoblock, BS Education
Product Developer

Derek Prater, MS Journalism
Product Developer

Copyright Notice

Important Notice to the Reader of this Publication

Preface

Overview

The overall goal of this Assessment Technologies Institute®, LLC (ATI) Content Mastery Series module is to provide nursing students with an additional resource for the focused review of "Mental Health Nursing" content relevant to NCLEX-RN® preparation and entry level nursing practice. Content within this review module is provided in a key point plus rationale format in order to focus recall and application of relevant content. Unit and chapter selections are reflective of the mental health nursing-relevant content categories and explanations of the NCLEX-RN® test plan, the ATI "Mental Health Nursing" assessment test plans, and standard nursing curricular content. Each chapter begins with an overview of some of the topic-relevant nursing activities outlined by the NCLEX-RN® test plan in an effort to guide the learner's review and application of chapter content.

Contributors

ATI would like to extend appreciation to the nurse educators and nurse specialists who contributed content for this review module. The names of contributors are noted in the chapter bylines. We would also like to thank those talented individuals who reviewed, edited, and developed this module. In the summer and fall of 2005, two focus groups of committed nurse educators gave invaluable input and feedback regarding the format and purposes of review modules. Their input and ideas were instrumental to the development of this review module, and we are very appreciative. Additionally, we would like to recognize and extend appreciation to the multiple nursing students and educators who have contacted us in the past year with comments and ideas regarding the content of this review module. And finally, we want to recognize and express appreciation to all of the contributors, reviewers, production developers, and editors of previous editions of this Content Mastery Series module.

Suggestions for Effective Utilization

Δ   Understanding the organizational framework of this review module will facilitate focused review. Each unit focuses on a specific aspect of mental health nursing. Unit 1 focuses on "Foundations for Mental Health Nursing;" unit 2 focuses on "Traditional Nonpharmacological Therapies;" unit 3 focuses on "Psychopharmacological Therapies;" and unit 4 focuses on "Psychobiologic Disorders, Psychiatric Emergencies, and Mental Health Nursing Care of Special Populations." The chapters are organized with headings such as Key Points, Key Factors, Assessment, NANDA Nursing Diagnoses, and Nursing Interventions.

Δ   Some suggested uses of this review module include:

•   As a review of NCLEX-RN® relevant mental health nursing content in developing and assessing your readiness for the NCLEX-RN®.

•   As a focused review resource based on the results of an ATI "Mental Health Nursing" or "Comprehensive Predictor" assessment. "Topics to Review" identified upon completion of these assessments can be used to focus your efforts to a review of content within specific chapter(s) of this review module. For example, an identified "Topic to Review" of "Eating Disorders: Nursing Assessments" suggests that a review of chapter 23, "Eating Disorders" and completion of the application exercises at the end of the chapter would be helpful.

Δ   To foster long-term recall and development of an ability to apply knowledge to a variety of situations, learners are encouraged to take a comprehensive approach to topic review. Using this review module along with other resources (class notes, course textbooks, nursing reference texts, instructors, ATI DVD series), consider addressing questions for each aspect of mental health nursing.

•   For **"Foundations for Mental Health Nursing,"** ask questions such as:

◊   What assessments are performed for a client with a mental health disorder?

◊   How does the medical diagnosis relate to the nursing diagnosis of a mental health disorder?

◊ How is the nursing process used to care for the client with a mental health disorder?

◊ How can the nurse promote effective communication in the mental health setting?

◊ How is mental health nursing delivered in diverse practice settings?

◊ What interventions can the nurse plan and implement to deliver culturally competent care to the client with a mental health disorder?

• For **"Traditional Nonpharmacological Therapies,"** ask questions such as:

◊ What strategies can the nurse use in group and family therapy?

◊ How can the nurse teach the client stress management techniques?

◊ What interventions should the nurse plan and implement when caring for the client receiving electroconvulsive therapy?

• For **"Psychopharmacological Therapies,"** ask questions such as:

◊ What medications are used to treat anxiety and mood disorders, psychosis, a cognitive disorder, or attention deficit hyperactivity disorder?

◊ What teaching should be provided to the client receiving a medication for a mental health disorder?

◊ What side effects should the nurse watch for in the client receiving a medication for a mental health disorder?

• For **"Psychobiologic Disorders,"** ask questions such as:

◊ What are some risk factors for various mental health disorders?

◊ What assessment tools can be used to assess the client with a mood disorder?

◊ What nursing diagnoses have the highest priority for the client in the acute phase of schizophrenia?

◊ What nursing interventions should be planned and implemented for the client at risk for self-injury?

• For **"Psychiatric Emergencies,"** ask questions such as:

◊ What places the client at risk for experiencing a psychiatric emergency?

◊ What is the highest priority for the client at risk for suicide?

◊ How can the nurse intervene for a family experiencing violence?

• For **"Mental Health Nursing Care of Special Populations,"** ask questions such as:

◊ What are the special needs of the client who is grieving?

◊ What are the special health issues of adolescent and older adult clients?

◊   How does the nurse assess the adolescent for high-risk behavior?

◊   What interventions does the nurse plan and implement for the older adult client experiencing depression?

Δ   Complete application exercises at the end of each chapter after a review of the topic. Answer questions fully and note rationales for answers. Complete exercises initially without looking for the answers within the chapter or consulting the answer key. Use these exercises as an opportunity to assess your readiness to apply knowledge. When reviewing the answer key, in addition to identifying the correct answer, examine why you missed or answered correctly each item—was it related to ability to recall, recognition of a common testing principle, or perhaps attention to key words?

Feedback

All feedback is welcome – suggestions for improvement, reports of mistakes (small or large), and testimonials of effectiveness. Please address feedback to: comments@atitesting.com

Table of Contents

Unit 4 Psychobiologic Disorders, Psychiatric Emergencies, and Mental Health Nursing Care of Special Populations

Section: Psychobiologic Disorders

Section: Psychiatric Emergencies

Section: Mental Health Nursing Care of Special Populations

Unit 1   Foundations for Mental Health Nursing

Chapter 1:   Mental Health Assessment, Medical/Nursing Diagnoses, and Mental Health Nursing Interventions

Contributors: Susan Adcock, MS, RN
                Audrey Knippa, MS, MPH, RN

 NCLEX-RN® Connections:

Learning Objective: Review and apply knowledge within "**Mental Health Assessment, Medical/Nursing Diagnoses, and Mental Health Nursing Interventions**" in readiness for performance of the following nursing activities as outlined by the NCLEX-RN® test plan:

Δ Apply knowledge of mental health to the nursing process in providing care to the client/family/community in the mental health setting.

Δ Identify the components of a psychosocial assessment and a mental status examination.

Δ Assess the client's psychosocial and mental status using standardized tools.

Δ Apply knowledge of the DSM-IV-TR as it relates to nursing care of clients in mental health settings.

Δ Apply knowledge of the multiaxial system used to classify DSM-IV-TR diagnoses and other client concerns.

Δ Identify nursing diagnoses commonly used for clients with mental health disorders.

Δ Identify nursing interventions used in the mental health setting.

 Key Points

Δ **Medical Diagnoses and Nursing Diagnoses**

• The Diagnostic and Statistical Manual of Mental Disorders, 4th Edition, text revision (DSM-IV-TR), published by the American Psychiatric Association, is used to identify **medical diagnoses** for clients with mental health disorders.

• A **nursing diagnosis** specifically describes the client's actual or potential reaction to a health problem that the nurse is licensed and skilled to treat.

Δ Evaluation of the client includes a psychosocial assessment, mental status examination, and an assessment of physical condition.

Key Factors

Δ   Use the nursing process and a **holistic approach** (e.g., biological, social, psychological, and spiritual aspects) to care for clients in mental health settings.

Δ   Use various methods to assess clients (e.g., observation, interviewing, physical examination, collaboration).

Δ   Start the nursing process by collecting **subjective data (the psychosocial history)** and **objective data (the mental status exam)** from the client.

Assessment

Δ   **Psychosocial History**

  • Perception of own health, beliefs about illness and wellness

  • Activity/leisure activities – how the client passes time

  • Use/abuse of substances

  • Stress level and coping abilities – usual coping strategies, support systems

  • Social supports/patterns – role in family, whom the client identifies as support (e.g., family members, friends, coworkers), with whom the client lives

  • Cultural beliefs and influences on health and wellness

  • Spirituality/religious beliefs and practices

Δ   **The Mental Status Examination**

  • Assess the client's cognitive, social, and psychological functioning with a mental status examination.

  • Various members of the health care team collect the following data for the mental status examination:

    ◊   Level of consciousness.

    ◊   Physical appearance and behavior.

    ◊   Mood – information about the emotion the client feels, such as euphoric mood.

    ◊   Affect – objective expression of mood, such as flat affect (e.g., lack of facial expression).

    ◊   Cognitive and intellectual abilities:

      °   Orientation.

      °   Memory – remote, recent, immediate.

      °   Level and fund of knowledge.

      °   Ability for calculation.

- ° Ability to think abstractly.

- ° Insight – objective assessment of the client's perception of illness.

- ° Judgment – based on the client's answer to a hypothetical question, such as: "What would you do if there were a fire in your room?"

- ◊ Speech – rate and features such as quality and quantity, hesitation, and volume.

- ◊ Thought process – processing differences, such as rapid change of topic (flight of ideas) and use of nonsense words (e.g.,"hipsnippity").

- ◊ Thought content – presence of delusions, hallucinations, and other ideas the client presents during the interview.

- • A **screening** mental status examination can be performed using the Mini-Mental State Examination as a tool.

∆ Use the **DSM-IV-TR** in the mental health setting to identify diagnoses and diagnostic criteria to guide assessment, identify nursing diagnoses, and to plan, implement, and evaluate care. For example:

Medical Diagnosis	Diagnostic Criteria (not inclusive)	Signs and Symptoms	NANDA Nursing Diagnoses
Major depressive disorder	• Symptoms cause significant distress or impair important areas of functioning. • Five or more serious symptoms are present most of the day for most waking hours over the same 2-week period.	• Inability to perform occupational/ family role • Reduced problem-solving skills • Decreased cognitive functioning	• Ineffective coping • Ineffective role performance
Generalized anxiety disorder	• Symptoms of excessive anxiety or worry occur most days over a 6-month period. • The client is unable to control these symptoms.	• Insomnia • Unwarranted fears • Excessive worrying • Poor self-image	• Ineffective coping • Disturbed sleep pattern

Δ Multiaxial System

- The DSM-IV-TR uses a multiaxial system to assess clients in the mental health setting. It assesses for abnormal behavior, comorbid medical conditions, conditions within the environment, and level of functioning (e.g., social, psychological, and environmental conditions).

  ◊ **Axis I** – all mental health diagnoses except for those found in Axis II

  ◊ **Axis II** – any personality disorder diagnoses and mental retardation

  ◊ **Axis III** – any general medical diagnoses (e.g., asthma)

  ◊ **Axis IV** – pertinent psychosocial problems and problems concerning the client's living conditions

  ◊ **Axis V** – global assessment of functioning (GAF) – an assessment of present and past-year functioning. The GAF rates the client's level of functioning in the areas of work performance, social abilities, and psychological ability on a scale of 1 to 100.

    ° Scores of 80 to 100 generally indicate normal or near-normal function.

    ° Scores of 60 to 80 indicate moderate problems.

    ° Scores 40 and below indicate serious mental disability and/or functioning impairments.

    ° Present and past-year GAF scores are compared to track the client's level of functioning. For example, a GAF of "50/80" indicates that the client presently has a GAF score of 50, with a previous score of 80 in the past year.

Nursing Interventions

Mental Health Nursing Interventions	
Counseling	• Using therapeutic communication skills • Assisting with problem solving • Crisis intervention • Stress management
Milieu therapy	• Orienting the client to the physical setting • Identifying rules and boundaries of the setting • Ensuring a safe environment for the client • Selecting activities for the client that meet physical and mental health needs
Promotion of self-care activities	• Offering assistance with self-care tasks • Allowing time for the client to complete self-care tasks • Setting incentives to promote client self-care
Psychobiological interventions	• Administering prescribed medications • Providing teaching to the client/family • Monitoring for side effects and effectiveness of therapy
Health teaching	• Identifying physical and mental health education needs of the client • Teaching social and coping skills
Health promotion and health maintenance	• Assisting the client with cessation of smoking
Case management	• Coordinating holistic care to include medical, mental health, and social services

Primary Reference:

Varcarolis, E. M., Carson, V. B., & Shoemaker, N. C. (2006). *Foundations of psychiatric mental health nursing: A clinical approach* (5th ed.). St. Louis, MO: Saunders.

Additional Resources:

Brannon, G. E. (2006, November 15). History and mental status examination. *eMedicine*. Retrieved November 20, 2006, from http://www.emedicine.com/med/topic3358.htm

NANDA International (2004). *NANDA nursing diagnoses: Definitions and classification 2005-2006*. Philadelphia: NANDA.

Chapter 1: Mental Health Assessment, Medical/Nursing Diagnoses, and Mental Health Nursing Interventions

Application Exercises

1. While performing a mental status examination on a client, the nurse notices that the client's facial expression constantly appears angry. This information should be recorded as part of the client's

    A. behavior.

    B. appearance.

    C. affect.

    D. thought process.

2. During a mental status examination, a client who is hospitalized states that she is in the hospital "to help out with the other patients." The nurse should record this information as

    A. poor insight.

    B. decreased level of knowledge.

    C. decreased judgment.

    D. poor remote memory.

3. Which of the following are examples of subjective assessment data? (Select all that apply.)

    ___ "I have a wife and three sons."

    ___ "I just want to sleep all day."

    ___ "My mother died when I was born."

    ___ "I want to get rid of the pain of living."

    ___ "I am a bad father most of the time."

4. A nurse is caring for a client diagnosed with paranoid schizophrenia, asthma, generalized anxiety disorder, and borderline personality disorder. Which of the following diagnoses should the nurse expect to find included in Axis II of this client's DSM-IV-TR axis diagnoses?

    A. Paranoid schizophrenia

    B. Asthma

    C. Generalized anxiety disorder

    D. Borderline personality disorder

5. Match each framework below with the appropriate description.

_____ Nursing diagnosis

_____ Medical diagnosis

_____ Nursing outcome criterion

_____ Nursing intervention

_____ Nursing assessment

A. Encouragement of activities to increase client's self-esteem

B. Major depressive disorder, single episode

C. Client expression of feelings of worthlessness, such as: "I'm not as good as anyone else."

D. Chronically low self-esteem related to a history of abusive relationships as evidenced by expressions of shame

E. Client identification of one support person that he can call if he feels suicidal

6. A client is admitted to an acute care mental health facility. The following medical diagnoses and psychosocial information are available at the time of admission: hypothyroidism, mild mental retardation, bipolar I disorder. The client's highest level of functioning from a global assessment of functioning (GAF) performed a year ago was 45. Today, the highest level of functioning on the same scale is 15. The client has been fighting with other clients frequently at the group home. How should the nurse enter all of this information into the multiaxial system of the DSM-IV-TR?

Axis I:

Axis II:

Axis III:

Axis IV:

Axis V:

Chapter 1: Mental Health Assessment, Medical/Nursing Diagnoses, and Mental Health Nursing Interventions

Application Exercises Answer Key

1. While performing a mental status examination on a client, the nurse notices that the client's facial expression constantly appears angry. This information should be recorded as part of the client's

    A. behavior.

    B. appearance.

    C. affect.

    D. thought process.

Description of the client's facial expression is described as affect. Facial expression is not described in the areas of behavior, appearance, or thought process.

2. During a mental status examination, a client who is hospitalized states that she is in the hospital "to help out with the other patients." The nurse should record this information as

    A. poor insight.

    B. decreased level of knowledge.

    C. decreased judgment.

    D. poor remote memory.

The nurse's objective assessment of the client's insight reflects the client's understanding of her current situation and medical condition. Knowledge, judgment, and memory are other objective cognitive assessments. None reflect the client's understanding of the responsibility for, or analysis of, the current situation.

3. Which of the following are examples of subjective assessment data? (Select all that apply.)

_____ "I have a wife and three sons."

__X__ **"I just want to sleep all day."**

_____ "My mother died when I was born."

__X__ **"I want to get rid of the pain of living."**

__X__ **"I am a bad father most of the time."**

Subjective data includes psychosocial information about the client's thoughts and feelings that can only be described by the client. Objective data is based on observable or verifiable facts.

4. A nurse is caring for a client diagnosed with paranoid schizophrenia, asthma, generalized anxiety disorder, and borderline personality disorder. Which of the following diagnoses should the nurse expect to find included in Axis II of this client's DSM-IV-TR axis diagnoses?

      A. Paranoid schizophrenia

      B. Asthma

      C. Generalized anxiety disorder

      D. Borderline personality disorder

Personality disorders and mental retardation are included in Axis II. Paranoid schizophrenia and generalized anxiety disorder are found in Axis I. Asthma and other general medical conditions are found in Axis III.

5. Match each framework below with the appropriate description.

__D__ Nursing diagnosis   A. Encouragement of activities to increase client's self-esteem

__B__ Medical diagnosis   B. Major depressive disorder, single episode

__E__ Nursing outcome criterion   C. Client expression of feelings of worthlessness, such as: "I'm not as good as anyone else."

__A__ Nursing intervention   D. Chronically low self-esteem related to a history of abusive relationships as evidenced by expressions of shame

__C__ Nursing assessment   E. Client identification of one support person that he can call if he feels suicidal

6. A client is admitted to an acute care mental health facility. The following medical diagnoses and psychosocial information are available at the time of admission: hypothyroidism, mild mental retardation, bipolar I disorder. The client's highest level of functioning from a global assessment of functioning (GAF) performed a year ago was 45. Today, the highest level of functioning on the same scale is 15. The client has been fighting with other clients frequently at the group home. How should the nurse enter all of this information into the multiaxial system of the DSM-IV-TR?

Axis I: **Bipolar I disorder**

Axis II: **Mild mental retardation**

Axis III: **Hypothyroidism**

Axis IV: **Has been fighting with other clients frequently at group home**

Axis V: **GAF 15/45**

Axis I includes most mental health clinical disorders, except those placed on Axis II. Axis II disorders include personality disorders and mental retardation. Axis III includes general medical disorders and problems. Axis IV includes pertinent psychosocial information or problems with living conditions. Axis V includes GAF for present assessment and previous assessment within 1 year of present.

Unit 1   Foundations for Mental Health Nursing

Chapter 2:   Legal and Ethical Issues in Mental Health Nursing
                Contributor: Susan Adcock, MS, RN

 NCLEX-RN® Connections:

Learning Objective: Review and apply knowledge within "**Legal and Ethical Issues in Mental Health Nursing**" in readiness for performance of the following nursing activities as outlined by the NCLEX-RN® test plan:

Δ   Apply knowledge of mental health when discussing civil rights and ethical issues as they apply to clients in the mental health setting.

Δ   Identify treatment options/decisions with the client/family/significant other/staff.

Δ   Inform clients regarding their right to treatment, right to refuse treatment, and right to informed consent.

Δ   Maintain client confidentiality in the mental health facility.

Δ   Identify the client's rights as they apply to seclusion and restraint issues.

Δ   Evaluate and document care provided to ensure client safety.

 Key Points

Δ   The nurse who works in the mental health setting is responsible for practicing **ethically, competently, safely**, and in a manner **consistent with all local, state, and federal laws**.

Δ   **Legal Rights of Clients in the Mental Health Setting**

•   Clients who have been diagnosed and/or hospitalized with a mental health disorder are guaranteed the same civil rights as any other citizen. This includes:

◊   The right to humanitarian treatment and care (e.g., medical and dental care).

◊   The right to vote.

◊   The right to due process of law with the right to press legal charges against another person.

- Clients also have various specific rights, including:

  ◊ Informed consent and the right to refuse treatment.

  ◊ Confidentiality.

  ◊ A written plan of care/treatment and participation in the planning and review of that plan.

  ◊ Communication with persons outside the mental health facility, including family members, attorneys, and other health care professionals.

  ◊ Respect and dignity in all treatment and care.

  ◊ Freedom from harm related to physical or pharmacologic restraint, seclusion, and any physical or mental abuse or neglect.

- Some legal issues regarding health care may be decided in court using a specialized civil category called a **tort**. Torts can be used to decide **liability** issues, as well as **intentional** issues that may involve criminal penalties, such as abuse of a client.

- State laws may vary greatly. The nurse must be aware of specific laws regarding client care within the state or states in which the nurse practices.

Δ **Ethical Issues for Clients in the Mental Health Setting**

- In comparison to laws, statutes, and regulations (enacted by local, state, or federal government), ethical issues are philosophical ideas regarding right and wrong.

- Nurses are frequently confronted with ethical dilemmas regarding client care (bioethical issues).

- Since ethics are philosophical and involve values and morals, there is frequently no clear-cut simple answer in ethical dilemmas.

- **Ethical principles** must be used to decide ethical issues. These include:

Ethical Principle	Definition	Example
Beneficence	This relates to the quality of doing good and can be described as charity.	The nurse helps a newly admitted client with psychosis feel safe in the environment of the mental health facility.
Autonomy	This refers to the client's right to make his own decisions. But the client must also accept the consequences of those decisions. The client must also respect the decisions of others.	Rather than giving advice to the client who has difficulty making decisions, the nurse helps the client explore all alternatives and arrive at a choice.

Ethical Principle	Definition	Example
Justice	This is defined as fair and equal treatment for all.	During a treatment team meeting, the nurse leads a discussion regarding whether or not two clients who broke the same facility rule were treated equally.
Fidelity	This relates to loyalty and faithfulness to the client and to one's duty.	Although the nurse's shift is over, he stays on the unit for an extra 30 min to assist a client with bipolar disorder who received distressing news that her mother had died.
Veracity	This refers to being honest when dealing with the client.	A client states, "You and that other staff member were talking about me, weren't you?" The nurse truthfully replies, "We were discussing ways to help you relate to the other clients in a more positive way."

Key Factors

Δ **Confidentiality**

- The client's right to privacy is protected by the Health Insurance Portability and Accountability Act (HIPAA) of 2003.

- Information about the client, verbal and in writing, must only be shared with those who are responsible for implementing the client's treatment plan.

- Information may be shared with other persons not involved in the client treatment plan by client consent only.

- It is important to gain an understanding of the federal law and of various state laws as they relate to confidentiality in specific health care facilities/ agencies.

- Specific mental health issues include disclosing HIV status, the duty to warn and protect third parties, and the reporting of child and elder abuse.

Δ **Resources for Solving Ethical Client Issues**

- Code of Ethics for Nurses with Interpretive Statements (revised in 2001 by the American Nurses Association)

- Patient Care Partnership (formerly the Patients' Bill of Rights)

- The nurse practice act of a specific state

- Legal advice from attorneys

- Facility policies
- Other members of the health care team, including facility bioethics committee (if available)
- Members of the clergy and other spiritual or ethical counselors

Δ **Types of Commitment to a Mental Health Facility**

- **Voluntary commitment** – The client or client's guardian chooses commitment to a mental health facility in order to obtain treatment. A voluntarily committed client has the right to apply for release. This client is considered competent, and so has the right to refuse medication and treatment.

- **Involuntary commitment** – The client enters the mental health facility against her will for an indefinite period of time. The need for commitment could be determined by a judge of the court or by another agency. The number of physicians required to certify that the client's condition requires commitment varies from state to state.

  ◊ **Emergency commitment** – a type of involuntary commitment in which the client is hospitalized to prevent harm to self or others. Emergency commitment is usually temporary (a few days), but time may be added if it is determined that the client is too ill for discharge.

  ◊ Involuntary commitment may also be either **temporary** or **long term,** depending on the client's condition. Temporary commitment may be for observation of the client's mental status. The amount of time spent in a facility for either temporary or long-term commitment can vary widely depending on state statute.

  ◊ Clients admitted under **involuntary commitment** are still considered **competent** and have the **right to refuse treatment**, unless they have gone through a legal competency hearing and have been judged incompetent. The client who has been judged incompetent has a temporary or permanent guardian, usually a family member if possible, appointed by the court. The guardian can sign informed consent for the client. The guardian is expected to consider what the client would want if he were still competent.

Δ **Client Rights Regarding Seclusion and Restraint**

- Nurses must know and follow federal/state/facility policies that govern the use of restraints.
- Use of seclusion rooms and/or restraints may be authorized for clients in some cases.
- In general, seclusion and/or restraint should be ordered for the **shortest duration necessary and only if less restrictive measures are not sufficient**. They are for the physical protection of the client or the protection of other clients or staff.

- A client may voluntarily request temporary seclusion in cases where the environment is disturbing or seems too stimulating.

- Restraints can be either physical or chemical, such as neuroleptic medication to calm the client.

- Seclusion and/or restraint must never be used for:

  ◊ Convenience of the staff.

  ◊ Punishment for the client.

  ◊ Clients who are extremely physically or mentally unstable.

  ◊ Clients who cannot tolerate the decreased stimulation of a seclusion room.

- When all other less restrictive means have been tried to prevent a client from harming self or others, the following must occur in order for seclusion or restraint to be used:

  ◊ The treatment must be ordered by the primary care provider **in writing**.

  ◊ Only in an emergency may the charge nurse place a client in seclusion or restraint; in this situation, a written physician's order must be obtained within a specified period of time (usually 15 to 30 min).

  ◊ The order must specify the duration of treatment.

  ◊ The provider must rewrite the order, specifying the type of restraint, every 24 hr or other amount of time specified by facility policy.

  ◊ The client's condition must be assessed and documented frequently (e.g., constant monitoring, every 30 min).

  ◊ Required assessment must include safety, physical needs, and comfort.

Δ Tort Law in the Mental Health Setting

- Although intentional torts can occur in any health care setting, they are particularly likely to occur in mental health settings due to the increased likelihood of violence and client behavior that can be challenging to facility staff.

Intentional Tort	Example
False imprisonment	Confining a client to a specific area, such as a seclusion room, is false imprisonment if the reason for such confinement is for the convenience of the staff.
Assault	Making a threat to a client's person, such as approaching the client in a threatening manner with a syringe in hand, is considered assault.
Battery	Touching a client in a harmful or offensive way is considered battery. This would occur if the nurse threatening the client with a syringe actually grabbed the client and gave an injection.

Δ Documentation

Δ **Documentation** – It is vital to clearly and objectively document information related to violent or other unusual episodes. The nurse should document:

- Client behavior in a clear and objective manner.

  ◊ Example: The client suddenly began to run down the hall with both hands in the air, screaming obscenities.

- Staff response to disruptive, violent, or potentially harmful behavior, such as suicide threats or potential or actual harm to others. Include time lines and extent of response.

  ◊ Example: The client states, "I'm going to pound (other client) into the ground." Client has picked up a chair and is standing 3 ft from other client with chair held over his head in both hands. Client is immediately told, "Put down the chair and back away from (the other person)." Other client moved away to safe area. Five other staff members respond to verbal call for help within 30 sec and stood several yards from client. Client then put the chair down, quietly turned around, walked to his room, and sat on the bed.

Primary Reference:

Varcarolis, E. M., Carson, V. B., & Shoemaker, N. C. (2006). *Foundations of psychiatric mental health nursing: A clinical approach* (5th ed.). St. Louis, MO: Saunders.

Additional Resources:

NANDA International (2004). *NANDA nursing diagnoses: Definitions and classification 2005-2006*. Philadelphia: NANDA.

Chapter 2: Legal and Ethical Issues in Mental Health Nursing

Application Exercises

1. True or False: A client who is admitted involuntarily to an acute care mental health facility automatically loses his right to informed consent for medical procedures or treatments.

   False

2. True or False: An example of the principle of justice is allowing a hospitalized client to refuse to attend a scheduled counseling session with her clear understanding that she must accept the consequences for not attending.

   ~~False~~
   ~~True~~ False

3. True or False: A nurse is committing battery against a client by forcefully holding the client and insisting that he swallow a pill. The nurse tells the client that he will be punished if he does not do it.

   True

4. Which of the following is an example of a client who requires emergency admission to a mental health facility?

   A. A client with schizophrenia who has frequent hallucinations
   B. A client with symptoms of depression who attempted suicide a year ago
   Ⓒ A client with psychosis who assaulted a homeless man with a metal rod
   D. A client with bipolar disease who paces quickly down the sidewalk talking to himself

5. A client tells a student nurse, "Don't tell anyone, but I hid a sharp knife under my mattress in order to protect myself from my roommate, who is always yelling at me and threatening me." Thinking about the principles of client confidentiality and veracity, the student makes a correct decision to

    A. keep the client's communication confidential but talk to the client daily, using therapeutic communication to convince him to admit to hiding the knife.

    B. keep the client's communication confidential, but watch the client and his roommate closely.

    C. tell the client that this must be reported to health care staff because it concerns health and safety.

    D. report the incident but do not inform the client of having the intention to do so.

6. A nurse decides to put a client with psychosis in seclusion overnight because the unit is very short-staffed and the client frequently fights with other clients. This is an example of

    A. beneficence.

    B. a tort.

    C. a facility policy.

    D. justice.

Chapter 2: Legal and Ethical Issues in Mental Health Nursing

Application Exercises Answer Key

1. True or False: A client who is admitted involuntarily to an acute care mental health facility automatically loses his right to informed consent for medical procedures or treatments.

   False: Even though a client is involuntarily committed, he still has the right to informed consent, unless he has been judged legally incompetent. A legal guardian will be appointed to give informed consent for a client who is legally incompetent.

2. True or False: An example of the principle of justice is allowing a hospitalized client to refuse to attend a scheduled counseling session with her clear understanding that she must accept the consequences for not attending.

   False: This question illustrates the ethical principle of autonomy, which means that the client has the right to make choices but must also be responsible for the consequences of those choices. Justice illustrates the principle that all clients must be treated equally.

3. True or False: A nurse is committing battery against a client by forcefully holding the client and insisting that he swallow a pill. The nurse tells the client that he will be punished if he does not do it.

   True: Clients have the right to refuse treatment. Forcing a client to take a medication by physical or verbal threats is unlawful and also unethical. If a client refuses to take medication, the nurse should document the refusal and consult the client's treatment plan.

4. Which of the following is an example of a client who requires emergency admission to a mental health facility?

   A. A client with schizophrenia who has frequent hallucinations

   B. A client with symptoms of depression who attempted suicide a year ago

   C. A client with psychosis who assaulted a homeless man with a metal rod

   D. A client with bipolar disease who paces quickly down the sidewalk talking to himself

   The client who is a current danger to self or others is a candidate for emergency admission. The presence of hallucinations, symptoms of depression without recent suicide attempt or intent to commit suicide, or other mental health symptoms does not constitute a clear reason for emergency commitment.

5. A client tells a student nurse, "Don't tell anyone, but I hid a sharp knife under my mattress in order to protect myself from my roommate, who is always yelling at me and threatening me." Thinking about the principles of client confidentiality and veracity, the student makes a correct decision to

> A. keep the client's communication confidential but talk to the client daily, using therapeutic communication to convince him to admit to hiding the knife.
>
> B. keep the client's communication confidential, but watch the client and his roommate closely.
>
> **C. tell the client that this must be reported to health care staff because it concerns health and safety.**
>
> D. report the incident but do not inform the client of having the intention to do so.

This is a serious safety issue that must be reported to staff. Using the principle of veracity, the student tells this client truthfully what must be done regarding the issue.

6. A nurse decides to put a client with psychosis in seclusion overnight because the unit is very short-staffed and the client frequently fights with other clients. This is an example of

> A. beneficence.
>
> **B. a tort.**
>
> C. a facility policy.
>
> D. justice.

A civil wrong that violates a client's civil rights is a tort, in this case, false imprisonment. The decision is neither beneficence (doing good for a client) nor justice (fair and equal treatment). If this were indeed a facility policy, it would certainly be substandard, and the nurse could still be held responsible for following it.

Unit 1   Foundations for Mental Health Nursing

Chapter 3:   Developing and Maintaining a Therapeutic Nurse-Client Relationship
Contributor: Carole A. Shea, PhD, RN, FAAN

 NCLEX-RN® Connections:

Learning Objective: Review and apply knowledge within "**Developing and Maintaining a Therapeutic Nurse-Client Relationship**" in readiness for performance of the following nursing activities as outlined by the NCLEX-RN® test plan:

Δ   Apply knowledge of therapeutic communication when establishing nurse-client relationships.

Δ   Supervise client behavior to impose boundaries on inappropriate behavior (e.g., unsafe or hostile behaviors).

 Key Points

Δ   **Therapeutic encounters** can occur in any nursing setting if the nurse is sensitive to the client's needs and has effective communication skills.

Δ   The **therapeutic nurse-client relationship** differs from social and intimate relationships. A therapeutic nurse-client relationship is:

- **Purposeful and goal-directed**.

- Well-defined with **clear boundaries**.

- **Structured** to meet the client's needs.

- Characterized by an interpersonal process that is safe, confidential, reliable, and consistent.

Δ   The **role** of the nurse is to:

- Consistently focus on the client's ideas, experiences, and feelings.

- Identify and explore the client's needs and problems.

- Discuss problem-solving alternatives with the client.

- Help to develop the client's strengths and new coping skills.

- Encourage positive behavior change in the client.

- Assist the client to develop a sense of autonomy and self-reliance.

- Portray genuineness, empathy, and a positive regard toward the client.

Δ   Therapeutic relationships:

- Contribute to the well-being of those who are seriously mentally ill, as well as higher-functioning clients, although the treatment goals will differ.

- Take time to establish, but even time-limited therapeutic encounters can produce very positive effects.

- Have a positive impact on the success of treatment.

Δ   Supervision by peers or the clinical team enhances the nurse's ability to examine her own thoughts and feelings, maintain boundaries, and continue to learn from client relationships.

Key Factors

Δ   Factors that Help Develop the Therapeutic Relationship

Nurse Factors	Client Factors
• Consistent approach to interaction • Adjustment of pace to client's needs • Attentive listening • Positive initial impressions • Comfort level in the session • Balance of control • Self-awareness of own thoughts and feelings	• Trustful attitude • Willingness to talk • Active participation • Consistent availability

Δ   The nurse-client relationship progresses in overlapping phases:

Phases and Tasks of a Therapeutic Relationship		
Phase	Nurse's Tasks	Client's Tasks
Orientation	• Introduce self to the client and state purpose. • Set the contract: meeting time, place, frequency, duration, and termination date. • Discuss confidentiality. • Build trust by establishing expectations and boundaries. • Set goals with the client. • Explore the client's ideas, issues, and needs. • Enforce limits on testing or inappropriate behaviors. • Explore the meaning of testing behaviors.	• Meet with the nurse. • Agree to the contract. • Understand the limits of confidentiality. • Understand the expectations and limits of the relationship. • Participate in setting goals. • Begin to explore own thoughts, experiences, and feelings. • Explore the meaning of own behaviors.

Phases and Tasks of a Therapeutic Relationship		
Phase	Nurse's Tasks	Client's Tasks
Working	• Maintain relationship according to the contract. • Collect data to plan and evaluate therapeutic measures. • Encourage the client's problem solving. • Promote the client's self-esteem. • Facilitate the client's expression of needs and issues. • Foster positive behavioral change. • Explore and deal with resistance and other defense mechanisms. • Recognize transference and countertransference issues. • Reassess the client's problems and goals and revise as necessary. • Support the client's adaptive alternatives and use of new coping skills. • Raise the issue of termination.	• Explore problematic areas of life. • Reconsider usual coping behaviors. • Examine own worldview and self-concept. • Describe major conflicts and various defenses. • Experience intense feelings and learn to cope with anxiety reactions. • Test new behaviors. • Begin to develop awareness of transference situations. • Identify unconscious motivations. • Try alternative solutions.
Termination	• Provide opportunity for the client to discuss thoughts and feelings about termination and loss. • Discuss the client's previous experience with separations and loss. • Elicit the client's feelings about the therapeutic work in the nurse-client relationship. • Summarize goals and achievements. • Review memories of work in the sessions. • Express own feelings about sessions to validate the experience with the client. • Discuss ways for the client to incorporate new healthy behaviors in life. • Maintain limits of final termination.	• Discuss thoughts and feelings about termination. • Examine previous separation and loss experiences. • Explore meaning of the therapeutic relationship. • Review goals and achievements. • Discuss plans to continue new behaviors. • Express feelings of loss related to termination. • Make plans for the future. • Accept termination as final.

Δ   Boundaries

- Boundaries must be established in order to maintain a safe and professional nurse-client relationship.

- Blurred boundaries occur if the relationship begins to meet the needs of the nurse rather than those of the client, or if the relationship becomes social rather than therapeutic.

- The nurse must work to maintain a consistent level of involvement with the client, to reflect on boundary issues frequently, and to maintain awareness of how behaviors can be perceived by others (clients, family members, other health team members).

- **Transference** and **countertransference**

	Example	Nursing Implications
Transference occurs when the client views a member of the health care team as having characteristics of another person who has been significant to the client's personal life.	The client may see the nurse as being like his mother and thus may demonstrate some of the same behaviors with the nurse as he did with his mother.	The nurse should be aware that transference by a client is more likely to occur with a person in authority, such as a member of the health care team in a mental health facility.
Countertransference occurs when the health care team member displaces characteristics of people in her past onto a client.	The nurse may feel defensive and angry with a client for no apparent reason if the client reminds her of a friend who often elicited those feelings.	The nurse should be aware that clients who induce very strong feelings in the nurse may be objects of countertransference.

Primary Reference:

Varcarolis, E. M., Carson, V. B., & Shoemaker, N. C. (2006). *Foundations of psychiatric mental health nursing: A clinical approach* (5th ed.). St. Louis, MO: Saunders.

Additional Resources:

Forchuk, C., et al. (2000). The developing nurse-client relationship: Nurse's perspective. *Journal of American Psychiatric Nurses Association, 6*(1), 3-10.

NANDA International (2004). *NANDA nursing diagnoses: Definitions and classification 2005-2006*. Philadelphia: NANDA.

Chapter 3: Developing and Maintaining a Therapeutic Nurse-Client Relationship

Application Exercises

1. A client says to the nurse, "Why should I talk to you? Everybody knows talking doesn't help!" Which of the following is the nurse's best response?

   A. "Why don't you let me be the judge of that?"

   B. "Your doctor said talking is part of your therapy."

   C. "Why do you think that talking won't help?"

   D. "I'm here to talk with you about your concerns."

2. A nurse notices that one of her clients follows her around the unit and tries to engage her in conversation. The client's behavior is an example of

   A. stalking.

   B. close rapport.

   C. inability to accept limits.

   D. a sign of loneliness.

3. Therapeutic relationships differ from social relationships in that

   A. the purpose is to communicate.

   B. the focus is on the client.

   C. both parties get some benefit.

   D. they are not time-limited.

4. The termination phase centers on issues related to

   A. separation and loss.

   B. transference and countertransference.

   C. anxiety and anger.

   D. testing new behaviors.

5. A nurse tells a colleague that she feels she is the only one who truly understands one of the clients, and that the client has been treated unfairly by the rest of the health care team. This situation is best described as

      A. positive regard.

      B. transference.

      C. boundary blurring.

      D. a therapeutic nurse-client relationship.

Scenario: A client has been referred to a substance abuse unit for 5 days of detoxification and treatment. She has been taking cocaine, methamphetamine, and heroin, or "whatever is available," for several years. This is her first time in an inpatient treatment facility.

---

6. What should the nurse do when she meets the client for the first counseling session?

7. The client agrees to participate in five counseling sessions. When it is time for the second session, the nurse arrives on time, but the client does not come to the room where the session is scheduled. What should the nurse do?

8. The client's two young children come to visit their mother. What interventions should the nurse implement to assist the client in having a positive experience with her children?

Chapter 3: Developing and Maintaining a Therapeutic Nurse-Client Relationship

Application Exercises Answer Key

1. A client says to the nurse, "Why should I talk to you? Everybody knows talking doesn't help!" Which of the following is the nurse's best response?

    A. "Why don't you let me be the judge of that?"

    B. "Your doctor said talking is part of your therapy."

    C. "Why do you think that talking won't help?"

    D. "I'm here to talk with you about your concerns."

    The correct answer is a broad opening that focuses on the client's feelings and needs. Option A minimizes the client's ability to make decisions and is obstructive to open expression of feelings. Option B changes the focus of the interview to the primary care provider's orders. Option C implies criticism of the client's response, which tends to put the client on the defense.

2. A nurse notices that one of her clients follows her around the unit and tries to engage her in conversation. The client's behavior is an example of

    A. stalking.

    B. close rapport.

    C. inability to accept limits.

    D. a sign of loneliness.

    Limits must be set so that one client will not monopolize the nurse's time. This may be a boundary issue for the client and nurse. There is no evidence that this is a stalking behavior, a sign of close rapport with the nurse, or that the client is lonely.

3. Therapeutic relationships differ from social relationships in that

>   A. the purpose is to communicate.
>   **B. the focus is on the client.**
>   C. both parties get some benefit.
>   D. they are not time-limited.

Therapeutic relationships between the nurse and client focus on the client and his needs. Communication is not limited to therapeutic relationships; it is also found in social relationships. The focus of the therapeutic relationship is to benefit the client. Therapeutic relationships have time limits and usually end when the client leaves the facility.

4. The termination phase centers on issues related to

>   **A. separation and loss.**
>   B. transference and countertransference.
>   C. anxiety and anger.
>   D. testing new behaviors.

Separation and loss issues are a hallmark of the therapeutic relationship's termination phase. Transference and countertransference are phenomena which may occur in the nurse-client relationship and may occur within any phase of the relationship. While anxiety and anger may be expressed during the termination phase, other feelings, such as positive regard, are just as likely to be present during this phase. Testing new behaviors occurs during the working phase.

5. A nurse tells a colleague that she feels she is the only one who truly understands one of the clients, and that the client has been treated unfairly by the rest of the health care team. This situation is best described as

>   A. positive regard.
>   B. transference.
>   **C. boundary blurring.**
>   D. a therapeutic nurse-client relationship.

In this situation, countertransference between the nurse and client may cause blurring of boundaries. There is no evidence to suggest positive regard. Transference occurs when the client sees characteristics in an authority figure that were present in a significant person in her past. This situation does not describe a therapeutic nurse-client relationship.

Scenario: A client has been referred to a substance abuse unit for 5 days of detoxification and treatment. She has been taking cocaine, methamphetamine, and heroin, or "whatever is available," for several years. This is her first time in an inpatient treatment facility.

6. What should the nurse do when she meets the client for the first counseling session?

Find the client and ask her to go to a quiet place to talk.
Tell the client the purpose of the session and explain the nurse's role.
Try to establish a contract.
Set the time, place, frequency, and duration of the sessions.
Discuss confidentiality and termination
Say, "This is your time to talk about yourself, your thoughts, your feelings, and how this experience is going for you. I'm here to listen to whatever you want to talk about."

7. The client agrees to participate in five counseling sessions. When it is time for the second session, the nurse arrives on time, but the client does not come to the room where the session is scheduled. What should the nurse do?

Wait in the room to see if the client comes to the session later. This shows consistency. After about 15 min, try to find the client and remind her about the session by stating, "We still have 30 min left. I'll wait in the room for you." This shows a positive regard for the client while reinforcing the limits. It is possible that this client is showing resistance and testing limits to see if the nurse really cares about her.

8. The client's two young children come to visit their mother. What interventions should the nurse implement to assist the client in having a positive experience with her children?

In anticipation of the visit, help the client to identify her expectations and needs.
Engage the client in role playing a typical communication exchange between her and her children.
Assist the client to set one realistic goal for the visit.
At her next session, ask the client to describe the visit and assist her to assess her responses and goal achievement.

Unit 1   Foundations for Mental Health Nursing

Chapter 4:   Effective Communication in Mental Health Nursing
Contributor: Carole A. Shea, PhD, RN, FAAN

 NCLEX-RN® Connections:

Learning Objective: Review and apply knowledge within "**Effective Communication in Mental Health Nursing**" in readiness for performance of the following nursing activities as outlined by the NCLEX-RN® test plan:

Δ   Apply knowledge of therapeutic relationships to initiate and sustain client/family relationships.

Δ   Model behaviors such as genuineness, respectfulness, and empathy to foster trust in the nurse-client therapeutic relationship.

Δ   Use effective communication to interact with and assist the client/family to increase their insight into the client's behavior.

Δ   Assess communication needs of the client/family within the mental health setting.

Δ   Promote and support client and family efforts to express feelings (e.g., anger, sadness).

Δ   Evaluate communication effectiveness with the client and family.

 Key Points

Δ   **Communication** is a **complex process** of sending, receiving, and comprehending messages between two or more people.

Δ   The nurse uses **therapeutic** communication skills with the client, family, and significant others.

Δ   **Therapeutic communication** helps the client to feel understood, explore interpersonal problems, discover healthy ways to cope, and experience a satisfying interpersonal relationship.

Δ   Therapeutic communication involves:

•   Establishing a therapeutic relationship.

•   Choosing a quiet, safe setting for the interview.

- Allowing enough time to engage in therapeutic communication.

- Using communication and interviewing techniques.

- Letting the client set the pace and determine the topics.

- Attending to the content and process of the client's communication.

- Using clinical supervision to improve communication and interviewing skills.

Δ   Nurses learn therapeutic communication skills by doing client-centered interviews, reviewing the interview process with a supervisor, and observing more experienced clinicians and role models in the health care setting.

Δ   The nurse must recognize and respond to both **verbal** and **nonverbal** communications.

Verbal Communication Content of the Message	Nonverbal Communication Process of the Message
• Vocabulary – These are the words that are used to communicate a message. • Denotative/connotative meaning – When communicating, it is important that meanings are shared by participants. Words that have multiple meanings may cause miscommunication when interpreted differently. • Clarity/brevity – The shortest, simplest types of communication are usually more effective. • Timing/relevance – Knowing when to communicate allows the receiver to be more attentive to the message.	• There are a wide range of personal behaviors that accompany expression of words and convey meaning. • Nonverbal communication includes: ◊ Sounds, tone, pitch, pacing, silence. ◊ Eye contact, eye cast. ◊ Posture. ◊ Personal appearance. ◊ Facial expressions. ◊ Gestures. ◊ Personal space.

Δ   Communications in which the content matches the process are congruent, make sense, and are clearly understood.

Δ   Communications in which the content conflicts with the process are confusing and contradictory, which leads to misunderstanding. For example, the nurse tells the client she is interested in hearing about the client's concerns, but her posture and tone of voice indicate that she is in a hurry.

Key Factors

Δ   The nurse should interpret all communication in the context of the client's gender, age, ethnicity, culture, class, sexual orientation, and spirituality.

Δ   **Active listening** and **attending** to verbal and nonverbal behaviors are the keys to facilitating effective communication with clients, family, and significant others.

Δ The nurse uses interactive, purposeful communication skills to:

- Elicit and attend to the client's thoughts, feelings, concerns, and needs.

- Express empathy and genuine concern for the client and family's issues.

- Obtain information and give feedback about the client's condition.

- Intervene to promote functional behavior and effective interpersonal relationships.

- Evaluate the client's progress toward desired goals and outcomes.

Δ Attending behaviors that enhance therapeutic communication include:

- **Eye contact**, which generally conveys interest and respect but varies by situation and culture.

- **Body language**, which demonstrates level of comfort and ease in the situation.

- **Vocal quality**, which enhances rapport and emphasizes special topics or issues.

- **Verbal tracking**, which provides neutral feedback by restating or summarizing the client's statements.

Δ **Effective and Ineffective Communication Skills and Techniques**

Effective Communication	Barriers to Communication
Silence that serves a function, such as time for meaningful reflection	Silence that conveys boredom, anger, or indifference
Active listening to hear, observe, and understand what the client communicates and to provide feedback based on the nurse's own thoughts and reactions	Inattentive listening or listening to just the client's words, taking the client's words at "face value," giving advice about the client's decisions
Clarification and validation of the client's messages to promote mutual understanding by paraphrasing, restating, reflecting, and exploring	Giving approval or disapproval of the client's thoughts, feelings, or behavior, which implies judgment and moralizing
Open-ended questions to facilitate spontaneous responses and interactive discussion	Closed-ended and "why" questions, which limit the client's responses and increase resistance or close down the interview process

Primary Reference:

Varcarolis, E. M., Carson, V. B., & Shoemaker, N. C. (2006). *Foundations of psychiatric mental health nursing: A clinical approach* (5th ed.). St. Louis, MO: Saunders.

Additional Resources:

NANDA International (2004). *NANDA nursing diagnoses: Definitions and classification 2005-2006*. Philadelphia: NANDA.

Chapter 4: Effective Communication in Mental Health Nursing

Application Exercises

1. Which of the following is a barrier to therapeutic communication?

>   A. Offering advice
>   B. Reflecting meaning
>   C. Listening attentively
>   D. Giving information

2. Effective communication with clients and families is based on

>   A. discussing topics the client feels comfortable talking about.
>   B. using silence to avoid unpleasant or difficult topics.
>   C. attending to verbal and nonverbal behaviors.
>   D. requiring the client to ask for feedback.

3. When a family asks for reassurance about a client's condition, which of the following is the nurse's best response?

>   A. "I think your son is getting better. What have you noticed?"
>   B. "I'm sure everything will be okay. It just takes time to heal."
>   C. "I'm not sure what's wrong. Have you asked the doctor about your concerns?"
>   D. "I understand you're concerned. Can you tell me what concerns you specifically?"

Scenario: A client comes to the primary care facility for her annual physical exam. While she is waiting to see the primary care provider, she says to the nurse, "I have so many aches and pains. I can't get out of bed in the morning. What do you think is wrong with me? Do I have cancer?"

---

4. What actions does the nurse need to take to establish an environment in which therapeutic communication can take place?

5. What is the nurse's best first response to this client's communication? Give a rationale for the chosen response.

6. After several minutes of talking with the nurse, the client says, "Well, that's enough about me and my problems. Tell me, are you married?" How should the nurse respond to this request for personal information? Give a rationale for your response.

7. What information about the conversation with this client should the nurse share with the client's primary care provider? What does the nurse need to do, if anything, before sharing information about the client with other health care providers?

Chapter 4: Effective Communication in Mental Health Nursing

Application Exercises Answer Key

1. Which of the following is a barrier to therapeutic communication?

   A. Offering advice
   B. Reflecting meaning
   C. Listening attentively
   D. Giving information

   Giving advice to a client should be avoided. Advice tends to interfere with the client's ability to make personal decisions and choices. The technique of reflection, on the other hand, encourages the client to make choices and is therapeutic. The skill of listening is an important therapeutic technique. Giving information informs the client of needed facts.

2. Effective communication with clients and families is based on

   A. discussing topics the client feels comfortable talking about.
   B. using silence to avoid unpleasant or difficult topics.
   C. attending to verbal and nonverbal behaviors.
   D. requiring the client to ask for feedback.

   Active listening and attending to verbal and nonverbal behaviors are the keys to effective communication. In-depth conversations are not necessary for effective communication; often very brief conversations are most effective. The purpose of effective silence is to allow the client time for reflection or to convey nonverbal support. Requiring the client to ask for feedback is not an effective technique.

3. When a family asks for reassurance about a client's condition, which of the following is the nurse's best response?

   A. "I think your son is getting better. What have you noticed?"
   B. "I'm sure everything will be okay. It just takes time to heal."
   C. "I'm not sure what's wrong. Have you asked the doctor about your concerns?"
   D. "I understand you're concerned. Can you tell me what concerns you specifically?"

   The therapeutic response reflects and accepts the family's feelings and allows them to clarify what they are feeling. Other responses interject the nurse's opinion and may cause the family to withhold their thoughts and feelings.

Scenario: A client comes to the primary care facility for her annual physical exam. While she is waiting to see the primary care provider, she says to the nurse, "I have so many aches and pains. I can't get out of bed in the morning. What do you think is wrong with me? Do I have cancer?"

4. What actions does the nurse need to take to establish an environment in which therapeutic communication can take place?

   To establish an environment conducive to therapeutic communication, the nurse should:

   Ensure privacy by pulling the curtains or closing the exam room door.
   Convey willingness to take time to be with the client by sitting beside the client.
   Focus attention on the client and what she is saying.

5. What is the nurse's best first response to this client's communication? Give a rationale for the chosen response.

   The nurse should choose an accepting attitude and ask an open-ended question, which would encourage open communication and give the client a chance to discuss her thoughts and feelings as well as troubling events. The nurse might respond, "You sound like you have many concerns. I've got time to talk with you now. Tell me what's been going on."

6. After several minutes of talking with the nurse, the client says, "Well, that's enough about me and my problems. Tell me, are you married?" How should the nurse respond to this request for personal information? Give a rationale for your response.

   The nurse should respond using appropriate self-disclosure to establish a bond with the client by stating, "Yes, I am married. Tell me something about your own marriage." The nurse needs to immediately refocus back on the client so that the interview can be therapeutic for the client.

7. What information about the conversation with this client should the nurse share with the client's primary care provider? What does the nurse need to do, if anything, before sharing information about the client with other health care providers?

   The nurse should share impressions of the client's state of mental and emotional well-being, as well as any specific concerns the client voiced about her health or life situation. The nurse needs to tell the client that information obtained during their interview that is relevant to the client's overall health will be shared with the health care team.

Unit 1   Foundations for Mental Health Nursing

Chapter 5:   Understanding Anxiety and Defense Mechanisms
Contributor: Meredith Flood, PhD, RN, APRN-BC

 NCLEX-RN® Connections:

Learning Objective: Review and apply knowledge within "**Understanding Anxiety and Defense Mechanisms**" in readiness for performance of the following nursing activities as outlined by the NCLEX-RN® test plan:

Δ   Apply knowledge of defense mechanisms in planning and implementing care for the client and family in the mental health setting.

Δ   Assess the client and family for stressors and ability to manage life situations.

Δ   Assess the client and family's coping mechanisms.

Δ   Help the client and family identify strategies to manage stress and illness.

Δ   Plan and provide care to assist the client and family to cope.

Δ   Evaluate and document the effectiveness of client and family coping.

 Key Points

Δ   **Stress** is a state produced by a change in the environment that is perceived as challenging, threatening, or damaging to one's well-being.

Δ   **Anxiety** is a universal human experience; dysfunctional behavior is often a defense mechanism against anxiety.

- Anxiety is a feeling of apprehension, uneasiness, uncertainty, or dread resulting from a real or perceived threat. The actual source of the threat is unknown or unrecognized. Anxiety attacks at a deeper level than does fear.

- The nursing theorist, Hildegard Peplau, identified anxiety as one of the most important concepts in psychiatric nursing. She developed a theoretical model delineating levels of anxiety and specific interventions to guide nurses in their care of clients experiencing anxiety.

Δ   **Fear** is a reaction to a specific danger.

Δ   **Defense mechanisms** are a major means of managing conflict and affect in response to anxiety. They are relatively unconscious and discrete from one another. Defense mechanisms are reversible and can be adaptive as well as pathological.

   •   Adaptive use of defense mechanisms helps people to achieve their goals in acceptable ways.

   •   Whether the use of defense mechanisms is adaptive or maladaptive is determined by their frequency, intensity, and duration.

Key Factors

Δ   **Healthy defenses** include altruism, sublimation, humor, and suppression. For example, a person who has feelings of anger and hostility toward his work supervisor **sublimates** those feelings by working out vigorously at the gym during his lunch period.

Δ   **Intermediate defenses** include repression (the foundation of defense mechanisms and the first-line defense against anxiety), displacement, reaction formation (overcompensation), somatization, undoing, and rationalization. An example of repression is the person who has a fear of the dentist's drill and continually "forgets" his dental appointment.

Δ   **Immature defenses** include passive aggression, acting-out behaviors, dissociation, devaluation, idealization, splitting, projection, and denial. Denial can be severe to the extent that it becomes psychotic. When this occurs, there is gross impairment in reality testing. For example, a person who abuses alcohol daily may completely deny that alcohol is a problem for her and may continue driving an automobile, even though she has a suspended license.

Δ   **Anxiety**

   •   Anxiety is viewed on a continuum with increasing levels of anxiety leading to decreasing ability to function.

      ◊   **Normal** – A healthy life force that is necessary for survival, normal anxiety motivates people to take action. For example, a potentially violent situation occurs on the mental health unit, and the nurse moves rapidly to defuse the situation. The anxiety experienced by the nurse during the situation helped him perform quickly and efficiently.

      ◊   **Acute (state)** – This level of anxiety is precipitated by an imminent loss or change that threatens one's sense of security. For example, the sudden death of a loved one precipitates an acute state of anxiety.

      ◊   **Chronic (trait)** – This level of anxiety is one that usually develops over time, often starting in childhood. The adult who experiences chronic anxiety may display that anxiety in physical symptoms, such as fatigue and frequent headaches.

Assessment

Δ   Assessment of a client's level of anxiety is basic to therapeutic intervention in any setting.

Levels of Anxiety	
Mild	• Mild anxiety occurs in the normal experience of everyday living. • It increases one's ability to perceive reality. • There is an identifiable cause of the anxiety. • Other characteristics include a vague feeling of mild discomfort, impatience, and apprehension.
Moderate	• Moderate anxiety occurs when mild anxiety escalates. • Slightly reduced perception and processing of information occurs, and selective inattention may occur. • Ability to think clearly is hampered, but learning and problem solving may still occur. • Other characteristics include concentration difficulties, tiredness, pacing, and increased heart rate and respiratory rate. • The client with this type of anxiety usually benefits from the direction of others.
Severe	• Perceptual field is greatly reduced with distorted perceptions. • Learning and problem solving are not possible. • Other characteristics include confusion, feelings of impending doom, and aimless activity. • The client with severe anxiety usually is not able to take direction from others.
Panic-level	• Panic-level anxiety is characterized by markedly disturbed behavior. • The client is not able to process what is occurring in the environment and may lose touch with reality. • The client experiences extreme fright and horror. • Other characteristics may include dysfunction in speech, inability to sleep, delusions, and hallucinations.

NANDA Nursing Diagnoses

Δ   Anxiety

Δ   Defensive coping

Δ   Readiness for enhanced coping

Nursing Interventions

Nursing diagnosis: *Anxiety* related to situational/maturational crisis as evidenced by tiredness, difficulty concentrating, and impaired attention	
Interventions	**Rationales**
Use active listening to demonstrate willingness to help and use specific communication techniques (e.g., open-ended questions, giving broad openings, exploring and seeking clarification).	These interventions encourage the client to express feelings, develop trust, and identify the source of the anxiety.
Provide a calm presence, recognizing the client's distress.	This assists the client to focus and start to problem solve.
Evaluate past coping mechanisms.	This will assist the client to identify adaptive and nonadaptive coping mechanisms.
Explore alternatives to problem situations.	This intervention offers options for problem solving.
Encourage participation in activities that may temporarily relieve feelings of inner tension (e.g., exercise).	This provides the client with an outlet for pent-up tension, promotes endorphin release, and improves mental well-being.

Nursing diagnosis: *Anxiety* related to change in role function and status	
Interventions	**Rationales**
Provide an environment that meets the physical and safety needs of the client.	This intervention minimizes risk to the client. The client may be unaware of needs (e.g., fluids, food, and sleep).
Provide a quiet environment with minimal stimulation.	This helps to prevent intensification of the current level of anxiety.
Use medications and restraint, but only after less restrictive interventions have failed to decrease anxiety to safer levels.	Medications and/or restraints may be necessary to prevent harm to the client and health care providers.
Encourage gross motor activities.	This provides the client with an outlet for pent-up tension, promotes endorphin release, and improves mental well-being.
Set limits by using firm, short, and simple statements. Repetition may be necessary.	Limit-setting can minimize risk to the client and health care providers. Clear, simple communication facilitates understanding.
Direct the client to acknowledge reality and focus on what is present in the environment.	Focusing on reality will assist with reducing the client's anxiety level.

Primary Reference:

Varcarolis, E. M., Carson, V. B., & Shoemaker, N. C. (2006). *Foundations of psychiatric mental health nursing: A clinical approach* (5th ed.). St. Louis, MO: Saunders.

Additional Resources:

NANDA International (2004). *NANDA nursing diagnoses: Definitions and classification 2005-2006*. Philadelphia: NANDA.

Chapter 5: Understanding Anxiety and Defense Mechanisms

Application Exercises

1. Match each defense mechanism below with the letter of the behavior that best illustrates it.

_____ Reaction formation

   A. A child is punished by his mother and sent to his room, where he begins to kick and break apart a favorite toy.

_____ Denial

   B. A woman who just lost her job, because she frequently was late for work, tells friends that it will be much better for her family if she stays home every day.

_____ Displacement

   C. A woman who just lost an election to a hated rival declares, "She is such a sweet person and I really like her!"

_____ Rationalization

   D. A heavy smoker diagnosed with lung cancer says, "I'm coughing because I have that cold that everyone has been getting."

_____ Sublimation

   E. A husband feels very angry with his wife, so he goes outside and begins energetically cutting up firewood with an axe.

2. A client in a primary care facility just learned that she must be admitted to the hospital for a breast biopsy. As the nurse tries to give her information about the procedure, he notices that the client is perspiring and pale. Her breathing is rapid at about 28/min, and she says, "You'll have to excuse me; I don't quite understand what you're trying to tell me." The nurse assesses the client's anxiety as

     A. mild.

     B. moderate.

     C. severe.

     D. panic.

3. The most appropriate nursing strategy when trying to give necessary information to a client with moderate anxiety is to

     A. discontinue giving information and reassure the client that everything will be okay.

     B. discontinue giving the information and instead encourage the client to talk about her feelings of anxiety.

     C. continue giving the information as before, and ignore the client's anxiety so that she will not be embarrassed.

     D. give the information again with simple language and in a calm manner.

Scenario: A father enters the emergency department with his son, who has just been hit by a car. The father was supposed to be watching the 6 year old while the child's mother was out shopping; however, the child slipped out of the house and wandered into the street in front of his home. At the hospital, the child is immediately sent to surgery and is in critical condition. The father, who is still in the emergency department waiting room, is very distraught and is wailing loudly. He demonstrates an inability to be still, his hands are shaking, and he is frequently dropping his keys. "It should have been me," he moans. Others in the waiting room are starting to appear anxious and are complaining about the disturbance.

4. What level of anxiety is the father experiencing? What data support this description?

5. The receptionist calls the emergency department nurse to the waiting room. What is the nurse's priority action in this situation?

6. Identify three nursing interventions for this family member.

Chapter 5: Understanding Anxiety and Defense Mechanisms

Application Exercises Answer Key

1. Match each defense mechanism below with the letter of the behavior that best illustrates it.

__C__ Reaction formation

A. A child is punished by his mother and sent to his room, where he begins to kick and break apart a favorite toy.

__D__ Denial

B. A woman who just lost her job, because she frequently was late for work, tells friends that it will be much better for her family if she stays home every day.

__A__ Displacement

C. A woman who just lost an election to a hated rival declares, "She is such a sweet person and I really like her!"

__B__ Rationalization

D. A heavy smoker diagnosed with lung cancer says, "I'm coughing because I have that cold that everyone has been getting."

__E__ Sublimation

E. A husband feels very angry with his wife, so he goes outside and begins energetically cutting up firewood with an axe.

Reaction formation involves keeping feelings that are unacceptable out of conscious awareness by showing the opposite behavior. A person in denial unconsciously ignores information that is unacceptable. In displacement, feelings of anger are shifted to someone or something other than the actual cause of the emotion. In rationalization, a person unconsciously makes excuses for behavior or feelings. Sublimation involves substituting acceptable activity for unacceptable feelings.

2. A client in a primary care facility just learned that she must be admitted to the hospital for a breast biopsy. As the nurse tries to give her information about the procedure, he notices that the client is perspiring and pale. Her breathing is rapid at about 28/min, and she says, "You'll have to excuse me; I don't quite understand what you're trying to tell me." The nurse assesses the client's anxiety as

        A. mild.

        B. moderate.

        C. severe.

        D. panic.

Moderate anxiety decreases problem solving and may hamper one's ability to understand information. Vital signs may increase somewhat, and the person is visibly anxious. In mild anxiety, the person's ability to understand information may actually increase. Severe anxiety causes restlessness, decreased perception, and an inability to take direction. During a panic attack, the person is completely distracted, unable to function, and may lose touch with reality.

3. The most appropriate nursing strategy when trying to give necessary information to a client with moderate anxiety is to

    A. discontinue giving information and reassure the client that everything will be okay.

    B. discontinue giving the information and instead encourage the client to talk about her feelings of anxiety.

    C. continue giving the information as before, and ignore the client's anxiety so that she will not be embarrassed.

    D. give the information again with simple language and in a calm manner.

Giving information simply and calmly will help the client grasp essential facts. Adding new topics of conversation or trying to make the client verbalize will distract her even more. Ignoring the anxiety and continuing to give information that has not been understood is not acceptable.

Scenario: A father enters the emergency department with his son, who has just been hit by a car. The father was supposed to be watching the 6 year old while the child's mother was out shopping; however, the child slipped out of the house and wandered into the street in front of his home. At the hospital, the child is immediately sent to surgery and is in critical condition. The father, who is still in the emergency department waiting room, is very distraught and is wailing loudly. He demonstrates an inability to be still, his hands are shaking, and he is frequently dropping his keys. "It should have been me," he moans. Others in the waiting room are starting to appear anxious and are complaining about the disturbance.

---

4. What level of anxiety is the father experiencing? What data support this description?

This man demonstrates severe anxiety. He has an extremely reduced attention span, psychomotor agitation, and he is yelling.

5. The receptionist calls the emergency department nurse to the waiting room. What is the nurse's priority action in this situation?

The priority action is to escort the father from the waiting area to a private room with less environmental stimulation. The father's anxiety level appears to be increasing. He is becoming potentially unsafe to himself and others. Several people are anxious about the disturbance.

6. Identify three nursing interventions for this family member.

Appropriate interventions include: staying with the family; providing a safe and secure environment; assessing for and responding to themes noted in his communication; using firm, short, simple statements to communicate with him; and addressing comfort and safety needs by providing fluids and nutrition.

Unit 1   Foundations for Mental Health Nursing

Chapter 6:   Creating and Maintaining a Therapeutic and Safe Environment

Contributor: Anne W. Ryan, MSN, MPH, RN-BC

 **NCLEX-RN® Connections:**

Learning Objective: Review and apply knowledge within "**Creating and Maintaining a Therapeutic and Safe Environment**" in readiness for performance of the following nursing activities as outlined by the NCLEX-RN® test plan:

Δ   Apply knowledge of mental health to provide a therapeutic environment for the client/family.

Δ   Assess the client's response to interventions.

Δ   Assess the client's ability to participate in community meetings.

Δ   Plan and provide care through collaboration with clients and the health care team.

Δ   Maintain safety by providing a structured environment.

 Key Points

Δ   **Therapeutic Milieu**

- Milieu therapy began as an effort to provide a safe, supportive, and therapeutic environment conducive to the treatment of children who were mentally ill.

- Management of the milieu means manipulating the total environment of the mental health unit in order to provide the least amount of stress while promoting the greatest benefit for all the clients.

- Within this therapeutic milieu of the mental health facility, the client is expected to learn adaptive coping, interaction, and relationship skills that can be generalized to other aspects of life.

- The nurse, as **manager of care**, is responsible for structuring and/or implementing many aspects of the therapeutic milieu within the unit.

- The structure of the therapeutic milieu often includes regular community meetings, which include both nursing staff and clients.

Key Factors

Δ   Characteristics of the Therapeutic Milieu

Physical setting	<ul><li>Unit should be clean and orderly.</li><li>Color scheme and overall design should be appropriate for the client's age (e.g., children, adolescents, adults).</li><li>The setting should include comfortable furniture for lounging and interacting with others, solitary spaces for reading and thinking alone, comfortable places conducive to meals, and quiet areas for sleeping.</li><li>Materials used for such features as floors should be attractive, easy to clean, and safe for walking.</li><li>Traffic flow considerations should be conducive to client and staff movement.</li></ul>
Members of the health care team	<ul><li>Promote independence for self-care and individual growth in clients.</li><li>Allow choices for clients within the daily routine and within individual treatment plans.</li><li>Treat clients as individuals.</li><li>Apply rules of fair treatment for all clients.</li><li>Model good social behavior for clients, such as respect for the rights of others.</li><li>Work cooperatively as a team to provide care.</li><li>Maintain boundaries with clients.</li><li>Maintain professional appearance and demeanor.</li><li>Promote safe and satisfying peer interactions among the clients.</li><li>Practice open communication techniques with health team members and clients.</li></ul>
Emotional climate	<ul><li>Promote feelings of self-worth and hope for the future.</li><li>Clients should feel safe from harm (self-harm, as well as harm from disruptive behaviors of other clients).</li><li>Clients should feel cared about and accepted by the staff and others.</li></ul>

Δ   The therapeutic milieu includes **safety** for both clients and staff within the environment.

- Physical safety

    ◊   The nurses' station and other areas should be set up for easy observation of clients by staff and access to staff by clients.

    ◊   Special safety features should be addressed for age/condition of clients (e.g., bathroom bars, wheelchair accessibility for disabled clients).

    ◊   Set up the following provisions to prevent client self-harm or harm by others:

    - No access to sharp or otherwise harmful objects.

    - Restriction of client access to out-of-bounds or locked areas.

    - Monitoring of visitors.

    - Restriction of alcohol and illegal drug access or use.

- ° Restriction of sexual activity among clients.

- ° Deterrence of elopement from facility.

- ° Rapid de-escalation of disruptive and potentially violent behaviors through planned interventions by trained staff.

◊ Seclusion rooms and restraints should be set up for safety and used only after all less restrictive measures have been tried. When used, there should be procedures and policies to prevent any client harm.

◊ Plan for safe access to recreational areas, occupational therapy, and meeting rooms.

◊ Teach fire, evacuation, and other safety rules to all staff.

- ° Have clear plans for keeping clients and staff safe in emergencies.

- ° Maintain staff skills, such as cardiopulmonary resuscitation, with in-service training.

◊ Considerations of room assignments on a 24-hr inpatient unit should include:

- ° Personalities of each roommate.

- ° The likelihood of nighttime disruptions for a roommate if one client has difficulty sleeping.

- ° Medical diagnoses, such as how two clients with severe paranoia might interact with each other.

Δ Nurses within a mental health unit must allow time for both **structured** and **unstructured** activity for clients and staff.

- • Structured activity may include time for:

  ◊ Community meetings.

  ◊ Group activities and individual therapy sessions.

  ◊ Recreational activities.

  ◊ Psychoeducational classes, such as learning about medication side effects.

- • Unstructured, flexible time may include time in which the nurse and other staff are able to observe clients and interact spontaneously within the milieu.

Δ Community Meetings

- The community meeting on the mental health unit should enhance the emotional climate of the therapeutic milieu by promoting:

  ◊ Interaction and communication between staff and clients.

  ◊ Decision-making skills for clients.

  ◊ A feeling of self-worth among clients.

  ◊ Discussions of common unit objectives, such as encouraging clients to meet treatment goals and plan for discharge.

- Meetings may be structured so that they are client-led with decisions made by the group as a whole.

Primary Reference:

Varcarolis, E. M., Carson, V. B., & Shoemaker, N. C. (2006). *Foundations of psychiatric mental health nursing: A clinical approach* (5th ed.). St. Louis, MO: Saunders.

Additional Resources:

Benson, W. D., & Briscoe, L. (2003). Jumping the hurdles of mental health care wearing cement shoes: Where does the inpatient psychiatric nurse fit in? *Journal of the American Psychiatric Nurses Association, 9*(4), 123-128.

NANDA International (2004). *NANDA nursing diagnoses: Definitions and classification 2005-2006*. Philadelphia: NANDA.

Chapter 6: Creating and Maintaining a Therapeutic and Safe Environment

Application Exercises

1. A new client is being admitted to the acute care mental health inpatient unit. The referral sheet indicates that the client is demonstrating delusional and paranoid behaviors. What considerations for making the client's room assignment should be included in the nurse's planning?

2. A registered nurse on an acute inpatient mental health unit is asked to develop an agenda for the biweekly community meeting in collaboration with a newly elected client president. How should the nurse approach this assignment?

3. A new registered nurse is being oriented to the acute mental health facility. The nurse has worked many years in general medical acute care facilities and is new to mental health nursing. The nurse asks, "I'm not sure exactly what a therapeutic milieu is. Could you explain it to me?" How should the orienting nurse respond?

4. A nurse is orienting a new client to an inpatient mental health unit. When explaining the unit's community meetings, the nurse should state which of the following to the client?

      A. "You and a group of other clients will meet to discuss your medication and treatment plans."

      B. "I never know what goes on at a community meeting, because the clients control the agenda."

      C. "You and the other clients will meet with staff to discuss activities, problems, and other things of interest to all."

      D. "You will meet alone with your therapist to discuss your treatment plan and problems you are having."

5. A client who is newly admitted to the acute care mental health unit has a DSM-IV-TR Axis I diagnosis of paranoid schizophrenia. The client is very frightened and delusional. During the client's first few days of treatment, which of the following aspects of the therapeutic milieu is most important?

      A. Socialization and communication skills

      B. Safety and structured activity

      C. Occupational therapy and other diversional activities

      D. Intensive group therapy

6. A new 24-hr residential treatment center for adult clients with chemical dependency has just been built. The nurse manager meets with newly hired members of the treatment team to plan the therapeutic milieu for the center. Which of the following are considerations for the therapeutic milieu? (Select all that apply.)

_____ Traffic flow patterns between the nurses' station and client lounge and dining areas

_____ Plan for structure of team and client group meetings

_____ Discussion of safety guidelines for clients who return from passes outside the facility

_____ Plan for staff involvement in unstructured client activities

_____ Discussion of a plan for handling potentially violent situations that might arise

_____ Performance evaluation of health care team members

Chapter 6: Creating and Maintaining a Therapeutic and Safe Environment

Application Exercises Answer Key

1. A new client is being admitted to the acute care mental health inpatient unit. The referral sheet indicates that the client is demonstrating delusional and paranoid behaviors. What considerations for making the client's room assignment should be included in the nurse's planning?

   The new client should be assigned to a room near the nurses' station, since the client is reported to be experiencing delusions and paranoia. Ideally, this would be a private room. If the new client must have a roommate, consideration should be given to the type of person assigned so that both clients will remain safe. The new client will need time to adjust to the new environment, and staff will want to monitor him frequently and unobtrusively for the first several days, assuring that the client's paranoia does not cause self-harm or harm to others.

2. A registered nurse on an acute inpatient mental health unit is asked to develop an agenda for the biweekly community meeting in collaboration with a newly elected client president. How should the nurse approach this assignment?

   Meet with the client president; review past procedures used for leading the meetings and unit goals for the meetings; use open communication techniques to answer any questions that the client may have; and discuss how she plans to handle the meeting. Review the past meeting's minutes; determine if there is any "unfinished business" that requires follow-up; discuss possible issues the nurse or the client president anticipates that other clients will bring up; and reinforce the importance of remaining on task and on time. The nurse should also demonstrate verbally and nonverbally that he values the input of the client president.

3. A new registered nurse is being oriented to the acute mental health facility. The nurse has worked many years in general medical acute care facilities and is new to mental health nursing. The nurse asks, "I'm not sure exactly what a therapeutic milieu is. Could you explain it to me?" How should the orienting nurse respond?

   The milieu refers to safety on the unit, as well as the physical setting, structure of activities, emotional climate, and the way the staff works as a team and with clients. Management of the milieu means manipulating the total environment of the mental health unit in order to provide the least amount of stress while promoting the greatest benefit for all of the clients.

4. A nurse is orienting a new client to an inpatient mental health unit. When explaining the unit's community meetings, the nurse should state which of the following to the client?

> A. "You and a group of other clients will meet to discuss your medication and treatment plans."
>
> B. "I never know what goes on at a community meeting, because the clients control the agenda."
>
> **C. "You and the other clients will meet with staff to discuss activities, problems, and other things of interest to all."**
>
> D. "You will meet alone with your therapist to discuss your treatment plan and problems you are having."

Community meetings include both staff and clients on a unit. Any topic of interest to the entire group may be discussed, including problems, future activities, and meeting new clients. Option A describes group therapy. Option B is an evasive answer, which gives the client no information about meetings. Option D describes individual therapy.

5. A client who is newly admitted to the acute care mental health unit has a DSM-IV-TR Axis I diagnosis of paranoid schizophrenia. The client is very frightened and delusional. During the client's first few days of treatment, which of the following aspects of the therapeutic milieu is most important?

> A. Socialization and communication skills
>
> **B. Safety and structured activity**
>
> C. Occupational therapy and other diversional activities
>
> D. Intensive group therapy

It is most important to plan for this client's safety; unit activities should be simple and structured at first. Other parts of the therapeutic milieu, such as socialization, occupational therapy, and group therapy would need to wait until the client is well enough to participate.

6. A new 24-hr residential treatment center for adult clients with chemical dependency has just been built. The nurse manager meets with newly hired members of the treatment team to plan the therapeutic milieu for the center. Which of the following are considerations for the therapeutic milieu? (Select all that apply.)

 __X__ **Traffic flow patterns between the nurses' station and client lounge and dining areas**

 __X__ **Plan for structure of team and client group meetings**

 __X__ **Discussion of safety guidelines for clients who return from passes outside the facility**

 __X__ **Plan for staff involvement in unstructured client activities**

 __X__ **Discussion of a plan for handling potentially violent situations that might arise**

 _____ Performance evaluation of health care team members

Traffic flow patterns, plans for structure of team and client group meetings, discussion of safety guidelines for clients who are returning from passes outside the facility, plans for staff involvement in unstructured client activities, and plans for handling potentially violent situations are all part of the total environment of the unit and thus of the therapeutic milieu. Performance evaluations of health care team members are personnel issues and not part of the environment in which the client is learning new skills.

Unit 1   Foundations for Mental Health Nursing

Chapter 7:   Mental Health Nursing in Diverse Practice Settings
Contributor: Christina D. Brazier, BSN, RN

 NCLEX-RN® Connections:

Learning Objective: Review and apply knowledge within "**Mental Health Nursing in Diverse Practice Settings**" in readiness for performance of the following nursing activities as outlined by the NCLEX-RN® test plan:

Δ   Describe the historical background for the diverse types of mental health practice settings available today.

Δ   Manage the client's care by making appropriate referrals and maintaining continuity of care.

Δ   Compare and contrast types of mental health facilities/agencies in both acute care and community care settings.

Δ   Explain the role of the nurse in varied mental health practice settings.

Δ   Provide the client/family/significant other with information on process and procedures for transfer to another type of health care facility/agency or for discharge home.

Δ   Identify community resources available to the mental health client/family/ significant other.

 Key Points

Δ   **History of Mental Health Care in the United States**

- Most clients with severe mental illness were treated solely in acute care inpatient facilities before the middle of the twentieth century.

- Congress passed a series of acts in 1946, 1955, and 1963 in response to the appalling condition of facilities for the mentally ill. This began a trend to deinstitutionalize mental health care.

- Clients who had lived in acute care mental health facilities for many years were discharged into the community at a time when community mental health facilities/agencies were often unprepared to deal with the influx.

- The concept of the **case manager** was introduced around 1970 to coordinate the various functions that care for all the individual needs of a client in a mental health setting.

- Starting around 1980, managed care through Health Maintenance Organizations (HMOs), Preferred Provider Organizations (PPOs), and others limited hospital stays for clients in a general medical setting.

    ◊ Managed Behavioral Healthcare Organizations (MBHOs) were later developed to coordinate care and limit stays in acute care facilities for clients needing mental health care.

    ◊ This began the trend to develop a continuum of acute care facilities, as well as community mental health facilities/agencies to provide for all levels of behavioral health care needs.

    ◊ Complete and accurate documentation of client needs and progress by nurses and other health care providers is necessary to assure quality client care for each individual.

- Factors that will affect the future of mental health care include:

    ◊ An increase in the aging population.

    ◊ An increase in cultural diversity within the United States.

    ◊ The expansion of technology, which may provide new settings for client care, as well as new ways to treat mental illness more effectively.

Δ **Acute Care Settings** for Mental Health Care

- This setting provides intensive treatment and supervision in locked units for clients with severe mental illness.

- Facilities help stabilize mental illness symptoms and promote a return to the community.

- Staff is made up of an interdisciplinary team with management provided by nurses.

- Facilities may be privately owned, with payment provided by private funds or insurance.

- Facilities may also be owned by one of the 50 states, with much of the funding provided for indigent clients. State-run facilities/agencies also often provide full-time acute care for forensic clients (those in a correctional setting) with severe mental illness.

- Case management programs assist with client transition to a community setting (as necessary) after discharge from the acute care facility.

Δ **Community Settings** for Mental Health Care

- Primary care is provided in community-based settings, which include clinics, schools and day care centers, partial hospitalization programs, drug and alcohol treatment facilities, forensic settings (county jails), psychosocial rehabilitation programs, telephone crisis counseling centers (suicide prevention), and home health care.

- Community care programs help to stabilize or improve the client's mental functioning within a community and teach, support, and make referrals in order to promote positive social activities.

- Nursing interventions in community settings provide for primary treatment and primary, secondary, and tertiary prevention of mental illness.

Key Factors

Δ **Client Care** In **Acute Mental Health** Care Settings

- Criteria to justify admission to an acute care facility include:

  ◊ Clear risk of the client's danger to self or others.

  ◊ Failure of community-based treatment.

  ◊ Dangerous decomposition of a client undergoing long-term treatment.

  ◊ Client having a medical need in addition to a mental illness.

- Goals of acute mental health treatment include:

  ◊ Prevention of the client harming self or others.

  ◊ Stabilizing mental health crises.

  ◊ Returning clients who are severally ill to some type of community care.

- **Interdisciplinary team members** in acute care include nurses, mental health technicians (who perform duties similar to assistive personnel in other health care facilities), psychologists, psychiatrists, other general health care providers, social workers, counselors, occupational and other specialty therapists, and pharmacists.

- The interdisciplinary team has the primary responsibility of planning and monitoring individualized treatment plans or clinical pathways of care, depending on the philosophy and policy of the facility.

- Plans for discharge to home or to a community facility/agency begin from the time of admission and continue with the implementation of the initial treatment plan or clinical pathway.

- Nurses in acute mental health facilities use the nursing process and a holistic approach to provide care. Nursing roles include:

  ◊ Overall management of each unit, including client activities and therapeutic milieu.

  ◊ Assuring safe administration and monitoring of all client medications.

  ◊ Implementation of individual client treatment plans.

  ◊ Documentation of the nursing process for each client.

  ◊ Managing crises as they arise.

Δ   **Client Care In Community Health Settings**

- Nurses are largely responsible for linking acute care with community care facilities/agencies.

- Intensive outpatient programs promote community reintegration for clients.

- Three levels of prevention are utilized by nurses when implementing community care interventions/teaching.

Level of Prevention	Interventions
Primary prevention promotes health and prevents mental health problems from occurring.	The nurse leads a group for parents of toddlers, discussing normal toddler behavior and ways to promote healthy development.
Secondary prevention focuses on early detection of mental illness.	The nurse performs screening for a group of parents with children who have developmental disorders.
Tertiary prevention focuses on rehabilitation and prevention of further problems in clients previously diagnosed.	The nurse leads a support group for clients who have completed a chemical dependency program.

- A continuum of community mental health facilities/agencies with treatment intensity levels from high to low should be available to allow clients to remain safe in the least restrictive environment possible.

- Community-based mental health programs include:

Community Setting	General Function and Examples of Care
Partial hospitalization programs	• These programs provide intense short-term treatment for clients who are well enough to go home every night and who have a responsible person at home to provide support and a safe environment. • Certain detoxification programs are a specialized form of partial hospitalization in that the client requires medical supervision, stress management, addiction counseling, and relapse prevention.
Assertive community treatment (ACT)	• This includes nontraditional case management and treatment by an interdisciplinary team for a caseload of clients with severe mental illness who are noncompliant with traditional treatment. • ACT helps to reduce reoccurrences of hospitalizations and provides assertive outreach, crisis intervention, independent living assistance, and linkage to necessary support services.

Community Setting	General Function and Examples of Care
Community mental health centers	These facilities provide a variety of services for a wide range of community clients, including: • Educational groups. • Medication dispensing programs. • Individual counseling programs.
Psychosocial rehabilitation programs	These provide a structured range of programs for clients in a mental health setting, including: • Residential services. • Adult day care programs for older adults.
Home care	Home care provides mental health assessment, interventions, and family support in the client's own home.

Δ   Roles for Nurses In Diverse Mental Health Practice Settings

Registered Nurse	Advanced Practice Nurse
Educational preparation: diploma, associate degree, or baccalaureate degree in nursing with additional on-the-job training and continuing education in mental health care	Educational preparation: advanced nursing degree in behavioral health (e.g., master's degree, doctorate, nurse practitioner, or clinical nurse specialist)
May work in either an acute care or community-based facility/agency.	May work in either an acute care or community-based facility/agency. Works independently, often supervising other individuals or groups.
Functions within a facility/agency using the nursing process to provide care and treatment, such as medication.	May have prescription privileges and is able to independently recommend interventions.
Manages care for a group of clients within a unit of the facility/agency.	May manage and administrate care for an entire facility/agency.

Δ   Nurses are **advocates** for clients with mental illness. Referral of clients and their families/significant other to organizations and agencies that provide additional resources can provide significant support to individuals. For example, the National Alliance for the Mentally Ill (NAMI) is a grassroots organization with the goals of improving quality of life for persons with mental illness and for providing research to better treat or eradicate mental illness.

Primary Reference:

Varcarolis, E. M., Carson, V. B., & Shoemaker, N. C. (2006). *Foundations of psychiatric mental health nursing: A clinical approach* (5th ed.). St. Louis, MO: Saunders.

Additional Resources:

Boyd, M. (2005). *Psychiatric nursing: Contemporary practice* (3rd edition). Philadelphia: Lippincott Williams & Wilkins.

Mohr, W. K. (2003). *Johnson's psychiatric-mental health nursing* (5th edition). Philadelphia: Lippincott Williams & Wilkins.

NANDA International (2004). *NANDA nursing diagnoses: Definitions and classification 2005-2006*. Philadelphia: NANDA.

Chapter 7: Mental Health Nursing in Diverse Practice Settings

Application Exercises

1. A staff nurse provides direct client care in an acute mental health facility. Which of the following aspects of care is the nurse most likely to perform?

   A. Assistance with bathing

   B. Assistance in finding a job

   C. Art therapy lesson

   D. Mental status assessment

2. Four clients have been living alone in studio apartments with regular visits from a nurse case worker. On today's visit, the nurse becomes very concerned about one of the four clients and arranges with the primary care provider for the client's admission to an acute care mental health unit. The nurse's concern relates to the client who

   A. recently burned her arm while using a hot iron at home.

   B. requests that her antipsychotic medication be changed due to some new side effects.

   C. says he is hearing a voice that tells him he is not worthy of living anymore.

   D. tells the nurse he experienced symptoms of severe anxiety before and during a job interview.

3. A nurse is working on promotion of healthy coping skills with older adult clients who had all previously been hospitalized for severe depression and are now in a residential care facility. This is an example of which of the following?

   A. Primary prevention

   B. Secondary prevention

   C. Tertiary prevention

   D. Mental status examination

4. Which of the following clients should the nurse consider referring to an assertive community treatment (ACT) group?

   A. A client in an acute care mental health facility who has fallen several times while running down the hallway

   B. A home client who keeps "forgetting" to come in for his monthly antipsychotic injection for schizophrenia

   C. A client in a day treatment program who says he is becoming more anxious during group therapy

   D. A client in a weekly grief support group who says she still misses her deceased husband who has been dead for 3 years

5. A client with severe mental illness, who will soon be ready for discharge from an acute mental health facility but still requires supervision much of the time, has a wife who works all day but is home by late afternoon. Which of the following accommodations would be the least restrictive while remaining safe for this client?

    A. Remaining in the 24-hr locked acute care facility

    B. Living at home with a weekly visit from a nurse case worker

    C. Attending a partial hospitalization program

    D. Living at home with a daily trip to a community mental health center

6. True or False: The best long-term goal for a 61-year-old client with severe mental illness, who has resided in a locked acute care facility for 2 years, is that she will be able to remain safe from harm on the acute care unit for the rest of her life.

7. True or False: The health care professional who typically manages client care on an acute care mental health unit is the psychiatrist.

Chapter 7: Mental Health Nursing in Diverse Practice Settings

Application Exercises Answer Key

1. A staff nurse provides direct client care in an acute mental health facility. Which of the following aspects of care is the nurse most likely to perform?

 A. Assistance with bathing

 B. Assistance in finding a job

 C. Art therapy lesson

 D. Mental status assessment

 One of many nursing responsibilities is to assess the client's mental status. A mental health technician or assistive personnel should perform physical care. The social worker provides care such as vocational assistance. An occupational or specialized activity therapist would provide art therapy.

2. Four clients have been living alone in studio apartments with regular visits from a nurse case worker. On today's visit, the nurse becomes very concerned about one of the four clients and arranges with the primary care provider for the client's admission to an acute care mental health unit. The nurse's concern relates to the client who

 A. recently burned her arm while using a hot iron at home.

 B. requests that her antipsychotic medication be changed due to some new side effects.

 C. says he is hearing a voice that tells him he is not worthy of living anymore.

 D. tells the nurse he experienced symptoms of severe anxiety before and during a job interview.

 A client who hears a voice telling him he is not worthy of living is at risk for self-harm, which is a criterion for admission. The other clients could deal with their problems with the nurse case worker or in a community mental health center with various members of the health care team.

3. A nurse is working on promotion of healthy coping skills with older adult clients who had all previously been hospitalized for severe depression and are now in a residential care facility. This is an example of which of the following?

    A. Primary prevention

    B. Secondary prevention

    C. Tertiary prevention

    D. Mental status examination

Tertiary prevention deals with preventing further problems in clients already diagnosed with mental illness. Primary prevention deals with preventing the initial onset of a mental health problem. Secondary prevention deals with early detection of disease. Mental status examination is a tool that the nurse could use to assess a client's problem, but it is not a type of prevention.

4. Which of the following clients should the nurse consider referring to an assertive community treatment (ACT) group?

    A. A client in an acute care mental health facility who has fallen several times while running down the hallway

    B. A home client who keeps "forgetting" to come in for his monthly antipsychotic injection for schizophrenia

    C. A client in a day treatment program who says he is becoming more anxious during group therapy

    D. A client in a weekly grief support group who says she still misses her deceased husband who has been dead for 3 years

An ACT group works with clients who are noncompliant with traditional therapy, such as the client in a home setting who keeps "forgetting" his injection. The client in acute care who has been running and falling should be helped by the treatment team on her unit. The client with anxiety might be referred to his counselor or mental health provider. The client who is grieving for her husband very likely needs no further referral; she may simply want to talk to the nurse about her grief.

5. A client with severe mental illness, who will soon be ready for discharge from an acute mental health facility but still requires supervision much of the time, has a wife who works all day but is home by late afternoon. Which of the following accommodations would be the least restrictive while remaining safe for this client?

   A. Remaining in the 24-hr locked acute care facility

   B. Living at home with a weekly visit from a nurse case worker

   C. Attending a partial hospitalization program

   D. Living at home with a daily trip to a community mental health center

   A partial hospitalization program can provide treatment during the day while allowing the client to spend nights at home, as long as a responsible family member is present. Staying in the acute care facility is not the best option if a community program is available. Being at home most of the day by himself is not a viable option if the client needs supervision. This client needs more supervision than just a daily trip to the community mental health center, which would not ensure adequate treatment.

6. True or False: The best long-term goal for a 61-year-old client with severe mental illness, who has resided in a locked acute care facility for 2 years, is that she will be able to remain safe from harm on the acute care unit for the rest of her life.

   False: Although some clients may remain inside an acute care facility for longer periods of time, the best long-term goal for this client would be for her to be discharged to some type of community care.

7. True or False: The health care professional who typically manages client care on an acute care mental health unit is the psychiatrist.

   False: A nurse typically manages client care on acute care mental health units.

Unit 1   Foundations for Mental Health Nursing

Chapter 8:   Culturally Aware Mental Health Nursing
Contributor: Carole A. Shea, PhD, RN, FAAN

 NCLEX-RN® Connections:

Learning Objective: Review and apply knowledge within "**Culturally Aware Mental Health Nursing**" in readiness for performance of the following nursing activities as outlined by the NCLEX-RN® test plan:

Δ   Recognize the impact of cultural, spiritual, and psychosocial factors when providing mental health care to clients.

Δ   Assess the client for needs related to culture (e.g., language barriers, education, personal space).

Δ   Provide written teaching materials in the client's language.

Δ   Assign appropriate interpreters to assist in helping the client/family/significant others understand mental health care.

Δ   Serve as interpreter for health care providers per facility policy.

Δ   Plan/provide mental health care that is sensitive to the client's culture (e.g., space and time orientation, care of the dying).

Δ   Evaluate and document how care was adapted to meet mental health/cultural needs.

 Key Points

Δ   **Culture** is a collection of learned, adaptive, and transmitted social values and beliefs that form the context from which a group interprets the human experience.

Δ   These values and beliefs can be shared by members of an ethnic, racial, social, or religious group.

Δ   Communication, dietary preferences, and dress are influenced by culture.

Δ   Nursing in a multicultural society, such as the United States, requires transcultural nursing care that is culturally competent. Effectiveness depends on the nurse's understanding of both personal culture and the client's culture.

Δ   Culture influences health beliefs, diagnoses and manifestation of symptoms, response to illness, health practices, and treatment of disease.

Δ   Different cultures subscribe to different theories about how mental health is defined, what causes mental illness, and which care providers and treatments will be effective.

Δ   Mental health and illness must be viewed within the context of the society and culture in which clients and families live.

Δ   Serious mental illnesses (e.g., schizophrenia, major depression, anxiety and stress-related disorders) are prevalent in every society and culture.

- Many cultures consider the **mind-body-spirit** to be a single entity; therefore, no distinction is made between physical and mental illness.

- Cultural-bound syndromes often have psychological and emotional components, which are manifested as physical symptoms.

- Western medicine considers complex **neurochemical disturbances** in the brain as the cause of serious mental disorders and dysfunctions.

- Mental illness carries a heavy stigma in most cultures, which affects willingness to seek and accept mental health care and follow a treatment regimen.

Key Factors

Δ   The nurse needs to understand her own cultural background and biases and the effect on the care provided to those from different cultures.

Δ   Nurses must be aware of, sensitive to, and appreciative of cultural differences to provide culturally competent mental health care.

Δ   Cultural Characteristics of Family Structure

- Communication and decision-making patterns depend on the family structure and cultural values.

- Clients/families may be reluctant to accept a mental illness diagnosis because of stigma and shame.

Δ   The goal of the culturally competent nurse is to adapt mental health nursing care to the client's needs and preferences.

Δ   The culturally competent nurse communicates with the client/significant other/family with respect for and understanding of different cultural verbal and nonverbal behaviors.

Δ   Barriers to providing culturally competent care include:

- Language and communication differences.

- Culturally inappropriate tests and tools, which lead to misdiagnosis.

- Ethnic variations in drug metabolism related to genetics.

Δ   People from different ethnic, racial, and minority backgrounds have less access to mental health services according to the U.S. Surgeon General's report (DHHS, 2001).

Assessment

Δ   In order to meet the client's cultural needs, a nurse must first perform a **cultural assessment** to identify those needs.

Δ   Perform the cultural assessment in a language that is common to both nurse and client, or employ an interpreter.

Δ   **Nonverbal Behaviors**

  •   The culturally competent nurse must understand how nonverbal behaviors vary among cultures. The nurse should take those variations into account when performing mental health assessments.

Nonverbal Behavior	Culture	Variation
Tone of voice	Asian	Soft tone of voice conveys respect.
	Italian and Middle Eastern	Loud tone of voice is typical.
Eye contact	American	Direct eye contact is expected; lack of eye contact implies the person is lying or embarrassed.
	Middle Eastern	Mutual avoidance of eye contact except in intimate relationships; direct eye contact may be seen as rude, hostile, or sexually aggressive.
	Asian	Direct eye contact may be seen as disrespectful.
	Native American	Direct eye contact may be thought to lead to soul loss or soul theft.
Tactile/touch	American	Touch is used during conversation between intimate partners or family members.
	Italian and Latin American	Frequent touch is a sign of concern, interest, and warmth.

Nonverbal Behavior	Culture	Variation
Use of space	Anglo-American/North Europeans (English, Swiss, Scandinavian, German)	Distance is kept during communication, except in intimate or family relationships.
	Italian, French, Spanish, Russian, Latin American, Middle Eastern	Closer personal contact and less distance between individuals during communication is usually preferred.

△ **Questions that may be asked include:**

- What do you call the problem you are having now?

- When did the problem start? Why then?

- What do you think caused the problem?

- What does the illness do to you? How does it work?

- How severe is the illness?

- What treatments have you tried? How do you think it should be treated?

- What are the chief problems the illness has caused you?

- What do you fear most about the illness?

△ **Cultural Variations to Stress and Anxiety**

- In response to stress, individuals exhibit symptoms of anxiety in ways that people of their culture can perceive as a sign of distress or needing help.

- A client can exhibit a culture-specific psychological syndrome. For example, *ataque de nervios* is a Latin American description of symptoms very similar to a panic attack, and *taijin kyofusho* is a Japanese culture-specific diagnostic label for symptoms of social phobia, shyness, and embarrassment.

NANDA Nursing Diagnoses

△ Relocation stress syndrome

△ Risk for relocation stress syndrome

△ Social isolation

△ Spiritual distress

△ Impaired verbal communication

Nursing Interventions

Δ **Religion/Spirituality/Death Rituals**

- Respect the religious/spiritual practices of the client.

- Death rituals vary among cultures, and the nurse must be prepared to facilitate such practices whenever possible.

Δ **Pain**

- Recognize that the way a client reacts to and displays pain varies by culture.

- Use an alterative to the pain scale (1 to 10), as it may not appropriately reflect pain evaluation for all cultures.

- Explore religious beliefs that may influence the meaning of pain.

Δ **Nutrition**

- Provide for food choices and preparation that are consistent with cultural beliefs.

- As possible, allow the client to consume foods that may be viewed as a treatment for illness.

- Communicate food intolerances/allergies that are related to ethnicity to the dietary staff.

Δ **Communication**

- Improve nurse-client communication when cultural variations exist.

- Use interpreters when the communication barrier is great enough to impact the exchange of information between the nurse and the client.

- Cautiously use nonverbal communication, as it may have very different meanings for the client and the nurse.

Δ **Family Patterns and Gender Roles**

- Include and communicate with the person who has the authority to make decisions in the family.

Δ **Culture and Life Transitions**

- Assist families as they mark rituals (rites of passage) that symbolize cultural values.

- Common events that are often expressed with cultural rituals are:

  ◊ Puberty.

  ◊ Pregnancy.

  ◊ Childbirth.

  ◊ Postpartum period.

  ◊ Dying and death.

Δ **Repatterning**

- Accommodate the client's cultural beliefs and values as much as is in the client's best interest.

- When a cultural value/behavior is a direct hindrance to the client's health/ wellness, the nurse should attempt to repattern that belief to one that is compatible with health promotion.

- With knowledge of cultural differences, the nurse can plan and implement appropriate interventions.

Primary Reference:

Varcarolis, E. M., Carson, V. B., & Shoemaker, N. C. (2006). *Foundations of psychiatric mental health nursing: A clinical approach* (5th ed.). St. Louis, MO: Saunders.

Additional Resources:

Campinha-Bacote, J. (2002). Cultural competence in psychiatric nursing: Have you "ASKED" the right questions? *Journal of the American Psychiatric Nurses Association, 8*, 183-187.

Galanti, G. (2006, October 22). *Cultural diversity in healthcare*. Retrieved November 1, 2006, from http://ggalanti.com/index.html

NANDA International (2004). *NANDA nursing diagnoses: Definitions and classification 2005-2006*. Philadelphia: NANDA.

Chapter 8: Culturally Aware Mental Health Nursing

Application Exercises

Scenario: A 37-year-old Spanish-speaking Mexican-American woman comes to the family clinic with her husband and three children. The oldest child, who speaks English, tells the nurse that his mother has stopped taking care of the baby and doesn't cook their meals. He says she just cries and wants to stay in bed all the time.

1. Based on the nurse's awareness and knowledge of Mexican-American culture, what generalizations could he make about this client's family structure, and how should they guide his interaction with the client and family members?

2. When are generalizations about specific cultural groups (e.g., Mexican-Americans) useful? When are they harmful?

3. If the nurse does not speak Spanish, how should he communicate with the identified client (the mother)? What are the pros and cons of communicating with the mother through the oldest child? When should the nurse seek the services of an interpreter? Why?

4. A 23-year-old Ukrainian man who speaks only his native language is hospitalized with major depression. The client's treatment plan includes expectations that he is to participate in various activities on the unit. The client refuses to leave his room. What steps can the nurse take to encourage the client to participate in unit activities?

5. Which of the following nonverbal behaviors of an American client most likely communicates openness and honesty to the nurse?

    A. A firm handshake

    B. Direct eye contact

    C. A friendly pat on the back

    D. Willingness to sit close

6. Culturally competent nursing care requires that the nurse have

    A. opportunities to experience cultural differences through travel.

    B. a world view that is tolerant and accepting of cultures.

    C. cultural awareness, knowledge, skills, encounters, and desire.

    D. scientific knowledge of sociocultural theories and concepts.

7. If a nurse and a client share the same religious background, the nurse should recognize that

    A. all members of the same religion share similar feelings about their religion.

    B. a shared religious background produces mutual regard for one another.

    C. the same religious beliefs may influence individuals differently.

    D. the differences and commonalities in their beliefs should be discussed.

8. A female Korean client who recently immigrated to the United States is hospitalized for major depression with several suicide attempts. After 2 months of hospitalized treatment, the client is no longer considered suicidal. However, she spends all of her time sitting by herself. She speaks no English and attends no group functions. An interpreter visits every morning to communicate the client's needs to health care staff, and the client takes an active part in treatment plan meetings with the interpreter present. Using this data, the nurse assigns a nursing diagnosis of

    A. self-care deficit.

    B. social isolation.

    C. chronic low self-esteem.

    D. ineffective coping.

Chapter 8: Culturally Aware Mental Health Nursing

Application Exercises Answer Key

Scenario: A 37-year-old Spanish-speaking Mexican-American woman comes to the family clinic with her husband and three children. The oldest child, who speaks English, tells the nurse that his mother has stopped taking care of the baby and doesn't cook their meals. He says she just cries and wants to stay in bed all the time.

1. Based on the nurse's awareness and knowledge of Mexican-American culture, what generalizations could he make about this client's family structure, and how should they guide his interaction with the client and family members?

   In general, Mexican-American families have a hierarchical structure with the husband as the head of the family. There is division of labor between the spouses, with the wife responsible for care of the children and household duties. The wife defers to the husband's decisions, but she may take charge of matters related to the family's health. Close interaction with the extended family is highly valued. Based on this generalization, the nurse should try to communicate his respect to the husband first as the head of the household and then address the needs of the client.

2. When are generalizations about specific cultural groups (e.g., Mexican-Americans) useful? When are they harmful?

   Generalizations are helpful in understanding behavior, but they should not be used to predict behavior (e.g., the expectation that a person will behave in a certain way because of his/her particular culture). Not all members of a cultural group exhibit the characteristics generally associated with that group. Generalizations become harmful when they lead to stereotypes that result in prejudice and discrimination.

3. If the nurse does not speak Spanish, how should he communicate with the identified client (the mother)? What are the pros and cons of communicating with the mother through the oldest child? When should the nurse seek the services of an interpreter? Why?

The nurse could try to use a few common phrases in Spanish first to establish the intent to communicate with the client directly. If this is not possible, the nurse should seek the services of a medical interpreter to exchange information that is necessary to make an accurate assessment of the client's concerns and the situation. The oldest child may have firsthand experience with the client's condition, and he may want to support his mother. However, it is not appropriate to let the child (or other family members) translate for the mother because of risks in miscommunication due to language and vocabulary difficulties and the need for confidentiality to promote open disclosure of possibly sensitive subjects.

4. A 23-year-old Ukrainian man who speaks only his native language is hospitalized with major depression. The client's treatment plan includes expectations that he is to participate in various activities on the unit. The client refuses to leave his room. What steps can the nurse take to encourage the client to participate in unit activities?

Progress from one-to-one interactions with minimal communication demands to group interactions with appropriate exchange of verbal communications. For example: Sit with the client in his room for a short time and then ask him to come out of the room to get a drink or snack from the kitchen. Suggest two activities and allow him to choose one. Gradually introduce him to another male client around his age, preferably someone who speaks the same language, if possible. Gradually engage him in an activity for two or three people. Use the interpreter to facilitate communication if necessary.

5. Which of the following nonverbal behaviors of an American client most likely communicates openness and honesty to the nurse?

    A. A firm handshake

    B. **Direct eye contact**

    C. A friendly pat on the back

    D. Willingness to sit close

Direct eye contact is expected by Americans; lack of direct eye contact implies dishonesty to many Americans. In general, touch and close physical contact are used by Americans in more intimate settings and may seem inappropriate during conversations with casual contacts.

6. Culturally competent nursing care requires that the nurse have

    A. opportunities to experience cultural differences through travel.

    B. a world view that is tolerant and accepting of cultures.

    C. cultural awareness, knowledge, skills, encounters, and desire.

    D. scientific knowledge of sociocultural theories and concepts.

Sensitivity toward other cultures, which includes tolerance and acceptance of cultural differences, is the basis of delivering culturally competent care. Travel, knowledge, encounters, desire, and simple awareness of different cultures may enhance cultural awareness but will not necessarily promote culturally competent care. Knowledge of theories and concepts also does not assure competent cultural nursing care.

7. If a nurse and a client share the same religious background, the nurse should recognize that

    A. all members of the same religion share similar feelings about their religion.

    B. a shared religious background produces mutual regard for one another.

    C. the same religious beliefs may influence individuals differently.

    D. the differences and commonalities in their beliefs should be discussed.

It would be stereotyping to assume that all members of a specific religion had the same beliefs. Feelings and ideas about religion and spiritual matters may be very diverse, even within a specific culture. Thus, all members of the same religion should be assessed for individual feelings and ideas. Mutual regard does not necessarily follow a shared religious background. Due to boundary issues, the nurse's beliefs are not part of a therapeutic client relationship; it is the client's beliefs that are important.

8. A female Korean client who recently immigrated to the United States is hospitalized for major depression with several suicide attempts. After 2 months of hospitalized treatment, the client is no longer considered suicidal. However, she spends all of her time sitting by herself. She speaks no English and attends no group functions. An interpreter visits every morning to communicate the client's needs to health care staff, and the client takes an active part in treatment plan meetings with the interpreter present. Using this data, the nurse assigns a nursing diagnosis of

    A. self-care deficit.

    B. social isolation.

    C. chronic low self-esteem.

    D. ineffective coping.

This client is socially isolated from other clients and group activities due to a language barrier. There is no data to show that she has a self-care deficit, low self-esteem, or ineffective coping.

Unit 2   Traditional Nonpharmacological Therapies

Chapter 9:   Psychoanalysis, Psychotherapy, and Behavioral Therapy

Contributors: Christina D. Brazier, BSN, RN
Susan Dawson, EdD, RN, APRN-BC

 NCLEX-RN® Connections:

Learning Objective: Review and apply knowledge within **"Psychoanalysis, Psychotherapy, and Behavioral Therapy"** in readiness for performance of the following nursing activities as outlined by the NCLEX-RN® test plan:

Δ   Apply knowledge of basic mental health principles in providing safety, client protection, and a therapeutic environment to clients participating in psychoanalysis, psychotherapy, and cognitive and behavioral therapies.

Δ   Provide and evaluate health teaching related to behavior management.

Δ   Support the client's efforts to participate in group psychotherapy/support groups.

Δ   Collaborate with other health care providers in providing care to clients with mental health needs.

Δ   Evaluate and document the client's response to behavioral management.

 Key Points

Δ   **Psychoanalysis** - Classical psychoanalysis is a therapeutic process of assessing unconscious thoughts/feelings and resolving conflict through talking to an analyst for many sessions and over months to years.

• Due to the length of psychoanalysis therapy and health insurance constraints, classical psychoanalysis is less likely to be used as the sole therapy of choice.

• Psychoanalysis was first developed by Sigmund Freud in order to resolve internal conflicts which, Freud contended, always occur from early childhood experiences.

• Defense mechanisms and past relationships are a common focus for therapy.

Δ   **Psychotherapy** involves more verbal therapist-to-client interaction than classic psychoanalysis.

- A trusting relationship is developed between the client and the therapist in order to explore the client's problems.

- **Cognitive-behavioral therapy**, one type of psychotherapy, is based on the cognitive model, which focuses on individual thoughts and behaviors to solve current problems.

  ◊ There are several approaches to cognitive-behavioral therapy, including cognitive therapy, rational emotive behavior therapy, and rational behavior therapy.

  ◊ Cognitive-behavioral therapy is based on the **cognitive model**, which focuses on individual thoughts and behaviors to solve current problems.

  ◊ Cognitive-behavioral therapy is used to treat depression, anxiety, eating disorders, and other problems that can be improved by changing the client's attitude toward life experiences.

Δ   **Behavioral Therapy**

- In protest of Freud's psychoanalytic theory, behavioral theorists such as Ivan Pavlov, John B. Watson, and B.F. Skinner felt that changing behavior was the key to treating problems such as anxiety and depression.

- Behavioral therapy is based on the theory that behavior is **learned** and has **consequences**. Abnormal behavior results from an attempt to avoid painful feelings. Changing abnormal or maladaptive behavior can occur without the need for insight into the underlying cause.

- Behavioral therapy is successfully used to treat clients with phobias, schizophrenia, addiction, and other problems.

- Behavioral theories are the foundation of behavioral modification programs used in mental health facilities today.

Key Factors

Δ   Both psychoanalysis and psychotherapy use similar therapeutic tools, such as:

- Free association, which is the spontaneous, uncensored verbalization of whatever comes to the client's mind.

- Dream analysis and interpretation.

- The concept of transference, which includes feelings the client has developed toward the therapist related to similar feelings toward significant persons in the client's early childhood.

Δ   Common classifications of psychotherapy include:

- Psychodynamic psychotherapy – utilizes the same tools as psychoanalysis but is oriented more to the client's present state rather than his early life.

- Short-term dynamic psychotherapy – 10 psychotherapy sessions or fewer that are designed for clients who are not severely ill.

- Interpersonal psychotherapy (IPT) – treats clients with specific problems and can improve interpersonal relationships, communication, role-relationship, and bereavement.

- Cognitive therapy – see cognitive-behavioral therapy, below.

Δ   **Use of Cognitive-Behavioral Therapy**

- The trained therapist uses therapeutic communication to change a client's irrational ideas to thoughts and feelings that are more objective and realistic.

- This therapy technique is a time-limited, active, structured, and directive way of helping people to identify distorted thoughts and to evaluate whether or not those thoughts (cognitions) are realistic.

- For example, a client who is depressed may say he is "a bad person" who has "never done anything good" in his life. Through therapy, the person may change his thinking to realize that he may have done some bad things, but he is not "a bad person."

Δ   **Use of Behavioral Therapy**

Behavioral Therapy		
Type	Definition	Use in Mental Health
Modeling	The therapist or others serve as role models for the client, who learns improved behavior by imitation.	Modeling has been used in the acute care milieu to help clients improve interpersonal skills. It has been used to treat phobias by modeling normal behavior to the feared stimuli.
Operant conditioning	Positive rewards are given for positive behavior (positive reinforcement).	Example: Tokens are given to clients for good behavior, and they can be exchanged by the client for a privilege, food, or other item.
Systematic desensitization	This is another type of behavior modification that is used to lessen the phobias of a specific client.	The therapist tailors gradual exposure to a feared situation or object in order to decrease fear and stress.

Behavioral Therapy		
Type	Definition	Use in Mental Health
Aversion therapy	A maladaptive behavior is paired with a punishment or unpleasant stimuli to change the behavior.	A therapist or treatment team may use unpleasant stimuli, such as bitter taste or mild electric shock, as punishment for behaviors such as alcoholism, violent behaviors, self-mutilation, and thumb sucking.
Meditation, guided imagery, diaphragmatic breathing, muscle relaxation, and biofeedback	Various techniques are used to decrease stress and to promote relaxation.	Some of these techniques can be easily taught to nurses and other health professionals to use in both mental health facilities and in general medical situations, such as diaphragmatic breathing for a client having a panic attack or for a female client in labor.

Δ   Specially trained behavioral health nurse practitioners and other advanced practice nurses, social workers, and psychologists with at least a master's degree and specified hours of training and practice may practice psychodynamic psychotherapy, as well as psychoanalysis and the other therapies discussed in this chapter.

Primary Reference:

Varcarolis, E. M., Carson, V. B., & Shoemaker, N. C. (2006). *Foundations of psychiatric mental health nursing: A clinical approach* (5th ed.). St. Louis, MO: Saunders.

Additional Resources:

Beck, J. S. (2006). *Questions & answers about cognitive therapy*. Academy of Cognitive Therapy. Retrieved November 4, 2006, from http://www.academyofct.org

Boyd, M. (2005). *Psychiatric nursing: Contemporary practice* (3rd ed.). Philadelphia: Lippincott Williams & Wilkins.

NANDA International (2004). *NANDA nursing diagnoses: Definitions and classification 2005-2006*. Philadelphia: NANDA.

Chapter 9: Psychoanalysis, Psychotherapy, and Behavioral Therapy

Application Exercises

Scenario: A newly admitted client on an acute locked mental health unit has many behavioral concerns. She refuses to attend group meetings and will not speak to other clients or attend activities on the ward. She enjoys one-to-one visits with staff and requests daily to take a walk out of the building with a staff member. This client's health provider/therapist suggested during a treatment team meeting that behavioral therapy would be an excellent way to change this client's negative behavior, and the client agreed to try to be more cooperative.

1. Explain how behavioral therapy could be used to help this client.

2. List two realistic short-term outcomes that would be appropriate for this client.

3. A client states that he is depressed and anxious because he has had to deal with role reversal with his spouse due to the permanent loss of his job because of a disability. Which of the following therapies would be most beneficial for this client?

      A. Behavioral therapy

      B. Psychoanalysis

      C. Psychodynamic psychotherapy

      D. Interpersonal psychotherapy

4. A client has come to an advanced-practice nurse who practices cognitive therapy. The client's 16-year-old son has run away from home several times in the past year, and the client feels her son's problems are her fault because she feels she is a poor mother. The nurse will use cognitive therapy by

        A. teaching the client meditation to promote relaxation.

        B. helping the client identify and change unrealistic thoughts.

        C. focusing on the client's unconscious thoughts related to her own early childhood.

        D. giving the client rewards for changing her behavior.

5. A client who is depressed will not get out of his bed in an acute care mental health facility. The nurse's best action is to

        A. give positive reinforcement for any activity.

        B. withhold rewards as long as the person stays in bed.

        C. structure the activities of daily living to require the client's active participation.

        D. insist that the client change his attitude and get up.

6. Match each type of therapy with the example that describes its use.

_____ Psychoanalysis	A. Staff gives a client tokens, which can be exchanged for food in a mental health facility store, when she attends group activities.
_____ Cognitive technique	B. The client discusses his dreams with the therapist.
_____ Operant conditioning	C. The client is encouraged to stop sucking his thumb by having a bitter liquid applied to his thumb.
_____ Aversion therapy	D. A client who feels very awkward in group social situations watches a video showing some positive ways to interact in groups.
_____ Modeling	E. A client who displayed violent behavior in the past and felt negative about herself learns to think and speak about herself in more positive terms.

Chapter 9: Psychoanalysis, Psychotherapy, and Behavioral Therapy

Application Exercises Answer Key

Scenario: A newly admitted client on an acute locked mental health unit has many behavioral concerns. She refuses to attend group meetings and will not speak to other clients or attend activities on the ward. She enjoys one-to-one visits with staff and requests daily to take a walk out of the building with a staff member. This client's health provider/therapist suggested during a treatment team meeting that behavioral therapy would be an excellent way to change this client's negative behavior, and the client agreed to try to be more cooperative.

1. Explain how behavioral therapy could be used to help this client.

   Tokens or certificates given in reward for any positive change of behavior could be used to purchase items that this client likes. A larger number of tokens or certificates could be used to walk outside with a staff member. Also, giving positive feedback and encouragement for positive behavior might also help.

2. List two realistic short-term outcomes that would be appropriate for this client.

   The client will attend three group meetings by the end of the week.
   The client will participate in two group activities by the end of the week.

3. A client states that he is depressed and anxious because he has had to deal with role reversal with his spouse due to the permanent loss of his job because of a disability. Which of the following therapies would be most beneficial for this client?

   A. Behavioral therapy

   B. Psychoanalysis

   C. Psychodynamic psychotherapy

   D. Interpersonal psychotherapy

   Interpersonal psychotherapy will assist this client to deal with his anxiety and depression, which has resulted from the interpersonal problem of role change. A behavioral viewpoint would focus on changing the client's behavior. Psychoanalysis and psychodynamic viewpoint would focus on examining unconscious information related to the client's concern.

4. A client has come to an advanced-practice nurse who practices cognitive therapy. The client's 16-year-old son has run away from home several times in the past year, and the client feels her son's problems are her fault because she feels she is a poor mother. The nurse will use cognitive therapy by

> A. teaching the client meditation to promote relaxation.
>
> **B. helping the client identify and change unrealistic thoughts.**
>
> C. focusing on the client's unconscious thoughts related to her own early childhood.
>
> D. giving the client rewards for changing her behavior.

Cognitive therapy assists the client to change irrational or unrealistic cognitions (thoughts) to thoughts that are more realistic. Teaching a relaxation technique or giving a reward for good behavior are types of behavioral therapy. Focusing on unconscious thoughts related to early childhood is a technique of psychoanalysis.

5. A client who is depressed will not get out of his bed in an acute care mental health facility. The nurse's best action is to

> **A. give positive reinforcement for any activity.**
>
> B. withhold rewards as long as the person stays in bed.
>
> C. structure the activities of daily living to require the client's active participation.
>
> D. insist that the client change his attitude and get up.

Giving positive reinforcement is a helpful technique in gradually changing negative behaviors. The other options are negative techniques, which are unlikely to encourage any positive behavior.

6. Match each type of therapy with the example that describes its use.

__B__	Psychoanalysis	A. Staff gives a client tokens, which can be exchanged for food in a mental health facility store, when she attends group activities.
__E__	Cognitive technique	B. The client discusses his dreams with the therapist.
__A__	Operant conditioning	C. The client is encouraged to stop sucking his thumb by having a bitter liquid applied to his thumb.
__C__	Aversion therapy	D. A client who feels very awkward in group social situations watches a video showing some positive ways to interact in groups.
__D__	Modeling	E. A client who displayed violent behavior in the past and felt negative about herself learns to think and speak about herself in more positive terms.

Unit 2   Traditional Nonpharmacological Therapies

Chapter 10:   Group and Family Therapy
Contributor: Christina D. Brazier, BSN, RN

 NCLEX-RN® Connections:

Learning Objective: Review and apply knowledge within "**Group and Family Therapy**" in readiness for performance of the following nursing activities as outlined by the NCLEX-RN® test plan:

Δ   Apply knowledge of basic mental health principles in providing safety, client protection, and a therapeutic environment to the client in group and family therapy.

Δ   Assess the factors that influence the functioning of the client's family.

Δ   Provide and evaluate health teaching related to behavior management.

Δ   Collaborate with other health care providers in providing care to clients with mental health needs.

Δ   Discuss group process, roles for group members and the group leader, and therapeutic factors that operate within groups.

Δ   Evaluate and document the client's response to behavioral/therapeutic interventions.

Δ   Facilitate group and family therapy sessions using behavioral management techniques.

Key Points

Δ   Therapy is an intensive treatment that involves open therapeutic communication with participants who are willing to be involved in therapy.

Δ   Although individual therapy is used as an important treatment for mental illness, group and/or family therapies are also indicated as part of the treatment plan for many clients in a mental health setting.

Δ   **Family Therapy**

•   A family is defined today as a group with reciprocal relationships in which members are committed to each other. Examples of a family vary widely and are often nontraditional, such as a family made up of a child living with her grown brother and his wife.

- Areas of functioning for families include management, boundaries, communication, emotional support, and socialization. Dysfunction can occur in any one or more areas, causing problems within the family.

- The nurse who functions as a family therapist is most likely to be an advanced practice nurse with special training in family therapy theory and techniques.

- Registered nurses work with families to provide teaching. For example, an RN might instruct a family on medication administration or ways to provide symptom management for a family member with a mental health disorder.

- Nurses also work to mobilize family resources, to improve communication, and to strengthen the family's ability to cope with the illness of one member.

Focus and Goals for Individual, Family, and Group Therapies		
Therapy	Focus	Goals
Individual	• Client needs and problems • The therapeutic relationship	• Make more positive individual decisions. • Make productive life decisions. • Develop a strong sense of self.
Family	• Family needs and problems within family dynamics • Improving family functioning	• Provide support for dealing with mental illness within the family. • Improve understanding among family members. • Maximize positive interaction among family members.
Group	• Helping individuals develop more functional and satisfying relations within a group setting	• Goals vary depending on type of group, but generally clients: ◊ Discover that members share some common feelings, experiences, and thoughts. ◊ Experience positive behavior changes as a result of group interaction and feedback.

Δ **Group Therapy**

- Group process is all verbal and nonverbal communication that occurs within the group during group sessions.

- Group norm is the way the group behaves during sessions and, over time, it provides structure for the group. For example, a group norm could be that members raise their hand to be recognized by the leader before they speak. Another norm could be that all members sit in the same places for each session.

- Hidden agenda – Some group members (or the leader) may have goals different than the stated group goals that may disrupt group processes. For example, three members may wish to humiliate another member whom they dislike.

- A subgroup is a small number of people within a larger group who function separately from that group.

- Groups may be open (new members added as old members leave) or closed (no new members added after the group is formed).

- A homogenous group is one in which all members share a certain chosen characteristic (e.g., all members are women or have problems with depression). Membership of heterogeneous groups is not based on a shared chosen personal characteristic. An example of a heterogeneous group is all clients on a given unit, including a mixture of males and females with a wide range of diagnoses.

Key Factors

Δ   All therapy sessions should:

- Provide open and clear communication, guidelines for the therapy session, and cohesiveness.

- Be goal directed.

- Give opportunities to develop interpersonal skills, resolve personal and/or family issues, and develop appropriate, satisfying relationships.

- Assist the client/family to maximize positive interactions, feel empowered to make positive decisions, and strengthen feelings of self-worth.

- Be respectful of all members.

- Make effective use of community support.

- Offer education and support.

Δ   Group therapy goals include:

- Sharing of common feelings and concerns.

- Sharing of stories and experiences.

- Diminishing feelings of isolation.

- Creating a community of healing and restoration.

- Providing a more cost-effective environment than that of individual therapy.

Δ   Group therapy may be used for varying age groups.

- For children, it is in the form of play while talking about a common experience.

- For the adolescent, it is especially valuable due to strong peer relationships in that age group.

- For the older adult, it helps to resocialize and share memories.

Phases of Group Development		
Initial Phase	The purpose and goals of the group are defined.	• The group leader (therapist) sets a tone of respect, trust, and confidentiality among members. • Members become acquainted with each other and with the therapist.
Working Phase	Power and control issues may dominate in this phase.	• The group leader uses therapeutic communication to encourage group work toward meeting goals. • Members take informal roles within the group, which may interfere with, or favor, group progress toward goals.
Mature Phase	The group develops its own norms and themes, and cohesiveness develops.	• The leader must continue to keep group members focused. • Members work as a team despite individual differences. • Work progresses toward objectives.
Termination Phase	This marks the end of group sessions.	• The leader summarizes work of the group and individual contributions. • Members prepare for the group to end and to move on.

Δ   Members of a group can take on any of a number of roles, including:

- Task roles – Members take on various tasks within the group process. An example of a task role is the recorder, who takes notes and/or recalls what has occurred during previous sessions.

- Maintenance roles – Members who take on these roles tend to help maintain the purpose and process of the group. For example, the harmonizer attempts to prevent conflict in the group.

- Individual roles – These roles tend to prevent teamwork, because individuals take on roles to promote their own agenda. Examples include the dominator, who tries to control other members, and the recognition seeker, who boasts about personal achievements.

Δ   Leadership for Various Therapy Groups

•   Leadership styles:

◊   Democratic – This style supports group interaction and decision making to solve problems.

◊   Laissez-faire – The group process progresses without any attempt by the leader to control the direction of the group.

◊   Autocratic – The leader completely controls the direction and structure of the group without allowing group interaction or decision making to solve problems.

•   Appropriate nursing leadership for various types of group therapy:

◊   A registered nurse may lead many types of groups, especially those groups in which a basic knowledge of group processes and of health care teaching is needed. Examples of these include stress management groups, chemical/alcohol dependency and dual diagnosis groups, and medication education groups.

◊   Advanced practice nurses, such as those specializing in cognitive-behavioral therapy, may lead the various types of groups described above and may also have the training to lead psychotherapy groups.

Δ   Characteristics of Families and Family Therapy

•   Families may have healthy (functional) characteristics or they may be dysfunctional in one or more of the areas of functioning. (Refer to the table on the next page.)

Area of Functioning	Healthy Families	Dysfunctional Families
Management	Adults of family agree on issues of power, rule making, how finances will be distributed, plans for the future, etc.	Management may be chaotic, with a child making management decisions at times.
Boundaries	Boundaries are distinguishable between family roles. Clear boundaries define roles of each member and are understood by all. Each family member is able to function well.	Enmeshed boundaries – Thoughts, roles, and feelings are so blended that individual roles are unclear. Rigid boundaries – Rules and roles are completely inflexible. These families tend to form isolated members.
Communication	There are clear, understandable messages between family members, and each member is encouraged to express individual feelings and thoughts.	One or more members use unhealthy patterns, such as: • Manipulating – Members use dishonesty to get what they want. • Distracting – There is no functional problem solving; instead one member inserts irrelevant information. • Blaming – Members blame others to shift focus away from their own inadequacies. • Placating – One member takes responsibility for problems in order to keep peace at all costs.
Emotional/Supportive	Emotional needs of family members are met most of the time, and members are concerned about each other. Conflict and anger do not dominate.	Negative emotions predominate most of time. Members are isolated and afraid and do not show concern for each other.
Socialization	All members interact, plan, and adopt healthy ways of coping. Children learn to function as family members, as well as members of society. Members are able to change as the family grows and matures.	Children who do not learn healthy socialization skills within the family are unable to adapt well to socialization roles of society.

- Other concepts related to family dysfunction include:

  ◊ Scapegoating – A member of the family with little power is blamed for problems within the family. For example, one child who has not completed his chores may be blamed for the entire family not being able to go on an outing.

  ◊ Triangulation – A third party is drawn into the relationship with two members whose relationship is unstable. For example, one parent may become strongly allied with a child, leaving the other parent relatively uninvolved with both.

  ◊ Multigenerational issues – These are emotional issues or themes within a family that continue for at least three generations (e.g., a pattern of addiction when the family is under stress, dysfunctional grief patterns, triangulation patterns, divorce).

- In family therapy, the focus is on the family as a system, rather than on each person as an individual.

Assessment

Δ Family assessments include focused interviews and use of various family assessment tools.

NANDA Nursing Diagnoses

Δ Defensive coping

Δ Interrupted family processes

Δ Readiness for enhanced family processes

Δ Deficient knowledge

Δ Parental role conflict

Δ Impaired parenting

Primary Reference:

Varcarolis, E. M., Carson, V. B., & Shoemaker, N. C. (2006). *Foundations of psychiatric mental health nursing: A clinical approach* (5th ed.). St. Louis, MO: Saunders.

Additional Resources:

Boyd, M. (2005). *Psychiatric nursing: Contemporary practice* (3rd ed.). Philadelphia: Lippincott Williams & Wilkins.

NANDA International (2004). *NANDA nursing diagnoses: Definitions and classification 2005-2006*. Philadelphia: NANDA.

Chapter 10: Group and Family Therapy

Application Exercises

1. A client is diagnosed with bipolar disorder and is active in individual and family therapy. An experienced nurse leads the family therapy session. The client expresses concern that his family does not understand his mental illness. The client's family expresses concern that the client may not be responding to the medication. What educational and therapeutic interventions should the nurse perform for the client and the family?

2. A nurse therapist leading a stress management group is using a democratic leadership style. What does that mean in terms of how the group process will proceed?

3. True or False: An example of a heterogeneous group is one in which all of the members have a history of alcohol abuse.

4. True or False: During the working phase of a group, members tend to challenge the leader and demonstrate other issues of power and control.

5. True or False: An example of an enmeshed family is one in which one member is always blamed for the family's problems.

6. The purpose of a group recently formed on an acute care mental health unit is to teach members self-management skills for their psychotropic medications. Three members of the group have decided that they want the group to plan future activities for the ward and are working hard to accomplish this goal. This is an example of which of the following?

        A. Group norm

        B. Group process

        C. Subgroup

        D. Hidden agenda

7. The teenage son in a family tells the family therapist that he plans ways to make his sister look bad so his parents will think of him as the better sibling. He does this in order to get his own way. This is an example of which of the following?

        A. Placation

        B. Manipulation

        C. Blaming

        D. Distraction

Chapter 10: Group and Family Therapy

Application Exercises Answer Key

1. A client is diagnosed with bipolar disorder and is active in individual and family therapy. An experienced nurse leads the family therapy session. The client expresses concern that his family does not understand his mental illness. The client's family expresses concern that the client may not be responding to the medication. What educational and therapeutic interventions should the nurse perform for the client and the family?

   Provide therapeutic and medication education.
   Assess further as to why the family feels the client is not responding to his medications.
   Address any client and family concerns and fears.
   Investigate and have both the client and family clarify their concerns.
   Help the client and family to find strengths on which to capitalize.
   Provide a nonmanipulative and decentralized communicative environment.
   Provide a safe environment for the client.

2. A nurse therapist leading a stress management group is using a democratic leadership style. What does that mean in terms of how the group process will proceed?

   A democratic leader supports group interaction and the decision making required to solve problems. The group should proceed with all parties feeling that they have input and some control of group decisions.

3. True or False: An example of a heterogeneous group is one in which all of the members have a history of alcohol abuse.

   False: This describes a homogeneous group. A heterogeneous group is one in which membership is not based on any specified shared personal characteristic.

4. True or False: During the working phase of a group, members tend to challenge the leader and demonstrate other issues of power and control.

   True: Power and control issues may dominate during the working phase.

5. True or False: An example of an enmeshed family is one in which one member is always blamed for the family's problems.

False: This example describes a family member who is a scapegoat. An enmeshed family is one in which rules and roles are blurred so that there are no clear distinctions between members.

6. The purpose of a group recently formed on an acute care mental health unit is to teach members self-management skills for their psychotropic medications. Three members of the group have decided that they want the group to plan future activities for the ward and are working hard to accomplish this goal. This is an example of which of the following?

   A. Group norm
   B. Group process
   C. Subgroup
   D. Hidden agenda

A hidden agenda is when some group members have a different goal than the stated group goals; this goal is often kept hidden from the other group members. The group norm is how the group behaves during sessions and over time. Group process is all verbal and nonverbal communication that occurs within the group during group sessions. A subgroup is a small number of people within a larger group who function separately from that group.

7. The teenage son in a family tells the family therapist that he plans ways to make his sister look bad so his parents will think of him as the better sibling. He does this in order to get his own way. This is an example of which of the following?

   A. Placation
   B. Manipulation
   C. Blaming
   D. Distraction

Manipulation refers to control by dishonest influence rather than through open and honest communication. Placation is a way to keep peace in the family. Blaming is done to move the focus to another to prevent being blamed for one's own actions; in this case, it is true that the son is blaming his sister, but he is doing it in order to get what he wants rather than to prevent being blamed himself. Distraction is a way to prevent looking at one's own faults by introducing other issues.

Unit 2 Traditional Nonpharmacological Therapies

Chapter 11: Stress Management

Contributor: Anne W. Ryan, MSN, MPH, RN-BC

 NCLEX-RN® Connections:

> **Learning Objective**: Review and apply knowledge within "**Stress Management**" in readiness for performance of the following nursing activities as outlined by the NCLEX-RN® test plan:
>
> Δ   Assess the client for factors that affect stress level (e.g., doubt, role change, pain, fatigue).
>
> Δ   Apply knowledge of basic mental health principles to plan and implement care for the client experiencing stress.
>
> Δ   Teach and promote stress-management techniques to reduce environmental stressors.
>
> Δ   Support the client's efforts to change and modify behavior.
>
> Δ   Evaluate and document the client's use of techniques to manage stress.

Key Points

Δ   **Stress** is the body's nonspecific response to any demand made upon it.

Δ   **Stressors** are physical or psychological factors that produce stress. Any stressor, whether it is perceived as "good" or "bad," produces the same biological response in the body.

Δ   Individuals need the presence of some stressors to provide interest and purpose to life; however, too much stress or too many stressors can cause distress.

Δ   Anxiety and anger are damaging stressors and cause distress.

Δ   General adaptation syndrome (GAS) is the body's response to an increased demand. This is also known as the "fight or flight" mechanism.

Δ   Stress management is the person's ability to experience appropriate emotions and cope with stress.

Δ   The person who manages stress in a healthy manner is flexible and uses a variety of coping techniques or mechanisms.

Δ   Responses to stress and anxiety are affected by factors such as age, gender, culture, life experiences, and lifestyle.

Δ   Life events, even happy or satisfying events, can cause an extreme amount of stress.

Δ   The effect of stressors is cumulative at any particular time. For example, the death of a family member may cause a high amount of stress. If the person experiencing that stress is also experiencing other stressful events at the same time (e.g., change in sleeping habits, trouble at work, moving to a new home), this could cause illness due to the cumulative effect of those stressors.

Key Factors

Δ   Physical and emotional problems associated with prolonged stress include:

- Chronic pain.

- Heart disease.

- Problems with diabetes control.

- Sleep disturbances.

- Weight gain or loss.

- Decreased ability to concentrate.

- Chronic anxiety.

Δ   Factors increasing a person's resilience or ability to resist the effects of stress include:

- Physical health.

- Strong sense of self.

- Religious or spiritual foundation.

- Optimism.

- Hobbies and other outside interests.

- Satisfying interpersonal relationships.

- Strong social support systems.

- Humor.

Assessment

Δ   Level of stress, as perceived by the client

Δ   Presence of support systems/other coping mechanisms

Δ   Thought patterns, such as having mostly negative thoughts

Δ   Behavioral patterns, such as appearing irritable much of the time

Δ   Energy/activity level, such as fatigue due to a major depressive episode

NANDA Nursing Diagnoses

Δ   Anxiety

Δ   Ineffective coping

Δ   Interrupted family processes

Δ   Fear

Nursing Interventions

Δ   **Cognitive-Behavioral Methods**

- Relaxation techniques

    ◊   Meditation includes formal meditation techniques, as well as prayer for those who believe in a higher power.

    ◊   Guided imagery – A leader guides the client through a series of images to promote relaxation. Images vary depending on the individual. For example, one client might imagine walking on a beach, while another client might imagine himself in a position of success.

    ◊   Breathing exercises are used to slow rapid breathing and promote relaxation.

    ◊   Progressive muscle relaxation (PMR) – A person trained in this method can help a client attain complete relaxation within a few minutes of time.

    ◊   Physical exercise (e.g., yoga, walking, biking) causes release of endorphins that lower anxiety, promote relaxation, and have antidepressant effects.

- Journal writing

    ◊   Journaling has been shown to allow for a therapeutic release of stress.

    ◊   This activity can help the client identify stressors and plan for the future with more hope.

- Cognitive reframing

  ◊ The client is helped to look at irrational cognitions (thoughts) in a more realistic light and to restructure the thoughts in a more positive way.

  ◊ As an example, a client may think he is "a terrible father to my daughter." A health professional, using therapeutic communication techniques, could help the person reframe that thought into a positive thought, such as, "I've made some bad mistakes as a parent, but I've learned from them and have improved my parenting skills."

- Priority restructuring

  ◊ The client learns to prioritize differently to reduce the number of stressors impacting her.

  ◊ For example, a person who is under stress due to feeling overworked might delegate some tasks to others rather than doing them all herself.

- Biofeedback

  ◊ A nurse or other health professional trained in this method can assist the client to gain voluntary control of such autonomic functions as heart rate or blood pressure.

- Assertiveness training

  ◊ The client learns to communicate in a more assertive manner in order to decrease psychological stressors.

  ◊ For example, one technique teaches the client to assert his feelings by describing a situation or behavior that causes stress, stating his feelings about the behavior/situation, and then requesting a change. The client states, "When you keep telling me what to do, I feel angry and frustrated. I need to try making some of my own decisions."

Primary Reference:

Varcarolis, E. M., Carson, V. B., & Shoemaker, N. C. (2006). *Foundations of psychiatric mental health nursing: A clinical approach* (5th ed.). St. Louis, MO: Saunders.

Additional Resources:

NANDA International (2004). *NANDA nursing diagnoses: Definitions and classification 2005-2006*. Philadelphia: NANDA.

Townsend, M. C. (2006). *Psychiatric mental health nursing: Concepts of care in evidence-based practice* (5th ed.). Philadelphia: F.A. Davis.

Chapter 11: Stress Management

Application Exercises

1. True or False: Being under stress is usually viewed as a positive experience, because the outcomes are positive.

2. True or False: Health is positively affected when coping is effective.

3. True or False: Stress responses are similar from one person to another.

Scenario: A client speaking to a nurse in a general medical clinic describes herself as feeling anxious and tired all the time. She cannot understand why, since she is very happy. She recently moved to the area to start a new job for a large corporation. She purchased a new and much larger home for herself and her three children ages 5, 8, and 12. The children were all moved into new schools successfully and are making new friends. The client's family and friends are all back in the previous city where she lived, but she has been so busy with work that she has not had time to phone or write to them. The client states she has not been able to sleep and has lost weight in the 2 months since the move.

---

4. List the stressors that impact this client.

5. What symptoms of increased stress are seen in this client?

6. Describe two stress-relieving activities the nurse could recommend that would not require the client to learn new techniques or see a therapist or specially trained professional.

7. A client says she is experiencing increased stress because her significant other is, "pressuring me and my kids to go live with him. I love him, but I'm not ready to do that." She also states that her significant other, "keeps nagging at my oldest son, which makes me mad, since he's my son after all." Which of the following is a coping strategy that the nurse might suggest for this client?

    A. Learn to reframe the situation.

    B. Use assertiveness techniques.

    C. Exercise regularly.

    D. Rely on the support of your mother.

8. A client who is under a great deal of stress tells the nurse, "I just don't know how to handle all my problems. So many things are going on that I don't do anything about because I'm not sure how to start or what to do." Based on this information, the nurse should plan for a client outcome regarding

    A. decision making.

    B. self-control regarding anxiety.

    C. acceptance of her health status.

    D. ability for self-care.

Chapter 11: Stress Management

Application Exercises Answer Key

1. True or False: Being under stress is usually viewed as a positive experience, because the outcomes are positive.

   False: Being under stress is usually viewed as a negative experience with outcomes that can be either positive or negative.

2. True or False: Health is positively affected when coping is effective.

   True: Ways in which effective coping positively affects health include: management of stress and increased ability to perform daily functions and to develop and maintain interpersonal relationships.

3. True or False: Stress responses are similar from one person to another.

   False: Stress responses vary and are different from person to person. Responses can be affected by factors such as age, gender, culture, life experiences, and lifestyle.

Scenario: A client speaking to a nurse in a general medical clinic describes herself as feeling anxious and tired all the time. She cannot understand why, since she is very happy. She recently moved to the area to start a new job for a large corporation. She purchased a new and much larger home for herself and her three children ages 5, 8, and 12. The children were all moved into new schools successfully and are making new friends. The client's family and friends are all back in the previous city where she lived, but she has been so busy with work that she has not had time to phone or write to them. The client states she has not been able to sleep and has lost weight in the 2 months since the move.

---

4. List the stressors that impact this client.

   **Recent move
   Purchase and move into new and larger home
   Putting three children into new schools
   Sudden decrease of support systems
   New job
   Lack of free time**

5. What symptoms of increased stress are seen in this client?

The client states that she feels anxious and tired all the time. She also has sleep disturbances and has had weight loss.

6. Describe two stress-relieving activities the nurse could recommend that would not require the client to learn new techniques or see a therapist or specially trained professional.

The client could be advised to increase physical exercise by doing things such as walking, swimming, or taking a class in aerobics or yoga. She could also begin to keep a journal. If she has learned meditation techniques in the past, she could try them again now.

7. A client says she is experiencing increased stress because her significant other is, "pressuring me and my kids to go live with him. I love him, but I'm not ready to do that." She also states that her significant other, "keeps nagging at my oldest son, which makes me mad, since he's my son after all." Which of the following is a coping strategy that the nurse might suggest for this client?

    A. Learn to reframe the situation.

    B. Use assertiveness techniques.

    C. Exercise regularly.

    D. Rely on the support of your mother.

Assertiveness techniques would assist this client to make her feelings known and to request a change of behavior without using blaming or other negative communications. Reframing the situation is not appropriate because the stressor does not seem to be caused by irrational thoughts. Exercise and talking to her mother might decrease the client's stress, but they would not change the situation.

8. A client who is under a great deal of stress tells the nurse, "I just don't know how to handle all my problems. So many things are going on that I don't do anything about because I'm not sure how to start or what to do." Based on this information, the nurse should plan for a client outcome regarding

    A. decision making.

    B. self-control regarding anxiety.

    C. acceptance of her health status.

    D. ability for self-care.

This client describes an inability to make decisions; she is experiencing negative feelings about herself and her life due to problems with decision making. The client does seem anxious, but there is no data to show that achieving self-control over anxiety would be beneficial. There is no data to prove relevance for either option C or D.

Unit 2   Traditional Nonpharmacological Therapies

Chapter 12:   Electroconvulsive Therapy

Contributor: Christina D. Brazier, BSN, RN

 NCLEX-RN® Connections:

Learning Objective: Review and apply knowledge within "**Electroconvulsive Therapy**" in readiness for performance of the following nursing activities as outlined by the NCLEX-RN® test plan:

Δ   Apply knowledge of basic mental health principles to plan and implement care for the client receiving electroconvulsive therapy.

Δ   Collaborate with other health care providers in providing care to the client with mental health needs.

Δ   Evaluate and document the client's response to behavioral/therapeutic interventions.

 Key Points

Δ   Electroconvulsive therapy (ECT) is an alternative somatic treatment that has been in use for 60 years and is still administered to 100,000 clients each year in the United States. ECT is the most controversial mental health treatment.

Δ   The exact mechanism of ECT is still unknown, but theories include:

•   ECT may enhance the effects of neurotransmitters in the brain, similar to the effect of tricyclic antidepressants.

•   The antidepressant effect of ECT may be caused by a sudden release of hypothalamic or pituitary hormones.

•   The sudden seizure effect on the brain may produce the benefits.

•   The seizure effect on the frontal lobe affects the client's mood.

Δ   Although some studies have shown that 80% of severely depressed clients demonstrate improvement after ECT, other studies indicate a high relapse rate.

Δ   Side effects of memory loss and confusion are distressing for some clients; however, proper administration of ECT can decrease some of the potential complications while providing important therapeutic effects.

Δ **Indications for ECT** include:

- Severe depression.

    ◊ In clients whose symptoms are not responsive to pharmacologic treatment

    ◊ In clients for whom the risks of other treatments outweigh the risks of ECT, such as clients who are pregnant and in their first trimester

    ◊ In clients who are actively suicidal and for whom there is need for a rapid response

- Certain types of schizophrenia not responsive to neuroleptic medications (e.g., catatonic schizophrenia, schizoaffective disorders).

- Acute manic episodes.

    ◊ In clients who are bipolar with rapid cycling (four or more episodes of acute mania within 1 year) and very destructive behavior. Both of these features tend to respond poorly to lithium therapy. These clients receive ECT and then a regimen of lithium therapy.

Δ The typical course of ECT treatment is three times a week for a total of six to 12 treatments.

Δ **Contraindications for ECT** – There are no absolute contraindications for this therapy if it is deemed necessary to save a client's life. However, some clients may have medical disorders that pose a high risk if ECT is used. These conditions include:

- Recent myocardial infarction.

- History of cerebrovascular accident.

- Cerebrovascular malformation.

- Intracranial mass lesion.

Δ Mental health conditions for which ECT has not been found useful include:

- Developmental disabilities.

- Chemical dependence.

- Personality disorders.

- Situational depression (e.g., a client who is grieving a recent loss).

Key Factors

Δ   Typical ECT Procedure

- The primary health care provider discusses the procedure (including all risks/benefits and a description of the procedure) with the client, and informed consent is obtained.

  ◊   A guardian must give consent for a client who has been judged incompetent. Some clients who have been declared incompetent require a court order.

  ◊   Some facilities require a separate informed consent for anesthesia, which would be obtained by an anesthesia provider.

- A history and physical examination, neurological examination, electrocardiogram (ECG), and laboratory tests (complete blood count and other tests ordered by the primary care provider or per facility protocol) must then be obtained.

- Any medications that affect the client's seizure threshold must be decreased or discontinued several days before the ECT procedure.

- MAOI antidepressants and lithium should be discontinued 2 weeks before the procedure.

- Severe hypertension should be controlled before the procedure, since a short period of hypertension occurs immediately after ECT is performed.

- Any cardiac conditions, such as dysrhythmias, should be monitored and treated before the procedure.

- ECT is performed early in the morning after the client has fasted for 8 to 12 hr.

- An intravenous line is inserted and maintained until full recovery.

- A bite guard should be used to prevent trauma to the oral cavity.

- Prior to the treatment, an anticholinergic such as atropine sulfate is given.

- An anesthesia provider administers a short-acting anesthetic, such as methohexital (Brevital) via IV.

- A muscle relaxant, such as succinylcholine, is then administered.

- Ventilatory assistance is provided, and the client receives 100% oxygen during the procedure; in addition, cardiac status, blood pressure, pulse oximetry, and pulse rate are monitored.

- Electrodes are applied to the scalp, either unilaterally or bilaterally. The exact number and placement of electrodes is decided by the mental health provider.

- A cuff is placed on one leg or arm to block the muscle relaxant so that seizure activity can be monitored in the limb distal to the cuff.

- The electrical stimulus dose is applied and seizure activity is monitored; the duration of the seizure is noted. Duration is usually 25 to 60 sec.

- After seizure activity has ceased, the anesthetic is stopped.

- When the client's condition warrants, the client is transferred to a recovery area where level of consciousness, cardiac status, vital signs, and oxygen saturation via pulse oximetry continue to be monitored.

- The client is usually awake and ready to transfer back to his regular mental health unit or other facility within 30 to 60 min after the procedure.

Δ Complications during and immediately following the procedure may include:

- Reactions to the anesthesia.

- Periods of apnea or airway obstruction and low oxygen saturation.

- ECG changes, such as heart rate and blood pressure changes. The baseline heart rate is expected to increase by 25% during the procedure and early recovery. Blood pressure may initially fall and then rise during the procedure. The elevated blood pressure should resolve shortly after the termination of the treatment.

- A temporary increase in intracranial pressure occurring immediately following the electrical stimulus.

- Headache, muscle soreness, and nausea occurring during and following the immediate recovery period.

- Confusion and short-term memory loss. Memory loss of longer duration, for weeks or months following the procedure, may also occur and may include:

  ◊ Retrograde amnesia (loss of memory of past events).

  ◊ Anterograde amnesia (inability to retain new memories).

Assessment

Δ The nurse assesses/monitors the client's vital signs and mental status before and after the ECT procedure.

Δ The nurse also assesses/monitors the client/family's understanding and knowledge of the procedure and provides teaching as necessary for both the client and the family.

NANDA Nursing Diagnoses

Δ Acute confusion

Δ Risk for injury

Δ Impaired memory

Nursing Interventions

Δ   The nurse assists with necessary teaching prior to and following informed consent being obtained by the mental health care provider.

Δ   The nurse continues to provide active listening and therapeutic communication prior to the procedure and during the course of ECT treatments.

Δ   The nurse who works in the ECT procedure area must be familiar with the procedure, with care for the client before, during, and after anesthesia, with cardiac and other monitoring, and with emergency procedures.

Δ   The nurse and other health care professionals must be ready to handle immediate adverse reactions, such as cardiac dysrhythmias.

Δ   During the recovery phase, the nurse needs to orient and reorient the client frequently, because confusion and short-term memory loss are common at this time.

Δ   The nurse on the inpatient acute care mental health unit should continue to monitor the client's vital signs as indicated and to monitor the client's mental status for memory loss.

Primary Reference:

Varcarolis, E. M., Carson, V. B., & Shoemaker, N. C. (2006). *Foundations of psychiatric mental health nursing: A clinical approach* (5th ed.). St. Louis, MO: Saunders.

Additional Resources:

Boyd, M. A. (2005). *Psychiatric nursing contemporary practice* (3rd ed.). Philadelphia: Lippincott Williams & Wilkins.

Mental Health America. (n.d.). *Electroconvulsive therapy (ECT)*. Retrieved November 12, 2006, from http://www.nmha.org/index.cfm?objectid=C7DF9906-1372-4D20-C8EFA62F651308AE

NANDA International (2004). *NANDA nursing diagnoses: Definitions and classification 2005-2006*. Philadelphia: NANDA.

New York State Office of Mental Health. (2004, January 20). *Electroconvulsive therapy review guidelines*. Retrieved November 12, 2006, from http://www.omh.state.ny.us/omhweb/ect/guidelines.htm

Chapter 12: Electroconvulsive Therapy

Application Exercises

Scenario: A client who has major depression and has not responded to antidepressive medications is admitted to an acute care mental health facility to receive several treatments of ECT. The client is voluntarily receiving ECT, but the client and his family have concerns regarding the treatment.

1. List care to be provided for the client and the client's family.

2. The client's family says, "We hear that people are really confused after ECT. Why should he have this treatment if he'll act like he has Alzheimer's afterward?" How should the nurse reply?

3. For which of the following should the nurse monitor during or immediately following ECT therapy? (Select all that apply.)

   _____ Hypotension or hypertension

   _____ Heart rate changes

   _____ Intestinal obstruction

   _____ Confusion

   _____ Nausea

4. Which of the following is a possible indication for ECT?

   A. Severe borderline personality disorder

   B. Depression and thoughts of suicide caused by the recent loss of a significant other

   C. Bipolar disorder with mania that has occurred six times in the past year

   D. Chronic paranoid schizophrenia and a moderate developmental disability

5. True or False: Retrograde amnesia may be present for weeks or months after a course of ECT ends.

6. True or False: A course of anticonvulsant medication is typically prescribed for a client several days prior to an ECT treatment.

Chapter 12: Electroconvulsive Therapy

Application Exercises Answer Key

Scenario: A client who has major depression and has not responded to antidepressive medications is admitted to an acute care mental health facility to receive several treatments of ECT. The client is voluntarily receiving ECT, but the client and his family have concerns regarding the treatment.

1. List care to be provided for the client and the client's family.

> **Assess the client's medical history.**
> **Collaborate with the mental health care provider regarding specific teaching for the ECT procedure as it applies to this client.**
> **Explain adverse reactions of the procedure to the client and family in short, easy-to-understand explanations.**
> **Be consistent when explaining procedures.**
> **Guide and teach the client and family on the orientation and reorientation process.**
> **Educate the client and family on safety precautions and maintenance of self-care needs.**
> **Listen to the client/family's concerns and fears.**
> **Help the client and the family to make and adhere to schedules for future ECT appointments.**

2. The client's family says, "We hear that people are really confused after ECT. Why should he have this treatment if he'll act like he has Alzheimer's afterward?" How should the nurse reply?

> **The person who has ECT is usually confused only for a short time immediately following the procedure. There may be some longer-term memory loss for a few weeks afterward, but it is not at all like that associated with Alzheimer's disease. The health care team members will be reorienting the client both in the recovery room and on the mental health unit, and the mental health care provider will be informed of any mental status effects from the procedure.**

3. For which of the following should the nurse monitor during or immediately following ECT therapy? (Select all that apply.)

   X   **Hypotension or hypertension**

   X   **Heart rate changes**

   _____   Intestinal obstruction

   X   **Confusion**

   X   **Nausea**

All of the above may potentially occur during or following ECT, with the exception of intestinal obstruction, which should not occur with this procedure.

4. Which of the following is a possible indication for ECT?

   A. Severe borderline personality disorder

   B. Depression and thoughts of suicide caused by the recent loss of a significant other

   C. Bipolar disorder with mania that has occurred six times in the past year

   D. Chronic paranoid schizophrenia and a moderate developmental disability

The client with bipolar disorder, rapid cycling, and destructive mania is a possible candidate for ECT. Clients who are not usually good candidates for ECT include those with personality disorders, situational depression, chemical dependency, or a developmental disability.

5. True or False: Retrograde amnesia may be present for weeks or months after a course of ECT ends.

True: The client may experience memory loss of past events following ECT.

6. True or False: A course of anticonvulsant medication is typically prescribed for a client several days prior to an ECT treatment.

False: The nurse could expect that any anticonvulsant medication the client might be taking would be decreased or discontinued prior to beginning ECT treatment, because it is necessary for the client to sustain a seizure during the treatment.

Unit 3   Psychopharmacological Therapies

Chapter 13:   Medications to Treat Anxiety Disorders

Contributor: Judith A. Harris, MSN, RNC

 NCLEX-RN® Connections:

Learning Objective: Review and apply knowledge within "**Medications to Treat Anxiety Disorders**" in readiness for performance of the following nursing activities as outlined by the NCLEX-RN® test plan:

Δ   Apply knowledge of mental health when caring for the client receiving psychopharmacological therapy for a mental health disorder.

Δ   Assess the client for expected and side/adverse effects of antianxiety medications.

Δ   Assess the client for actual/potential specific food-medication interactions.

Δ   Identify contraindications, actual/potential incompatibilities, and interactions between medications. Intervene appropriately.

Δ   Identify symptoms/evidence of an allergic reaction and respond appropriately.

Δ   Evaluate/monitor and document the therapeutic and adverse/side effects of antianxiety medications.

Δ   Provide client teaching on actions, therapeutic effects, potential side/adverse effects, and interactions of antianxiety medications.

 Key Points

Δ   The **major medications** used to treat anxiety disorders include:

•   The benzodiazepine **anxiolytics** – diazepam (Valium), alprazolam (Xanax), lorazepam (Ativan), chlordiazepoxide (Librium), oxazepam (Serax), and clonazepam (Klonopin).

•   Buspirone (BuSpar) – a nonbarbiturate anxiolytic.

•   Many of the **antidepressant medications**. (*Refer to chapter 14, Medications to Treat Mood Disorders: Depression.*) These include:

◊   Paroxetine (Paxil), an SSRI.

◊   Amitriptyline (Elavil), a tricyclic antidepressant (TCA).

◊   Phenelzine (Nardil), a monoamine oxidase inhibitor (MAOI).

◊   Venlafaxine (Effexor), a serotonin-norepinephrine reuptake inhibitor.

- Other classes of medications used to treat anxiety disorders include:

    ◊ **Antihistamines**, such as hydroxyzine (Vistaril).

    ◊ **Beta blockers**, such as propranolol (Inderal).

    ◊ **Anticonvulsants**, such as gabapentin (Neurontin).

Therapeutic Agents

△ **Diazepam (Valium)**: Sedative Hypnotic Anxiolytic – Benzodiazepine

- **Expected pharmacological action**

    ◊ This medication enhances the inhibitory effects of gamma-aminobutyric acid (GABA) in the central nervous system (CNS).

- **Therapeutic uses**

    ◊ Anxiety disorders, including panic disorder, social phobia, obsessive-compulsive disorder, generalized anxiety disorder, and posttraumatic stress disorder

    ◊ Seizure disorders

    ◊ Insomnia

    ◊ Muscle spasm

    ◊ Alcohol withdrawal (for prevention and treatment of acute symptoms)

    ◊ Induction of anesthesia

Side/Adverse Effects	Nursing Interventions/Client Education
CNS depression, such as sedation, light-headedness, ataxia, and decreased cognitive function	• Advise the client to observe for symptoms. Instruct the client to notify the primary care provider if symptoms occur. • Advise the client to avoid hazardous activities (e.g., driving, operating heavy equipment/machinery).
Anterograde amnesia – difficulty recalling events that occur after dosing	• Advise the client to observe for symptoms. Instruct the client to notify the primary care provider and stop the medication if symptoms occur.
Paradoxical response (e.g., insomnia, excitation, euphoria, anxiety, rage)	• Advise the client to observe for symptoms. Instruct the client to notify the primary care provider and stop the medication if symptoms occur.
Withdrawal symptoms, which occur infrequently with short-term use, such as anxiety, insomnia, diaphoresis, tremors, and light-headedness	• Advise the client who has been taking diazepam regularly and in high doses to taper the dose over several weeks.

Side/Adverse Effects	Nursing Interventions/Client Education
Acute toxicity/overdose • Oral toxicity (drowsiness, lethargy, confusion) • IV toxicity (respiratory depression, stupor, coma)	• For oral toxicity, gastric lavage can be used, followed by the administration of activated charcoal or saline cathartics. • For IV toxicity, administer flumazenil (Romazicon) to counteract sedation and reverse side effects. • Monitor the client's vital signs, maintain a patent airway, and provide fluids to maintain blood pressure. • Have resuscitation equipment available.

- **Contraindications/precautions**
  - ◊ Diazepam is a Pregnancy Risk Category D medication.
  - ◊ Benzodiazepines are classified under Schedule IV of the Controlled Substances Act.
  - ◊ Diazepam is contraindicated in clients with sleep apnea and/or respiratory depression.
  - ◊ Use diazepam cautiously in clients with substance abuse and liver disease.

Medication/Food Interactions	Nursing Interventions/Client Education
• CNS depressants (e.g., alcohol, barbiturates, opioids) • High risk of respiratory depression when two CNS depressants are taken concurrently	• Advise the client to observe for symptoms. Instruct the client to notify the primary care provider if symptoms occur. • Advise the client to avoid hazardous activities (e.g., driving, operating heavy equipment/machinery).

- **Therapeutic nursing interventions and client education**
  - ◊ Advise the client to take the medication as prescribed and to **avoid abrupt discontinuation of treatment** to prevent withdrawal symptoms.
  - ◊ When discontinuing benzodiazepines that have been taken regularly for long periods and in higher doses, taper the dose over several weeks.
  - ◊ Administer the medication with meals.
  - ◊ Advise the client to swallow sustained-released tablets and to avoid chewing or crushing the tablets.
  - ◊ Inform the client about the possible development of dependency during and after treatment and to notify the primary care provider if symptoms occur.

Δ   **Buspirone (BuSpar)**: Nonbarbiturate Anxiolytic

- **Expected pharmacological action**

    ◊   The exact antianxiety mechanism of this medication is unknown. This medication does bind to serotonin and dopamine receptors. There is no potential for abuse, and use of buspirone does not result in sedation or potentiate the effects of other CNS depressants.

- **Therapeutic uses**

    ◊   Long-term management of anxiety disorders

    ◊   Treatment of general anxiety disorder (GAD)

Side/Adverse Effects	Nursing Interventions/Client Education
CNS effects (e.g., dizziness, nausea, headache, light-headedness, agitation)	This medication does not interfere with activities, because it does not cause sedation.

- **Contraindications/precautions**

    ◊   Buspirone is not recommended for use in nursing mothers.

    ◊   Use buspirone cautiously in older adult clients and clients with liver and/or renal dysfunction.

    ◊   Buspirone is contraindicated for concurrent use with MAOI antidepressants or for 14 days after MAOIs are discontinued. Hypertensive crisis may result.

Medication/Food Interactions	Nursing Interventions/Client Education
Increase in the effects of buspirone with the concurrent use of erythromycin, ketoconazole, grapefruit juice	• Advise the client to avoid the use of these antimicrobial agents. • Advise the client to avoid drinking grapefruit juice.

- **Therapeutic nursing interventions and client education**

    ◊   Advise the client to take the medication with meals to prevent gastric irritation.

    ◊   Advise the client that effects do not occur rapidly and may take **a week** to start, and several more for the full benefit to be felt.

    ◊   This medication should not be used when rapid results are needed or on a PRN basis.

Δ **Paroxetine (Paxil)**: Nonbarbiturate Anxiolytic – SSRI

- **Expected pharmacological action**
  - ◊ Paroxetine selectively inhibits serotonin reuptake, allowing more serotonin to stay at the junction of the neurons.
  - ◊ It does not block uptake of dopamine or norepinephrine.
  - ◊ Paroxetine produces CNS excitation rather than sedation.
  - ◊ The medication has a long effective half-life; about 4 weeks is necessary to produce therapeutic medication levels

- **Therapeutic uses**
  - ◊ Generalized anxiety disorder (GAD)
  - ◊ Panic disorder – decreases both the frequency and intensity of panic attacks and also prevents anticipatory anxiety about attacks
  - ◊ Obsessive-compulsive disorder (OCD) – reduces symptoms by increasing serotonin
  - ◊ Social phobia
  - ◊ Posttraumatic stress disorder
  - ◊ Depressive disorders

Side/Adverse Effects	Nursing Interventions/Client Education
Early adverse effects (first few days/weeks): nausea, diaphoresis, tremor, fatigue, drowsiness	• Advise the client that these effects should soon subside. • Instruct the client to report symptoms to the primary care provider. • Instruct the client to take the medication as prescribed.
Later adverse effects (after 5 to 6 weeks of therapy): sexual dysfunction (e.g., impotence, delayed or absent orgasm, delayed or absent ejaculation, decreased sexual interest), weight gain, headache	• Instruct the client to report problems with sexual function (may be managed with dose reduction, medication holiday, changing medications).
Serotonin syndrome • Agitation, confusion, disorientation, anxiety, hallucinations, hyperreflexia, fever, diaphoresis • Usually begins 2 to 72 hr after initiation of treatment (especially if combined with MAOI) • Resolves when the medication is discontinued	• Watch for and advise the client to report any of these symptoms, which could indicate a lethal problem. • Avoid the use of SSRIs with MAOI antidepressants.

Side/Adverse Effects	Nursing Interventions/Client Education
Extrapyramidal symptoms (rare) • Akathisia (restlessness, agitation) • Parkinsonian reactions • Dystonias – altered muscle tone (e.g., severe spasms of the upper body, back, eyes) • Tardive dyskinesia (involuntary twisting, writhing, worm-like movements of the tongue and face)	• Advise the client to watch for extrapyramidal reactions and report them to the primary care provider.
Withdrawal syndrome • Nausea, sensory disturbances, anxiety, tremor, dysphoria (e.g., malaise, unease) • Minimized by tapering the medication slowly	• Advise the client that, after a long period of use, the medication will be tapered slowly to avoid withdrawal symptoms. • The client should not discontinue use abruptly and should seek the advice of the primary care provider.
Bruxism: grinding and clenching of teeth, usually during sleep	• Bruxism should be reported to the primary care provider, who may: ◊ Switch the client to another class of medication. ◊ Treat bruxism with low-dose buspirone. ◊ Advise the client to use a mouth guard during sleep.

- **Contraindications/precautions**

  ◊ Paroxetine is contraindicated in clients taking MAOIs.

  ◊ Clients taking paroxetine should avoid alcohol.

  ◊ Use paroxetine cautiously in clients with liver and renal dysfunction, seizure disorders, or a history of gastrointestinal bleeding.

Medication/Food Interactions	Nursing Interventions/Client Education
Can cause serotonin syndrome when taken concurrently with MAOI antidepressants	Educate the client about this combination.

- **Therapeutic nursing interventions and client education**

  ◊ Instruct the client to report problems with sexual function (may be managed with dose reduction, medication holiday, changing medications).

  ◊ Advise the client to restrict calories and get exercise to minimize weight gain.

  ◊ Instruct the client to report bruxism (may be managed by changing medications, use of a mouthguard, administration of buspirone).

Nursing Evaluation of Medication Effectiveness

Δ   Effectiveness is evidenced by improvement in condition or easing of symptoms without occurrence of major side effects.

- Absence of panic attacks
- Decrease or absence of anxiety
- Normal sleep pattern, feeling rested
- Decreased muscle tension
- Increased ability to concentrate and stay focused
- Improvement in ability to participate in social and occupational interactions

Primary Reference:

Varcarolis, E. M., Carson, V. B., & Shoemaker, N. C. (2006). *Foundations of psychiatric mental health nursing: A clinical approach* (5th ed.). St. Louis, MO: Saunders.

Additional Resources:

Lehne, R. A. (2007). *Pharmacology for nursing care* (6th ed.). St. Louis, MO: Saunders.

NANDA International (2004). *NANDA nursing diagnoses: Definitions and classification 2005-2006*. Philadelphia: NANDA.

Chapter 13: Medications to Treat Anxiety Disorders

Application Exercises

1. A client has been prescribed diazepam (Valium) for generalized anxiety disorder. The client had originally told her primary care provider that she took no other medications. However, before leaving the clinic, she says to the nurse, "Oh, I forgot that I do take a sleeping pill at night for insomnia, and I also usually drink a glass of wine before bedtime to make sure I sleep." What should be the nurse's concerns about this information, and what interventions are necessary?

2. Which of the following is an antidote for benzodiazepine overdose or toxicity?

    A. Buspirone (BuSpar)

    B. Hydroxyzine (Vistaril)

    C. Flumazenil (Romazicon)

    D. Naloxone (Narcan)

3. A nurse knows that teaching has been effective if a client who is taking a benzodiazepine for long-term treatment of anxiety says,

    A. "I will only take the medication at bedtime."

    B. "I cannot take this drug if I am using a pain medication."

    C. "I will not stop taking the drug abruptly."

    D. "I will need to take this medication the rest of my life."

4. Buspirone is different from other antianxiety medications in that it

    A. has anticonvulsant effects.

    B. has muscle relaxant effects.

    C. will depress the central nervous system.

    D. does not cause physical or psychological dependence.

5. A client has been taking buspirone for 3 days for an anxiety disorder. He calls the community mental health facility and tells the nurse that the medication has not helped him to sleep at all and that he is still feeling anxious. How should the nurse reply?

6. A client has been taking paroxetine (Paxil) to treat an anxiety disorder for several weeks. The client calls the nurse to say that he has been grinding his teeth during the night, which causes pain in his mouth and insomnia for his wife. Which of the following measures may be used to manage bruxism (teeth grinding)? (Select all that apply.)

_____ Concurrent administration of buspirone

_____ Administration of a different SSRI

_____ Use of a mouth guard

_____ Changing to a different class of antianxiety medication

_____ Increasing the dose of paroxetine

Chapter 13: Medications to Treat Anxiety Disorders

Application Exercises Answer Key

1. A client has been prescribed diazepam (Valium) for generalized anxiety disorder. The client had originally told her primary care provider that she took no other medications. However, before leaving the clinic, she says to the nurse, "Oh, I forgot that I do take a sleeping pill at night for insomnia, and I also usually drink a glass of wine before bedtime to make sure I sleep." What should be the nurse's concerns about this information, and what interventions are necessary?

    Taking a benzodiazepine concurrently with other CNS agonists, including alcohol, can cause an overdose marked by increased sedation, lack of coordination, and confusion. Report this information to the primary care provider after telling the client that the information she mentioned is important information that should be known.

2. Which of the following is an antidote for benzodiazepine overdose or toxicity?

    A. Buspirone (BuSpar)

    B. Hydroxyzine (Vistaril)

    C. Flumazenil (Romazicon)

    D. Naloxone (Narcan)

    Flumazenil is a benzodiazepine receptor antagonist, which specifically reverses an overdose of benzodiazepines. Buspirone is a nonbarbiturate anxiolytic, and hydroxyzine is an antihistamine used for anxiety disorders. Naloxone is an opioid antagonist used to reverse an overdose of opioids, such as morphine sulfate.

3. A nurse knows that teaching has been effective if a client who is taking a benzodiazepine for long-term treatment of anxiety says,

    A. "I will only take the medication at bedtime."

    B. "I cannot take this drug if I am using a pain medication."

    C. "I will not stop taking the drug abruptly."

    D. "I will need to take this medication the rest of my life."

    Abrupt discontinuation of a benzodiazepine that the client has been taking for some time may cause withdrawal symptoms. The medication may need to be tapered for several weeks before discontinuing. The other options are not true about benzodiazepine therapy.

4. Buspirone is different from other antianxiety medications in that it

    A. has anticonvulsant effects.

    B. has muscle relaxant effects.

    C. will depress the central nervous system.

    D. does not cause physical or psychological dependence.

Buspirone does not affect the CNS in the same way as do benzodiazepines. It does not cause dependence or tolerance, does not have anticonvulsant or muscle relaxant effects, and does not promote drowsiness.

5. A client has been taking buspirone for 3 days for an anxiety disorder. He calls the community mental health facility and tells the nurse that the medication has not helped him to sleep at all and that he is still feeling anxious. How should the nurse reply?

The initial response to buspirone takes 1 week, but it may take several weeks to reach its therapeutic peak. The medication has no hypnotic effect, so it does not promote sleep. Try nonmedication measures to promote sleep (e.g., warm bath, soothing music, avoiding caffeine and alcohol before bedtime).

6. A client has been taking paroxetine (Paxil) to treat an anxiety disorder for several weeks. The client calls the nurse to say that he has been grinding his teeth during the night, which causes pain in his mouth and insomnia for his wife. Which of the following measures may be used to manage bruxism (teeth grinding)? (Select all that apply.)

    __X__   **Concurrent administration of buspirone**

    _____   Administration of a different SSRI

    __X__   **Use of a mouth guard**

    __X__   **Changing to a different class of antianxiety medication**

    _____   Increasing the dose of paroxetine

Concurrent administration of buspirone, use of a mouth guard, or changing to a different class of antianxiety medication are all ways to manage bruxism. Any SSRI may cause bruxism, so changing to another SSRI will not be effective. Increasing the dose of paroxetine would also not stop the problem.

Unit 3   Psychopharmacological Therapies

Chapter 14:   Medications to Treat Mood Disorders: Depression
Contributor: Judith A. Harris, MSN, RNC

 NCLEX-RN® Connections:

Learning Objective: Review and apply knowledge within "**Medications to Treat Mood Disorders: Depression**" in readiness for performance of the following nursing activities as outlined by the NCLEX-RN® test plan:

Δ   Apply knowledge of mental health when caring for the client receiving psychopharmacological therapy for depression.

Δ   Assess the client for expected and side/adverse effects of antidepressant medications.

Δ   Assess the client for actual/potential specific food-medication interactions.

Δ   Identify contraindications, actual/potential incompatibilities, and interactions between medications. Intervene appropriately.

Δ   Identify symptoms/evidence of an allergic reaction and respond appropriately.

Δ   Evaluate/monitor and document the therapeutic and adverse/side effects of antidepressant medications.

Δ   Provide client teaching on actions, therapeutic effects, potential side/adverse effects, and interactions of antidepressant medications.

 Key Points

Δ   Antidepressants used for treating depression include:

•   **Selective serotonin reuptake inhibitors (SSRIs)**, which are now considered first choice for depression. Therapeutic agents include:

◊   Fluoxetine (Prozac).

◊   Citalopram (Celexa).

◊   Escitalopram oxalate (Lexapro).

◊   Paroxetine (Paxil).

◊   Sertraline (Zoloft).

- **Tricyclic antidepressants (TCAs)**, which are the oldest class of antidepressants and are still prescribed for depressive disorders fairly frequently. Therapeutic agents include:

  ◊ Amitriptyline (Elavil).

  ◊ Imipramine (Tofranil).

  ◊ Doxepin (Sinequan).

  ◊ Nortriptyline (Aventyl).

- **Monoamine oxidase inhibitors (MAOIs)**, which are now considered second- or third-choice medications for depression due to their many adverse effects and food-medication interactions. Therapeutic agents include:

  ◊ Phenelzine (Nardil).

  ◊ Isocarboxazid (Marplan).

  ◊ Tranylcypromine (Parnate).

- **Atypical antidepressants**. Mechanisms include:

  ◊ Inhibiting dopamine uptake – bupropion (Wellbutrin).

  ◊ Inhibiting reuptake of serotonin and norepinephrine – venlafaxine (Effexor).

  ◊ Increasing release of serotonin and norepinephrine – mirtazapine (Remeron).

  ◊ Selectively inhibiting norepinephrine reuptake – reboxetine (not yet approved in the U.S.).

  ◊ Inhibiting moderate, selective reuptake of serotonin – trazodone (Desyrel).

Δ Clients starting antidepressant medication therapy for depression need to be advised that symptom relief can take **1 to 3 weeks** and possibly **2 to 3 months** for full benefits to be achieved (depending on the specific medication). Encourage continued compliance.

Δ Clients with major depression may require hospitalization with close observation and suicide precautions until the antidepressant medications reach their peak effects.

Therapeutic Agents

Δ **Fluoxetine (Prozac)**: SSRI

- **Expected pharmacological action**

  ◊ Fluoxetine selectively blocks reuptake of the monoamine neurotransmitter serotonin in the synaptic space, thereby intensifying the effects that can be produced.

- **Therapeutic uses**

  ◊ Depressive disorders

  ◊ Anxiety disorders including panic disorder, social phobia, obsessive-compulsive disorder, generalized anxiety disorder, and posttraumatic stress disorder

  ◊ Bulimia nervosa

Side/Adverse Effects	Nursing Interventions/Client Education
Sexual dysfunction (e.g., absent orgasm, impotence, decreased libido)	• Warn the client of possible side effects and to notify the primary care provider if the effects are intolerable. • Strategies to manage sexual dysfunction may include lowering the dosage, discontinuing medication temporarily (medication holiday), and using adjunct medications to increase sexual function (e.g., sildenafil [Viagra] and buspirone [BuSpar]). • Switch to an atypical antidepressant with fewer sexual dysfunction side effects (e.g., bupropion [Wellbutrin] and nefazodone [Serzone]).
Weight gain	• Monitor the client's weight gain. • Encourage the client to participate in regular exercise and to follow a healthy, low-calorie diet.
Serotonin syndrome (symptoms beginning 2 to 72 hr after starting treatment): • Mental confusion • Agitation • Anxiety • Hallucinations • Hyperreflexia • Fever • Tremors	• Advise the client to observe for symptoms. Instruct the client to notify the primary care provider and stop the medication if symptoms occur.
Withdrawal syndrome: • Headache • Nausea • Visual disturbances • Anxiety	• Instruct the client to taper the dose gradually when discontinuing the medication.
Hyponatremia – more likely in older adult clients taking diuretics	• Obtain baseline serum sodium and monitor the level periodically throughout treatment.

Side/Adverse Effects	Nursing Interventions/Client Education
Rash	• Rashes can be treated with an antihistamine or withdrawal of medication.
Sleepiness, faintness, light-headedness	• Advise the client that these side effects are not common, but they can occur. • The client should avoid driving if these side effects occur.

- **Contraindications/precautions**

    ◊ Fluoxetine is contraindicated for clients taking MAOIs.

    ◊ Use this medication cautiously in clients with liver and renal dysfunction, cardiac disease, seizure disorders, diabetes, ulcers, or a history of gastrointestinal bleeding.

Medication/Food Interactions	Nursing Interventions/Client Education
MAOIs increase the risk of serotonin syndrome.	• The client should not be administered an MAOI while taking fluoxetine. MAOIs should be discontinued for 14 days prior to starting an SSRI. If already taking fluoxetine, the client should wait 5 weeks before starting an MAOI.
Warfarin (Coumadin) – Fluoxetine can displace warfarin from bound protein and result in increased warfarin levels.	• Monitor the client's PT and INR levels. • Assess the client for signs of bleeding. • A dosage adjustment may be required.
TCAs and lithium – Fluoxetine can increase the levels of these medications.	• Concurrent use is not recommended.
NSAIDs and anticoagulants – Fluoxetine suppresses platelet aggregation and thus increases the risk of bleeding when used concurrently with these medications.	• Advise the client to monitor for signs of bleeding (e.g., bruising, hematuria) and to notify the primary care provider if they occur.

- **Therapeutic nursing interventions and client education**

    ◊ Advise the client to take the medication with meals/food and to take the medication on a daily basis to establish therapeutic plasma levels.

    ◊ Assist the client with medication regimen compliance by informing the client that therapeutic effects may not be experienced for **1 to 3 weeks** and that it might take **2 to 3 months** for full benefits to be achieved.

    ◊ Instruct the client to continue therapy after improvement in symptoms. Sudden discontinuation of the medication can result in relapse.

    ◊ Advise the client that therapy usually continues for 6 months after resolution of symptoms and may continue for 1 year or longer.

    ◊ Older adult clients taking diuretics should be monitored for sodium levels. Obtain baseline sodium levels and monitor periodically.

Δ   **Amitriptyline (Elavil)**: TCA

• **Expected pharmacological action**

◊ Amitriptyline blocks reuptake of the monoamine neurotransmitters norepinephrine and serotonin in the synaptic space, thereby intensifying the effects that they produce.

• **Therapeutic uses**

◊ Depressive disorders

◊ Depressive episodes of bipolar disorders

Side/Adverse Effects	Nursing Interventions/Client Education
Orthostatic hypotension	• Instruct the client about the signs of postural hypotension (light-headedness, dizziness). Advise the client to sit or lie down if these occur. Orthostatic hypotension can be minimized by getting up slowly. • Take orthostatic blood pressures, waiting at least 1 min between lying down and sitting or standing. If a significant change in BP and HR is noted, withhold the medication and notify the primary care provider.
Anticholinergic effects: • Dry mouth • Blurred vision • Photophobia • Acute urinary retention • Constipation • Tachycardia	• Instruct the client on ways to minimize anticholinergic effects. • Advise the client to chew sugarless gum, eat foods high in fiber, and increase water intake to at least 6 to 8 glasses (8 oz) of water/day. • Teach the client to monitor HR and report noteworthy increases. • Advise the client to notify the primary care provider if symptoms are intolerable.
Cardiac toxicity (usually only at excessive dosing)	• Obtain the client's baseline ECG and monitor ECG during treatment.
Sedation	• This side effect usually diminishes over time. • Advise the client to avoid hazardous activities, such as driving, if sedation is excessive. • Advise the client to take the medication at bedtime to minimize daytime sleepiness and to promote sleep.
Toxicity evidenced by dysrhythmias, mental confusion, and agitation, followed by seizures and coma	• Give the client who is acutely ill only a 1-week supply of the medication. • Monitor the client for signs of toxicity. • Notify the primary care provider if signs of toxicity occur.

- **Contraindications/precautions**
    - ◊ Amitriptyline is a Pregnancy Risk Category C medication.
    - ◊ Use amitriptyline cautiously in clients with seizure disorders; coronary artery disease; diabetes; liver, kidney, or respiratory disorders; urinary retention or obstruction; or hyperthyroidism.

Medication/Food Interactions	Nursing Interventions/Client Education
MAOIs – Concurrent use causes hypertension.	Avoid concurrent use of TCAs and MAOIs.
Antihistamines and other anticholinergic agents cause additive anticholinergic effects.	Avoid concurrent use of TCAs and antihistamines.
Epinephrine, norepinephrine (direct-acting sympathomimetics) – There is an increased amount of these medications in the synaptic space because uptake is blocked by TCAs, which leads to an increased intensity of their effects.	Avoid concurrent use of TCAs and these medications.
Ephedrine, amphetamine (indirect-acting sympathomimetics) – There is a decreased response to these medications due to the inhibition of their uptake and their inability to get to the site of action in the nerve terminal.	Avoid concurrent use of TCAs and these medications.
Alcohol, benzodiazepines, opioids, and antihistamines cause additive CNS depression when used concurrently.	Advise the client to avoid other CNS depressants.

- **Therapeutic nursing interventions and client education**
    - ◊ Instruct the client to take this medication as prescribed on a daily basis to establish therapeutic plasma levels.
    - ◊ Assist with medication regimen compliance by informing the client that therapeutic effects may not be experienced for **1 to 3 weeks** and that it might take **2 to 3 months** for full benefits to be achieved.
    - ◊ Instruct the client to continue therapy after improvement in symptoms. Sudden discontinuation of the medication can result in relapse.
    - ◊ Advise the client that therapy usually continues for 6 months after resolution of symptoms and may continue for 1 year or longer.
    - ◊ Suicide prevention can be facilitated by prescribing only a week's worth of medication for an acutely ill client, and then only prescribing 1 month's worth of medication at a time.
    - ◊ Instruct the client to minimize anticholinergic side effects by:
        - ° Sipping fluids, chewing gum, and sucking on hard candy to decrease dry mouth.
        - ° Avoiding hazardous activities if visual disturbances occur.

- ° Wearing sunglasses outside to prevent photophobia.
- ° Voiding just before taking the medication to minimize urinary retention.
- ° Increasing intake of dietary fiber and fluids to prevent constipation.
- ° Avoiding strenuous exercise in warm weather due to the suppression of sweating.

Δ Phenelzine (Nardil): MAOI

- **Expected pharmacological action**
  - ◊ Phenelzine blocks MAO-A in the brain, thereby increasing the amount of norepinephrine (NE) and serotonin available for transmission of impulses. An increased amount of NE and serotonin at nerve endings intensifies responses and relieves depression.

- **Therapeutic uses**
  - ◊ Treatment of choice for atypical depression
  - ◊ Bulimia nervosa
  - ◊ Obsessive-compulsive disorder (OCD)

Side/Adverse Effects	Nursing Interventions/Client Education
CNS stimulation (e.g., anxiety, agitation, hypomania, mania)	• Advise the client to observe for symptoms. Instruct the client to notify the primary care provider if symptoms occur.
Orthostatic hypotension	• Instruct the client about the signs of postural hypotension (light-headedness, dizziness). Advise the client to sit or lie down if these occur. Orthostatic hypotension can be minimized by getting up slowly. • Monitor the client's blood pressure (and heart rate for the hospitalized client). Take orthostatic blood pressures, waiting at least 1 min between lying down and sitting or standing. If a significant change in BP and HR is noted, withhold the medication and notify the primary care provider.
Hypertensive crisis resulting from intake of dietary tyramine – severe hypertension as a result of intensive vasoconstriction and stimulation of the heart • Headache • Nausea • Increased HR • Increased BP	• Hypertensive crisis is managed by inducing rapid vasodilation. This is accomplished with IV phentolamine, a rapid-acting alpha-adrenergic blocker. Hypertensive crisis can also be treated with sublingual nifedipine. • Provide continuous cardiac monitoring and respiratory support as indicated.

- **Contraindications/precautions**

  ◊ Phenelzine is a Pregnancy Risk Category C medication.

  ◊ Phenelzine is contraindicated in clients taking SSRIs, clients with pheochromocytoma, heart failure, cardiovascular or cerebral vascular disease, or severe renal insufficiency.

  ◊ Use phenelzine cautiously in clients with diabetes and seizure disorders.

Medication/Food Interactions	Nursing Interventions/Client Education
Ephedrine, amphetamine (indirect-acting sympathomimetics) – These medications promote the release of NE and can lead to hypertensive crisis.	• Advise the client not to use any medications with sympathomimetic actions. • Instruct the client that OTC decongestants and cold remedies frequently contain medications with sympathomimetic action.
TCAs – Concurrent use can lead to hypertensive crisis.	• Use MAOIs and TCAs cautiously.
SSRIs – Concurrent use can lead to serotonin syndrome.	• Concurrent use should be avoided.
Antihypertensives cause additive hypotensive effects.	• Monitor the client's blood pressure. • Notify the primary care provider if there is a significant drop in the client's blood pressure. Reduce the client's dose of the antihypertensive if necessary.
Meperidine (Demerol) – Concurrent use can lead to hyperpyrexia.	• An alternative analgesic should be used.
Tyramine-rich foods – Hypertensive crisis can occur; the client will most likely experience headache, nausea, and increased heart rate and blood pressure. Foods containing high amounts of tyramine include ripe avocados or figs, fermented or smoked meats, liver, dried or cured fish, most cheeses, some beer and wine, and protein dietary supplements.	• Assess the client for the ability to follow strict adherence to dietary restrictions. • Inform the client of symptoms and to notify the primary care provider if they occur. • Provide the client with written instructions regarding foods and beverages to be avoided. • Advise the client to avoid taking any medications without approval of the primary care provider.
Vasopressors (e.g., **phenylethylamine, caffeine**) – Concurrent use may result in hypertension.	• Advise the client to avoid foods that contain these agents (e.g., caffeinated beverages, chocolate, fava beans, ginseng).

- **Therapeutic nursing interventions and client education**

  ◊ Instruct the client to take the medication on a daily basis to establish therapeutic plasma levels.

  ◊ Assist with medication regimen compliance by informing the client that therapeutic effects may not be experienced for **1 to 3 weeks** and that it might take **2 to 3 months** for full benefits to be achieved.

◊ Instruct the client to continue therapy after improvement in symptoms. Sudden discontinuation of the medication can result in relapse.

◊ Advise the client that therapy usually continues for 6 months after resolution of symptoms and may continue for 1 year or longer.

◊ Give clients a list of tyramine-rich foods so hypertensive crises can be avoided.

◊ Advise the client to avoid taking any other prescription or nonprescription medications unless approved by the primary care provider.

Δ **Bupropion (Wellbutrin)**: Atypical Antidepressant

- **Expected pharmacological action**

  ◊ Bupropion acts by inhibiting dopamine uptake.

- **Therapeutic uses**

  ◊ Depressive disorders

  ◊ Aid to quit smoking

Side/Adverse Effects	Nursing Interventions/Client Education
Headache, dry mouth, constipation, increased HR, nausea, restlessness, weight loss	• Advise the client to observe for signs/symptoms and to notify the primary care provider if they are intolerable. • Treat headaches with a mild analgesic. • Advise the client to sip on fluids to treat dry mouth and to increase dietary fiber to prevent constipation.
Seizures	• Avoid administering to clients at risk for seizures, such as a client with a head injury. • Monitor clients for seizures and treat accordingly.

- **Contraindications/precautions**

  ◊ It is contraindicated for clients with a seizure disorder.

  ◊ It is contraindicated for clients taking MAOIs.

Medication/Food Interactions	Nursing Interventions/Client Education
MAOIs, such as **phenelzine (Nardil)**, increase the risk of toxicity.	MAOIs should be discontinued 2 weeks prior to beginning treatment with bupropion.

- **Therapeutic nursing interventions and client education**

  ◊ Instruct the client to take the medication on a daily basis to establish therapeutic plasma levels.

  ◊ Assist with medication regimen compliance by informing the client that therapeutic effects may not be experienced for **1 to 3 weeks** and that it might take **2 to 3 months** for full benefits to be achieved.

  ◊ Instruct the client to continue therapy after improvement in symptoms. Sudden discontinuation of the medication can result in relapse.

  ◊ Advise the client that therapy usually continues for 6 months after resolution of symptoms and may continue for 1 year or longer.

Nursing Evaluation of Medication Effectiveness

Δ Depending on therapeutic intent, the effectiveness of any of the antidepressants may be evidenced by:

- Improvement in depressive state as evidenced by elevated mood, greater alertness and activity level, improved appetite, and normal sleep pattern.

- Improvement of symptoms as evidenced by greater ability to perform ADLs and to interact socially with peers.

- Improvement of sleeping and eating habits.

Primary Reference:

Varcarolis, E. M., Carson, V. B., & Shoemaker, N. C. (2006). *Foundations of psychiatric mental health nursing: A clinical approach* (5th ed.). St. Louis, MO: Saunders.

Additional Resources:

German, D., & Lee, A. (Eds.) (2006). Mood disorders. *Nurse practitioners' prescribing reference, 13*(3), 81-90.

Lehne, R. A. (2007). *Pharmacology for nursing care* (6th ed.). St. Louis, MO: Saunders.

NANDA International (2004). *NANDA nursing diagnoses: Definitions and classification 2005-2006*. Philadelphia: NANDA.

Chapter 14: Medications to Treat Mood Disorders: Depression

Application Exercises

1. When a client is admitted with a diagnosis of overdose of bupropion (Wellbutrin), which of the following nursing diagnoses has the highest priority?

   A. Alteration in thought processes related to confusion

   B. Sleep pattern disturbances related to depression

   C. Potential for injury related to seizure activity

   D. Knowledge deficit of use and effects of antidepressants related to denial

2. Which of the following statements made by a client indicates to the nurse that the teaching regarding tricyclic antidepressants (TCAs) has been understood?

   A. "I will stay out of the sun because I might get a severe skin rash."

   B. "I may feel drowsy for a few weeks after starting this drug."

   C. "Since diarrhea is common with this drug, I will increase my dietary fiber."

   D. "To help control the nausea and vomiting, I will eat small, frequent meals."

3. A client is started on a TCA for depression. Which of the following should be included in the teaching plan?

   A. "Sit on the side of the bed before getting up; then stand up very slowly."

   B. "Eat four to six small meals throughout the day."

   C. "Be sure to eat foods high in potassium."

   D. "Elevate your legs whenever you sit down."

4. A nurse has completed medication teaching regarding fluoxetine (Prozac) with a client. Which of the following statements made by the client indicates an understanding of the adverse effects?

   A. "I will need extra sleep while I am taking this medication."

   B. "I have to drink extra fluid while I'm taking this medication."

   C. "It will take about 4 weeks before I notice effects from this medication."

   D. "I will control my caloric intake and get lots of exercise."

5. A client has taken two doses of fluoxetine for treatment of depression. A family member calls the clinic to tell the nurse that the client is very confused, sweating a lot, and "seeing things." Which of the following should the nurse communicate to the family member?

   A. "This is a common reaction with the first few doses of fluoxetine and will go away in a few hours."

   B. "This is a very serious reaction to the drug. The drug must be stopped immediately."

   C. "Your primary care provider will need to prescribe an MAOI to control these symptoms."

   D. "We will need to increase the drug dose to control these side effects."

6. A client is to be started on the MAOI phenelzine (Nardil). Which of the following should be monitored frequently?

   A. Blood pressure

   B. Breath sounds

   C. Body temperature

   D. Blood glucose

7. A client is to be started on an MAOI for treatment of depression. Identify eight foods that should be avoided during therapy.

Chapter 14: Medications to Treat Mood Disorders: Depression

Application Exercises Answer Key

1. When a client is admitted with a diagnosis of overdose of bupropion (Wellbutrin), which of the following nursing diagnoses has the highest priority?

>   A. Alteration in thought processes related to confusion
>
>   B. Sleep pattern disturbances related to depression
>
>   **C. Potential for injury related to seizure activity**
>
>   D. Knowledge deficit of use and effects of antidepressants related to denial

   Dose-dependent seizures are a serious side effect of bupropion. Alteration in thought processes related to confusion is not a side effect related to this medication. Sleep-pattern disturbances are related to depression rather than bupropion therapy. Knowledge deficit is a possible nursing diagnosis, but it is lower priority than the potential for injury.

2. Which of the following statements made by a client indicates to the nurse that the teaching regarding tricyclic antidepressants (TCAs) has been understood?

>   A. "I will stay out of the sun because I might get a severe skin rash."
>
>   **B. "I may feel drowsy for a few weeks after starting this drug."**
>
>   C. "Since diarrhea is common with this drug, I will increase my dietary fiber."
>
>   D. "To help control the nausea and vomiting, I will eat small, frequent meals."

   Sedation is an effect of TCAs during the first few weeks of therapy. Skin rash is a side effect of fluoxetine. Constipation, rather than diarrhea, is an anticholinergic side effect seen in TCAs. Nausea and vomiting are not expected adverse effects of TCAs.

3. A client is started on a TCA for depression. Which of the following should be included in the teaching plan?

>   **A. "Sit on the side of the bed before getting up; then stand up very slowly."**
>
>   B. "Eat four to six small meals throughout the day."
>
>   C. "Be sure to eat foods high in potassium."
>
>   D. "Elevate your legs whenever you sit down."

   Orthostatic hypotension is a common adverse effect of TCAs and is due to blockade of alpha-adrenergic receptors on blood vessels. Getting up slowly can minimize the dizziness and light-headedness that occur with orthostatic hypotension. The other statements are not included in the teaching plan for TCAs.

4. A nurse has completed medication teaching regarding fluoxetine (Prozac) with a client. Which of the following statements made by the client indicates an understanding of the adverse effects?

> A. "I will need extra sleep while I am taking this medication."
> B. "I have to drink extra fluid while I'm taking this medication."
> C. "It will take about 4 weeks before I notice effects from this medication."
> **D. "I will control my caloric intake and get lots of exercise."**

Weight gain is an adverse effect of fluoxetine. The other options are not related to adverse effects of this medication.

5. A client has taken two doses of fluoxetine for treatment of depression. A family member calls the clinic to tell the nurse that the client is very confused, sweating a lot, and "seeing things." Which of the following should the nurse communicate to the family member?

> A. "This is a common reaction with the first few doses of fluoxetine and will go away in a few hours."
> **B. "This is a very serious reaction to the drug. The drug must be stopped immediately."**
> C. "Your primary care provider will need to prescribe an MAOI to control these symptoms."
> D. "We will need to increase the drug dose to control these side effects."

These are symptoms of serotonin syndrome, which usually arises 2 to 72 hr after treatment has begun. It resolves when the medication is discontinued; however, the client may require hospitalization for serious symptoms.

6. A client is to be started on the MAOI phenelzine (Nardil). Which of the following should be monitored frequently?

> **A. Blood pressure**
> B. Breath sounds
> C. Body temperature
> D. Blood glucose

Because orthostatic hypotension is an adverse effect of MAOIs and because hypertensive crisis may also occur when taking this medication, it is important to monitor blood pressure. Breath sounds, body temperature, and blood glucose are not specifically monitored for the client taking an MAOI.

7. A client is to be started on an MAOI for treatment of depression. Identify eight foods that should be avoided during therapy.

Foods containing high amounts of tyramine include ripe avocados or figs, fermented or smoked meats, liver, dried or cured fish, most cheeses, some beer and wine, and protein dietary supplements.

Unit 3   Psychopharmacological Therapies

Chapter 15:   Medications to Treat Mood Disorders: Bipolar

Contributor: Judith A. Harris, MSN, RNC

NCLEX-RN® Connections:

Learning Objective: Review and apply knowledge within "**Medications to Treat Mood Disorders: Bipolar**" in readiness for performance of the following nursing activities as outlined by the NCLEX-RN® test plan:

Δ   Apply knowledge of mental health when caring for the client receiving psychopharmacological therapy for mania.

Δ   Assess the client for expected and side/adverse effects of mood stabilizers.

Δ   Assess the client for actual/potential specific food-medication interactions.

Δ   Identify contraindications, actual/potential incompatibilities, and interactions between medications. Intervene appropriately.

Δ   Evaluate/monitor and document the therapeutic and adverse/side effects of mood stabilizers.

Δ   Provide client teaching on actions, therapeutic effects, potential side/adverse effects, and interactions of mood stabilizers.

 Key Points

Δ   The two first-line medications most often used for long-term treatment of bipolar disorder are **lithium** and **valproic acid (Depakote)**.

Δ   Other medications used for bipolar disorder include:

•   **Atypical antipsychotics** – These can be useful in early treatment to promote sleep and to decrease anxiety and agitation. These medications also demonstrate mood-stabilizing properties. (*Refer to chapter 16, Medications to Treat Psychoses.*)

•   **Anxiolytics** – Clonazepam (Klonopin) and lorazepam (Ativan) can be useful in treating acute mania and managing the psychomotor agitation often seen in mania. (*Refer to chapter 13, Medications to Treat Anxiety Disorders.*)

•   **Antidepressants** – The depression of bipolar disorders may be treated with an antidepressant medication.

- **Anticonvulsants**.

  ◊ Carbamazepine (Tegretol) is used along with lithium or an antipsychotic to manage severely manic clients with treatment-resistant bipolar I disorder and clients with rapid cycling.

  ◊ Lamotrigine (Lamictal), another anticonvulsant medication, has been approved as a first-line medication to treat bipolar disorder since 2003. It has been useful for bipolar disorder that does not respond well to other medication therapy.

Therapeutic Agents

Δ **Lithium Carbonate (Lithane, Eskalith, and Others)**: Mood Stabilizer

- **Expected pharmacological action**

  ◊ Lithium produces neurochemical changes in the brain, including serotonin receptor blockade.

  ◊ Use of lithium causes evidence of decrease in neuronal atrophy and/or increase in neuronal growth.

- **Therapeutic uses**

  ◊ Lithium is used in the treatment of bipolar disorders. It controls episodes of acute mania and is used for long-term maintenance of clients with bipolar I disorder.

Side/Adverse Effects	Nursing Interventions/Client Education
Gastrointestinal effects (e.g., nausea, **diarrhea**, abdominal pain)	• Advise the client that symptoms are usually transient. • Administer medication with meals or milk.
Fatigue, muscle weakness, headache, memory loss, and confusion	• Advise the client that symptoms are usually transient. • Advise the client to rest.
Weight gain	• Manage with lowered-calorie diet and exercise.
Tremors, which can interfere with fine motor skills and can be exacerbated by factors such as stress and caffeine	• Beta-adrenergic blocking agents such as propranolol (Inderal) may be prescribed. • Reduce peak levels by using the lowest possible dosage, giving in divided doses, or using long-acting formulations.
Polyuria	• A potassium-sparing diuretic such as amiloride (Midamor) may be prescribed. • Instruct the client to maintain adequate fluid intake by drinking at least 8 to 10 glasses (8 oz) of water/day.

Side/Adverse Effects	Nursing Interventions/Client Education
Goiter and hypothyroid symptoms	• Obtain the client's baseline T_3, T_4, and TSH levels prior to starting treatment and then annually thereafter. • Advise the client to monitor for signs of hypothyroidism (e.g., cold, dry skin; decreased heart rate, weight gain). • Goiter and hypothyroid symptoms are reversible with discontinuation of lithium or administration of a thyroid hormone such as levothyroxine (Synthroid).
Degenerative kidney changes	• Keep the dosage as low as possible to maintain control of the disorder. • Assess kidney function at the start of therapy and then annually thereafter.

- **Signs and symptoms of lithium toxicity include**:

  ◊ Fine hand tremors progressing to coarse tremors.

  ◊ Mild gastrointestinal upset progressing to persistent upset.

  ◊ Slurred speech and muscle weakness progressing to mental confusion, muscle hyperirritability, poor coordination, and electroencephalogram changes.

  ◊ Severe toxicity – The client has decreasing level of consciousness to stupor and finally coma, seizures, severe hypotension, and severe polyuria with dilute urine. Death can occur from pulmonary complications.

- **Contraindications/precautions**

  ◊ Lithium is a Pregnancy Risk Category D medication. The client should avoid use during pregnancy.

  ◊ Discourage the client from breastfeeding if lithium therapy is necessary.

  ◊ In the client with decreased **renal function**, smaller doses of lithium may be needed. "Start low and go slow" is a phrase used for adjusting doses in lithium therapy.

  ◊ Use lithium cautiously in clients with heart disease, sodium depletion, and dehydration.

Medication/Food Interactions	Nursing Interventions/Client Education
Diuretics – Sodium is excreted with the use of diuretics. With decreased serum sodium, lithium excretion is decreased, leading to lithium toxicity.	• Monitor the client for signs of toxicity. • Advise the client to observe for signs/symptoms and to notify the primary care provider. • Encourage the client to maintain a diet adequate in sodium and to drink 8 to 12 glasses (8 oz) of water/day.
NSAIDs (e.g., **ibuprofen [Motrin] and celecoxib [Celebrex]**) – Concurrent use will cause renal reabsorption of lithium, leading to toxicity.	• Avoid use of NSAIDs to prevent toxic accumulation of lithium. • Aspirin does not cause this to occur, so it can be used for analgesia.
Anticholinergics (e.g., **antihistamines, tricyclic antidepressants**) – Abdominal discomfort can result from anticholinergic-induced urinary retention and polyuria.	• Advise the client to avoid medications with anticholinergic effects.

- **Therapeutic nursing interventions and client education**
  - ◊ Clients must maintain **adequate sodium and fluid intake** while taking lithium.
    - ° When serum sodium is decreased, lithium, which is a salt, takes the place of sodium in the body. The lithium that is not excreted builds up and causes lithium toxicity.
    - ° Excessive loss of salt and fluids, caused by vomiting, diarrhea, increased perspiration, or use of diuretics, will also increase retention of lithium.
    - ° Sodium supplements and additional fluid may be required in cases of sodium or fluid loss.
  - ◊ Monitor plasma lithium levels during treatment.
    - ° At initiation of treatment, the primary care provider monitors levels every 2 to 3 days and then every 1 to 3 months.
    - ° Therapeutic levels are between **0.4 and 1.3 mEq/L**.
    - ° Toxicity occurs with levels > **1.5 mEq/L**.
    - ° Serum levels > than 2.0 mEq/L constitute a life-threatening emergency.
  - ◊ Advise the client that effects of lithium begin within **5 to 7 days** and that it may take **2 to 3 weeks** to achieve full benefits.
  - ◊ Advise the client to report signs of toxicity and to take the medication as prescribed.
  - ◊ Encourage the client to comply with laboratory appointments needed to monitor lithium effectiveness and adverse effects.

◊ Encourage the client to comply with follow-up appointments to monitor thyroid and renal function.

◊ Treatment for lithium toxicity

　° Treatment for mild toxicity is cessation of the medication.

　° Treatment for severe toxicity includes gastric lavage and hastening medication elimination through infusion of mannitol (Osmitrol), urea, and aminophylline. In extreme cases, hemodialysis may be necessary.

Δ **Valproic Acid (Depakote)**: Antiepileptic

- **Expected pharmacological action**

  ◊ The mechanism of action of valproic acid is unknown, but it is believed to affect the function of the neurotransmitter gamma-aminobutyric acid (GABA) by increasing available levels in the brain.

- **Therapeutic uses**

  ◊ This medication is used to treat acute manic episodes associated with bipolar I disorder and is useful for rapid cycling mania.

Side/Adverse Effects	Nursing Interventions/Client Education
Gastrointestinal effects (e.g., nausea, vomiting, indigestion)	• Advise the client to take the medication with food. Enteric-coated formulation can prevent symptoms.
Hepatotoxicity (e.g., anorexia, abdominal pain, jaundice)	• Assess baseline liver function and monitor liver function periodically. • Advise the client to observe for signs/symptoms (e.g., anorexia, nausea, vomiting, abdominal pain, jaundice) and notify the primary care provider if symptoms occur. • Avoid using in children younger than 3 years old. • Medication should be prescribed in the lowest effective dose.
Pancreatitis, as evidenced by nausea, vomiting, and abdominal pain	• Advise the client to observe for symptoms and to notify the primary care provider immediately if these symptoms occur. • Monitor amylase levels. • Medication should be discontinued if pancreatitis develops.
Thrombocytopenia, due to reduced platelets and platelet aggregation	• Advise the client to observe for signs/symptoms, such as bruising, and to notify the primary care provider if these occur. • Monitor the client's platelet counts.

- **Contraindications/precautions**
  - ◊ Valproic acid is a Pregnancy Risk Category D medication.
  - ◊ Discourage the client from breastfeeding while taking valproic acid.
  - ◊ This medication is contraindicated in clients with liver disorders, because it is metabolized by the liver.

Medication/Food Interactions	Nursing Interventions/Client Education
Valproic acid reduces platelets and therefore should not be taken with other medications that affect blood clotting, such as **warfarin (Coumadin), ticlopidine (Ticlid), and NSAIDs,** such as aspirin.	• Educate the client regarding over-the-counter medications to avoid. • Teach signs/symptoms of covert bleeding (e.g., bruising, fatigue).
Valproic acid can decrease the elimination of **lamotrigine, (Lamictal), ethosuximide (Zarontin), diazepam (Valium), zidovudine (AZT) and phenobarbital**, thus increasing the blood concentration of these medications.	• Monitor medication levels as appropriate. • Teach the client to watch for signs of excess. • Adjust the dosage of medications as needed.

- **Therapeutic nursing interventions and client education**
  - ◊ Advise the client to take medications as prescribed and not to stop medications without consulting the primary care provider.
  - ◊ Advise the client who is traveling to carry extra medication to avoid interruption of medications in case he becomes stranded.

Nursing Evaluation of Medication Effectiveness

- Δ Absence or decrease of acute manic or depressive episodes
- Δ Relief of acute manic symptoms (e.g., flight of ideas, obsessive talking, agitation) or depressive symptoms (e.g., fatigue, poor appetite, psychomotor retardation)
- Δ Improvement in ability to perform self-care and ADLs
- Δ Improvement in ability to interact socially with peers

Primary Reference:

Varcarolis, E. M., Carson, V. B., & Shoemaker, N. C. (2006). *Foundations of psychiatric mental health nursing: A clinical approach* (5th ed.). St. Louis, MO: Saunders.

Additional Resources:

German, D., & Lee, A. (Eds.) (2006). Mood disorders. *Nurse practitioners' prescribing reference, 13*(3), 81-90.

Lehne, R. A. (2007). *Pharmacology for nursing care* (6th ed.). St. Louis, MO: Saunders.

NANDA International (2004). *NANDA nursing diagnoses: Definitions and classification 2005-2006*. Philadelphia: NANDA.

Chapter 15: Medications to Treat Mood Disorders: Bipolar

Application Exercises

1. A client who has been on lithium therapy for 6 months has recently developed symptoms of mild arthritis. He tells the nurse that he wants to start taking the NSAID ibuprofen (Advil) for his pain. Which of the following is the nurse's best response?

   A. "That is a good choice. Stronger analgesics would not be good for you."

   B. "Regular aspirin would be a better choice, because Advil can raise your lithium level too high."

   C. "You will have to stop taking the lithium if you take any pain medication."

   D. "The Advil will make your lithium level fall too low, and your symptoms may come back."

2. A client is started on valproic acid (Depakote) for treatment of bipolar disorder. Which of the following laboratory studies should be monitored regularly?

   A. AST/ALT and LDH

   B. Creatinine and BUN

   C. WBC and granulocyte counts

   D. Serum sodium and potassium

3. Which of the following medications, if given concurrently with lithium, could produce a toxic effect?

   A. Insulin

   B. Prednisone

   C. Digoxin (Lanoxin)

   D. Furosemide (Lasix)

4. A client with bipolar I disorder has been well controlled with valproic acid (Depakote). She wants children and asks the clinic nurse if she could become pregnant. Which of the following is the nurse's best response?

   A. "If you watch your diet very closely, you may be able to discontinue the medication so that you can become pregnant."

   B. "You should avoid becoming pregnant, because your chances of carrying the baby to term are very slight."

   C. "There is an increased risk of birth defects if you become pregnant while taking this medication."

   D. "Since you have been on this medication for so long, your chances of having a healthy baby are excellent."

5. A client who has been taking valproic acid for 2 years calls the nurse and reports flu-like symptoms for the past 4 to 5 days. He says he has nausea, some vomiting, does not feel like eating, and has constant abdominal pain. Which of the following should the nurse communicate to the client?

    A. "You must contact your primary care provider right away, as this may indicate a very serious side effect of your medication."

    B. "The flu is going around, so take plenty of fluids and call back if you don't feel better in a few days."

    C. "Call your primary care provider to ask for a prescription for an antiemetic, because vomiting can cause toxicity of this drug."

    D. "Stay home from work, get lots of rest, and drink ginger ale to help settle your stomach."

6. True or False: For a client with bipolar I disorder who is taking lithium, a serum lithium level of 1.8 mEq/L is within normal limits.

7. True or False: A client taking lithium is experiencing fine hand tremors. The client should stop taking her medication because she is experiencing a toxic effect.

Chapter 15: Medications to Treat Mood Disorders: Bipolar

Application Exercises Answer Key

1. A client who has been on lithium therapy for 6 months has recently developed symptoms of mild arthritis. He tells the nurse that he wants to start taking the NSAID ibuprofen (Advil) for his pain. Which of the following is the nurse's best response?

> A. "That is a good choice. Stronger analgesics would not be good for you."
>
> **B. "Regular aspirin would be a better choice, because Advil can raise your lithium level too high."**
>
> C. "You will have to stop taking the lithium if you take any pain medication."
>
> D. "The Advil will make your lithium level fall too low, and your symptoms may come back."

NSAIDs increase renal lithium reabsorption; aspirin does not increase lithium levels. Option A is incorrect because ibuprofen increases lithium levels. Stronger analgesics are not necessary for mild arthritis. Option C is incorrect because not all pain medications are contraindicated with concurrent use of lithium. The client can safely take aspirin. Option D is incorrect because ibuprofen may cause the client's lithium level to rise to toxic levels.

2. A client is started on valproic acid (Depakote) for treatment of bipolar disorder. Which of the following laboratory studies should be monitored regularly?

> **A. AST/ALT and LDH**
>
> B. Creatinine and BUN
>
> C. WBC and granulocyte counts
>
> D. Serum sodium and potassium

Liver function tests should be monitored, because valproic acid is metabolized in the liver and hepatotoxicity may result. It is not vital to test creatinine and BUN (kidney function tests), WBC and granulocyte counts (tests to monitor for infection), or serum sodium and potassium (electrolytes).

3. Which of the following medications, if given concurrently with lithium, could produce a toxic effect?

    A. Insulin

    B. Prednisone

    C. Digoxin (Lanoxin)

    D. Furosemide (Lasix)

Furosemide, a loop diuretic, promotes sodium loss and lithium retention, possibly increasing serum levels. Insulin, prednisone, and digoxin do not interact with lithium.

4. A client with bipolar I disorder has been well controlled with valproic acid (Depakote). She wants children and asks the clinic nurse if she could become pregnant. Which of the following is the nurse's best response?

    A. "If you watch your diet very closely, you may be able to discontinue the medication so that you can become pregnant."

    B. "You should avoid becoming pregnant, because your chances of carrying the baby to term are very slight."

    C. "There is an increased risk of birth defects if you become pregnant while taking this medication."

    D. "Since you have been on this medication for so long, your chances of having a healthy baby are excellent."

Female clients who become pregnant while taking valproic acid have an increased risk of delivering a baby with a neural tube defect, such as spina bifida. Valproic acid is a Pregnancy Risk Category D medication. Lithium and carbamazepine (Tegretol), two other commonly used medications for bipolar disorder, are also Pregnancy Risk Category D medications.

5. A client who has been taking valproic acid for 2 years calls the nurse and reports flu-like symptoms for the past 4 to 5 days. He says he has nausea, some vomiting, does not feel like eating, and has constant abdominal pain. Which of the following should the nurse communicate to the client?

    A. "You must contact your primary care provider right away, as this may indicate a very serious side effect of your medication."

    B. "The flu is going around, so take plenty of fluids and call back if you don't feel better in a few days."

    C. "Call your primary care provider to ask for a prescription for an antiemetic, because vomiting can cause toxicity of this drug."

    D. "Stay home from work, get lots of rest, and drink ginger ale to help settle your stomach."

The symptoms mentioned may indicate that the client has pancreatitis, a potentially fatal inflammation of the pancreas that can occur in a client taking valproic acid. This client needs to be seen by his primary care provider.

6. True or False: For a client with bipolar I disorder who is taking lithium, a serum lithium level of 1.8 mEq/L is within normal limits.

False: A serum lithium level above 1.5 mEq/L is considered in the toxic range.

7. True or False: A client taking lithium is experiencing fine hand tremors. The client should stop taking her medication because she is experiencing a toxic effect.

False: Fine hand tremors are an expected side effect of lithium. This side effect may either subside or continue during lithium therapy. However, if the tremors begin to increase and become coarse, early lithium toxicity is a possibility.

Unit 3   Psychopharmacological Therapies

Chapter 16:   Medications to Treat Psychoses
                Contributor: Judith A. Harris, MSN, RNC

 NCLEX-RN® Connections:

> **Learning Objective**: Review and apply knowledge within "**Medications to Treat Psychoses**" in readiness for performance of the following nursing activities as outlined by the NCLEX-RN® test plan:
>
> Δ   Apply knowledge of mental health when caring for the client receiving psychopharmacological therapy for psychosis.
>
> Δ   Assess the client for expected and side/adverse effects of antipsychotic medications.
>
> Δ   Assess the client for actual/potential specific food-medication interactions.
>
> Δ   Identify contraindications, actual/potential incompatibilities, and interactions between medications. Intervene appropriately.
>
> Δ   Identify symptoms/evidence of an allergic reaction and respond appropriately.
>
> Δ   Evaluate/monitor and document the therapeutic and adverse/side effects of antipsychotic medications.
>
> Δ   Provide client teaching on actions, therapeutic effects, potential side/adverse effects, and interactions of antipsychotic medications.

 Key Points

Δ   **Schizophrenia** is the primary reason for the administration of antipsychotic medications. (*Refer to chapter 26, Schizophrenia.*)

•   The clinical course of schizophrenia usually involves acute exacerbations with intervals of semiremission.

•   Medications are used to treat:

◊   **Positive symptoms** related to behavior, thought, and speech (e.g., agitation, delusions, hallucinations, tangential speech patterns).

◊   **Negative symptoms** (e.g., social withdrawal, lack of emotion, lack of energy [anergia]).

Δ   The goals of psychopharmacological treatment for schizophrenia are to:

- Suppress acute episodes.

- Prevent acute recurrence.

- Maintain the highest possible level of functioning.

Δ   Other disorders with psychotic symptoms, such as schizoaffective disorder, are also treated with antipsychotic medications.

Δ   **Conventional Antipsychotic Agents**

- The conventional antipsychotic medications suppress mainly the **positive** symptoms of psychosis.

- These medications are reserved for clients who are:

    ◊   Using them successfully and can tolerate the side effects.

    ◊   Violent or particularly aggressive.

- Conventional antipsychotic medications include:

    ◊   Low-potency agents: chlorpromazine (Thorazine), thioridazine (Mellaril).

    ◊   Medium-potency agents: molindone (Moban).

    ◊   High-potency agents: haloperidol (Haldol), fluphenazine decanoate (Prolixin).

Δ   The **atypical** antipsychotic agents are now medications of choice for clients receiving initial treatment and for treating breakthrough episodes in clients on conventional medication therapy, because they are more effective with fewer adverse effects.

- Advantages of atypical antipsychotic agents include:

    ◊   Relief of both the **positive** and **negative** symptoms of the disease.

    ◊   A decrease in affective symptoms (e.g., depression, anxiety) and suicidal behaviors.

    ◊   Improvement of neurocognitive defects, such as poor memory.

    ◊   Fewer or no extrapyramidal symptoms (EPS), including tardive dyskinesia, due to less dopamine blockade.

    ◊   Less anticholinergic adverse effects, with the exception of clozapine (Clozaril), which has a high incidence of anticholinergic effects. This is because most of the atypical antipsychotics cause little or no blockade of cholinergic receptors.

    ◊   Less relapse.

- Atypical antipsychotic medications include: risperidone (Risperdal), olanzapine (Zyprexa), quetiapine (Seroquel), aripiprazole (Abilify), ziprasidone (Geodon), and clozapine (Clozaril).

Therapeutic Agents

Δ   **Chlorpromazine (Thorazine)**: Conventional Antipsychotic

• **Expected pharmacological action**

◊ The typical antipsychotic medications block dopamine (D_2), acetylcholine, histamine, and norepinephrine (NE) receptors in the brain and periphery.

◊ Inhibition of psychotic symptoms is believed to be a result of D_2 blockade in the brain.

Receptor Sites Affected	Therapeutic Use	Adverse Effects
Blockade of the D_2 receptors for dopamine	Decreases dopamine. and reduces the positive symptoms of psychosis (e.g., delusions and hallucinations), which are thought to be a result of overactivity of dopamine in the limbic system.	• Extrapyramidal symptoms (EPS): acute dystonia, parkinsonism, akathisia, and tardive dyskinesia • Increased prolactin leading to gynecomastia (breast enlargement) in men and menstrual irregularities and galactorrhea (milk production) in women
Blockade of muscarinic receptors for acetylcholine, which affects the parasympathetic nervous system	There is no therapeutic use in psychosis.	• Anticholinergic side effects (e.g., blurred vision, dry mouth, urinary retention, constipation, tachycardia)
Blockade of alpha$_1$ receptors for NE and histamine	There is no therapeutic use in psychosis.	• Orthostatic hypotension • Dizziness • Reflex tachycardia • Ejaculatory dysfunction
Blockade of alpha$_2$ receptors for NE	There is no therapeutic use in psychosis.	• Sexual dysfunction • Priapism
Blockade of H$_1$ receptors for histamine	It is unclear whether or not therapeutic use is obtained for clients with psychosis.	• Sedation • Weight gain
5-HT$_2$ receptors for serotonin	Produces antipsychotic effects, as well as relief from depression.	• Weight gain • Hypotension • Ejaculatory dysfunction
Gamma-aminobutyric acid **(GABA) receptors**	Increase in GABA reduces symptoms of schizophrenia.	• Lowered seizure threshold in clients with existing seizure disorder

- **Therapeutic uses**
  - ◊ Schizophrenia
  - ◊ Bipolar disorders
  - ◊ Tourette's syndrome
  - ◊ Delusional disorders
  - ◊ Schizoaffective disorder
  - ◊ Dementia and other organic mental syndromes
  - ◊ Huntington's chorea
  - ◊ Prevention of nausea/vomiting through blocking of dopamine in the chemoreceptor trigger zone of the medulla

Side/Adverse Effects	Nursing Interventions/Client Education
Early EPS • Acute dystonia (e.g., severe spasms of the tongue and jaw spreading to the face, neck, and back) • Parkinsonism (e.g., bradykinesia, rigidity, shuffling gait, drooling, tremors) • Akathisia (e.g., inability to stand still or sit, pacing)	• EPS may develop within hours of first dose. • Severe cases should be treated with IM or IV doses of an anticholinergic medication (e.g., benztropine [Cogentin], diphenhydramine [Benadryl]). • Symptoms usually appear within 1 month of initiation of therapy. Manage symptoms with anticholinergic medications (e.g., benztropine [Cogentin], diphenhydramine [Benadryl]). Symptoms usually resolve within a few months. • Medication can be discontinued to determine if symptoms return. If symptoms persist, the client can be switched to an atypical antipsychotic agent, such as risperidone (Risperdal). • Effects usually develop within 2 months of the initiation of treatment. • Manage symptoms with a beta-blocker, benzodiazepine, or anticholinergic medication or switch to low-potency agent.
Late EPS – tardive dyskinesia (TD) (e.g., twisting or wormlike movement of the tongue and face, lip smacking, uncontrollable movements of the limbs, movements of the trunk, such as hip jerks and twisting pelvic movements)	• There is no treatment for TD, and discontinuing the medication may not stop the symptoms. • The client should be on the lowest dosage possible to control symptoms. • Evaluate the client after 12 months of therapy and then every 3 months thereafter. If signs of TD appear, the client should be switched to an atypical agent. • Screening exam is the AIMS test (Abnormal Involuntary Movement Scale).

Side/Adverse Effects	Nursing Interventions/Client Education
Neuroleptic malignant syndrome – an uncommon effect that is potentially fatal when it occurs (e.g., sudden high-grade fever, blood pressure fluctuations, dysrhythmias, muscle rigidity, change in level of consciousness developing into coma)	• Stop the antipsychotic medication. • Monitor the client's vital signs. • Apply cooling blankets. • Administer antipyretics (e.g., aspirin, acetaminophen). • Increase the client's fluid intake. • Administer benzodiazepines to control anxiety. • Administer dantrolene (Dantrium) to induce muscle relaxation. • Wait 2 weeks before resuming therapy; consider switching to an atypical agent.
Anticholinergic effects (e.g., dry mouth, visual disturbances, acute urinary retention, constipation, tachycardia)	• Assess the client for urinary retention. • Monitor the client's I&O. • Advise the client to chew sugarless gum, eat foods high in fiber, and increase water intake to at least 8 to 10 glasses (8 oz) per day. • Teach the client to monitor heart rate and report noteworthy increases. These effects are more likely with low-potency agents.
Orthostatic hypotension and tachycardia	• Monitor baseline and orthostatic vital signs during the first weeks of treatment. • The client should develop a tolerance in 2 to 3 months. • Instruct the client about signs of postural hypotension (e.g., light-headedness, dizziness). If these occur, advise the client to sit or lie down. Orthostatic hypotension can be minimized by getting up slowly from a lying or sitting position.
Sedation	• Administer the dose at bedtime. • The effect should diminish within a week. • Advise the client not to drive until sedation has subsided.
Neuroendocrine effects (e.g., gynecomastia, galactorrhea, menstrual irregularities)	• Advise the client to observe for symptoms and to notify the primary care provider if they occur.
Seizures – greatest risk in clients with an existing seizure disorder	• Advise the client to report seizure activity to the primary care provider. • An increase in antiseizure medication may be necessary.

Side/Adverse Effects	Nursing Interventions/Client Education
Sexual dysfunction – common in both males and females	• Advise the client of possible side effects. • Encourage the client to report side effects to the primary care provider. • The client may need a lower dosage or to be switched to a high-potency agent.
Skin effects – photosensitivity resulting in severe sunburn, contact dermatitis from handling medications	• Advise the client to avoid excessive exposure to sunlight, to use sunscreen, and to wear protective clothing. • Advise the client to avoid direct contact with medication.
Agranulocytosis – a rare but dangerous toxic effect	• Advise the client to observe for signs of infection (e.g., fever, sore throat) and to notify the primary care provider if these occur. If signs of infection appear, obtain the client's baseline WBC count and discontinue the medication if laboratory tests indicate the presence of infection.
Severe dysrhythmias	• Obtain the client's baseline ECG and potassium level prior to treatment and periodically throughout the treatment period. • Avoid concurrent use with other medications that prolong QT interval.

- **Contraindications/precautions**
  - ◊ This medication is contraindicated for clients in a coma and for clients with severe depression, Parkinson's disease, prolactin-dependent cancer of the breast, or severe hypotension.
  - ◊ Use cautiously in clients with glaucoma, paralytic ileus, prostate enlargement, heart disorders, liver or kidney disease, and seizure disorders.

Medication/Food Interactions	Nursing Interventions/Client Education
Anticholinergic agents – Concurrent use with other anticholinergic medications will increase effects.	• Advise the client to avoid over-the-counter medications that contain anticholinergic agents (e.g., sleep medications, antihistamines).
CNS depressants (e.g., **alcohol, opioids, antihistamines**) – Additive CNS depressant effects will occur with concurrent use.	• Advise the client to avoid alcohol and other medications that cause CNS depression. • Advise the client to avoid hazardous activities, such as driving.
Levodopa (Dopar) – By activating dopamine receptors, levodopa counteracts the effects of antipsychotic agents.	• Clients receiving antipsychotic medications for treatment of psychiatric disorders should not use levodopa or other direct dopamine receptor agonists concurrently.

- **Therapeutic nursing interventions and client education**

  ◊ Initial therapy usually requires high doses that should be divided throughout the day. Maintenance doses should be kept at the lowest effective dose and can be given once a day at bedtime.

  ◊ Clients should be carefully assessed to distinguish between EPS and worsening of the psychotic disorder.

  ◊ Early EPS symptoms can be controlled with the use of anticholinergics, beta-blockers, and benzodiazepines. If symptoms are intolerable, the client can be switched to a low-potency or an atypical antipsychotic agent.

  ◊ Advise the client that antipsychotic medications do not cause addiction.

  ◊ Advise the client to take the medication as prescribed and to take it on a regular schedule.

  ◊ Instruct the client in ways to minimize anticholinergic side effects, including:

    ° Sipping fluids and sucking on hard candy to decrease dry mouth.

    ° Avoiding hazardous activities if visual disturbances occur.

    ° Wearing sunglasses outside to prevent photophobia.

    ° Voiding just before taking the medication to minimize urinary retention.

    ° Increasing intake of dietary fiber and fluids to prevent constipation.

    ° Avoiding strenuous exercise in warm weather due to suppression of sweating.

  ◊ Advise the client that these agents begin working within 1 to 2 days, but full effectiveness may not be seen for 2 to 4 weeks.

  ◊ Advise the client that liquid preparations should be protected from sunlight.

  ◊ Advise the client to avoid skin contact with liquid preparations to avoid dermatitis.

  ◊ Administer the medication in equally divided doses until the effective dose is attained. When the effective dose is determined, advise the client to take the total dose at bedtime to decrease sedative side effects.

  ◊ Consider depot preparations for clients with difficulty maintaining a medication regimen. Inform the client that lower doses can be used with depot preparations, which will decrease the risk of developing tardive dyskinesia.

Δ **Risperidone (Risperdal)**: Atypical Antipsychotic

- **Expected pharmacological action**

  ◊ The primary actions of atypical antipsychotic medications result from blocking **serotonin** and, to a lesser degree, **dopamine** receptors. These medications also block receptors for norepinephrine, histamine, and acetylcholine.

  ◊ This medication is available in tablets, oral solution, oral disintegrating tablets, and a long-acting injectable form (Risperdal Consta).

- **Therapeutic uses**

  ◊ Risperidone relieves both positive and negative symptoms, which begin to subside less than 1 week after the start of therapy.

  ◊ It is used to treat symptoms of psychosis seen in other mental health disorders, such as the mania of bipolar I disorder.

  ◊ Risperidone has recently (2006) been approved for treatment of irritability in autistic youth age 5 to 16 years, including the symptoms of aggression, temper tantrums, and rapidly changing mood.

Side/Adverse Effects (usually mild and infrequent)	Nursing Interventions/Client Education
Headache, sleepiness, anxiety	• Monitor for these adverse effects and report their occurrence to the primary care provider.
Weight gain (seen in up to 18% of clients taking risperidone)	• Advise the client to follow a healthy, low-calorie diet, engage in regular exercise, and monitor weight gain.
Prolonged QT interval on ECG	• The client should not take other medications that prolong QT interval. • The client should report risperidone use to other health providers prescribing medications. • ECG may be monitored.
Symptoms of agitation, dizziness, sedation, and sleep disruption	• Monitor for these adverse effects and report their occurrence to the primary care provider. • The client may need to be switched to an alternative medication.
Orthostatic hypotension (may occur during the first few weeks of administration)	• Monitor baseline and orthostatic vital signs during the first weeks of treatment. • Educate the client about signs of postural hypotension (e.g., light-headedness, dizziness). Advise the client to sit or lie down if these occur. Orthostatic hypotension can be minimized by getting up slowly from a lying or sitting position.
May cause mild EPS, such as tremor	• Monitor for and teach clients to recognize EPS symptoms. • Use AIMS test to screen for EPS.

- **Contraindications/precautions**

  ◊ Risperidone is a Pregnancy Risk Category C medication.

  ◊ The client should avoid the use of alcohol when taking this medication.

  ◊ Use cautiously in clients with cardiovascular or cerebrovascular disease, seizures, or diabetes mellitus. Clients with diabetes mellitus should have a baseline fasting blood sugar, and blood glucose should be monitored carefully.

  ◊ Risperidone should not be used for dementia-related psychosis. Use of this medication may lead to cerebrovascular accident.

Medication/Food Interactions	Nursing Interventions/Client Education
If taken with clozapine, blood levels of clozapine may increase, thus increasing the chance of adverse effects.	Monitor medication therapy carefully.
Risperidone may potentiate the effects of antihypertensive medications, especially in the first few weeks of treatment.	Monitor vital signs and concurrent medication therapy.

Δ   **Other Atypical Antipsychotic Agents**

Medication	Formulations	Comments
Olanzapine (Zyprexa)	• Tablets • Oral solution • Short-acting injectable	• There is a moderate incidence of anticholinergic effects and EPS associated with the use of olanzapine. • Major adverse effects include significant weight gain, drowsiness, insomnia, and restlessness.
Quetiapine (Seroquel)	• Tablets	• Quetiapine causes mild anticholinergic effects. • There is a low incidence of EPS. • Major adverse effects include weight gain, headache, and drowsiness.

Medication	Formulations	Comments
Aripiprazole (Abilify)	• Tablets • Oral solution	• There is a low incidence of mild anticholinergic effects and EPS associated with the use of aripiprazole. • Major adverse effects include headache, anxiety, insomnia, and gastrointestinal upset.
Ziprasidone (Geodon) – This medication affects both dopamine and serotonin, so it can be used for clients with concurrent depression.	• Capsules • Short-acting injectable	• There is a low incidence of anticholinergic effects associated with the use of ziprasidone. • This medication may cause mild EPS. • Major adverse effects include ECG changes and QT prolongation.
Clozapine (Clozaril) – The first atypical antipsychotic developed, it is no longer considered a first-line medication for schizophrenia due to its adverse effects.	• Tablets	• There is a high incidence of anticholinergic effects associated with the use of clozapine. • This medication does not cause EPS. • It can cause agranulocytosis in up to 1% of those who take it. • Other major adverse effects include seizure risk, significant weight gain, excessive salivation, and tachycardia.

- **Therapeutic nursing interventions and client education**

    ◊ Advise the client that low doses of atypical antipsychotic medications are given initially and are then gradually increased.

    ◊ Advise the client that clozapine has less likelihood of causing EPS symptoms, including tardive dyskinesia.

    ◊ Advise the client to observe for signs of diabetes mellitus(e.g., increased thirst, urination), infection (e.g., fatigue, fever), and weight gain. Advise the client to report these signs to the primary care provider.

Nursing Evaluation of Medication Effectiveness

Δ   Improvement of symptoms (e.g., prevention of acute psychotic symptoms, absence of hallucinations, delusions, anxiety, hostility)

Δ   Improvement in ability to perform ADLs

Δ   Improvement in ability to interact socially with peers

Δ   Improvement of sleeping and eating habits

Primary Reference:

Varcarolis, E. M., Carson, V. B., & Shoemaker, N. C. (2006). *Foundations of psychiatric mental health nursing: A clinical approach* (5th ed.). St. Louis, MO: Saunders.

Additional Resources:

Lehne, R. A. (2007). *Pharmacology for nursing care* (6th ed.). St. Louis, MO: Saunders.

NANDA International (2004). *NANDA nursing diagnoses: Definitions and classification 2005-2006*. Philadelphia: NANDA.

Chapter 16: Medications to Treat Psychoses

Application Exercises

Scenario: A 24-year-old client with paranoid schizophrenia has been treated successfully on an outpatient basis for the past 3 years. Now his condition is deteriorating and inpatient treatment at an acute care mental health facility has been recommended by his primary care provider. The client is very suspicious of the nursing staff, and he has auditory hallucinations in which a voice tells him to "hurt those evil people before they hurt you." He also has pressured speech and speaks mostly using clang associations (meaningless rhymes). His appearance indicates a lack of grooming and hygiene. His behavior is usually aggressive toward others, but his face shows no emotion, even though he sounds angry. The primary care provider has placed this client on risperidone (Risperdal) oral disintegrating tablets, which he receives once daily.

1. Which of the client's symptoms indicate a need for an atypical antipsychotic agent rather than a conventional (typical) medication?

2. Why is this client receiving tablets that disintegrate on the tongue with or without water versus regular tablets that are swallowed?

3. Which of the following symptoms of schizophrenia are effectively treated by the traditional, typical antipsychotics? (Select all that apply.)

_____ Auditory hallucinations

_____ Withdrawal from social situations

_____ Delusions of grandeur

_____ Loose associations

_____ Lack of energy

_____ No motivation to initiate tasks, such as grooming

_____ Pressured speech

4. A client with schizophrenia experiences blurred vision. Which of the following types of receptor blockade results in this adverse effect?

        A. D_2 receptors

        B. Muscarinic receptors

        C. Alpha$_1$ receptors

        D. H_1 receptors

5. Extrapyramidal symptoms (EPS) resulting from typical antipsychotic medications include which of the following? (Select all that apply.)

      _____ Cardiac dysrhythmias

      _____ Parkinson-like symptoms

      _____ Involuntary pelvic and hip movements

      _____ GI pain with nausea, vomiting, and diarrhea

      _____ Muscle spasm in the neck

      _____ Restlessness, jitteriness

      _____ Dehydration caused by polyuria

6. Which of the following client statements indicates understanding of the nurse's teaching regarding antipsychotic medications?

        A. "I will be able to stop taking the drug as soon as I feel better."

        B. "If I feel sleepy I will stop taking the drug and call my health provider."

        C. "My symptoms can come back if I don't take the medication exactly as ordered."

        D. "These drugs are highly addictive and must be withdrawn slowly."

7. A client who has been on an antipsychotic medication for several years begins to exhibit lip smacking, tongue protrusion, and facial grimaces. Which of the following should the nurse suspect?

        A. Parkinsonism

        B. Tardive dyskinesia

        C. Antiadrenergic effects

        D. Anticholinergic effects

Chapter 16: Medications to Treat Psychoses

Application Exercises Answer Key

Scenario: A 24-year-old client with paranoid schizophrenia has been treated successfully on an outpatient basis for the past 3 years. Now his condition is deteriorating and inpatient treatment at an acute care mental health facility has been recommended by his primary care provider. The client is very suspicious of the nursing staff, and he has auditory hallucinations in which a voice tells him to "hurt those evil people before they hurt you." He also has pressured speech and speaks mostly using clang associations (meaningless rhymes). His appearance indicates a lack of grooming and hygiene. His behavior is usually aggressive toward others, but his face shows no emotion, even though he sounds angry. The primary care provider has placed this client on risperidone (Risperdal) oral disintegrating tablets, which he receives once daily.

1. Which of the client's symptoms indicate a need for an atypical antipsychotic agent rather than a conventional (typical) medication?

   The negative symptoms of psychosis are more readily treated by atypical antipsychotics, such as risperidone, than by typical antipsychotics, such as chlorpromazine (Thorazine). Negative symptoms for this client include his lack of grooming and hygiene and his flat affect (no facial emotion shown). The other symptoms mentioned are positive symptoms of psychosis.

2. Why is this client receiving tablets that disintegrate on the tongue with or without water versus regular tablets that are swallowed?

   A client who is suspicious of others and who is so ill that he is unable to behave rationally is at high risk for nonadherence to his treatment regimen. The orally disintegrating tablets dissolve easily in the oral cavity and should help prevent him from "cheeking" his medication and later disposing of it. Another alternative would be to administer this client's medication intramuscularly until he is able to take it orally.

3. Which of the following symptoms of schizophrenia are effectively treated by the traditional, typical antipsychotics? (Select all that apply.)

  __X__ **Auditory hallucinations**

  _____ Withdrawal from social situations

  __X__ **Delusions of grandeur**

  __X__ **Loose associations**

  _____ Lack of energy

  _____ No motivation to initiate tasks, such as grooming

  __X__ **Pressured speech**

Auditory hallucinations, delusions of grandeur, loose associations, and pressured speech are all positive symptoms of schizophrenia that can be successfully treated with typical antipsychotics, such as chlorpromazine. Withdrawal from social situations, lack of energy, and no motivation to initiate tasks are examples of negative symptoms. The newer atypical antipsychotics can successfully treat both positive and negative symptoms.

4. A client with schizophrenia experiences blurred vision. Which of the following types of receptor blockade results in this adverse effect?

  A. D_2 receptors

  B. Muscarinic receptors

  C. Alpha$_1$ receptors

  D. H_1 receptors

Blurred vision is an example of an anticholinergic adverse effect caused by blockade of muscarinic receptors for acetylcholine. Other anticholinergic effects include dry mouth, constipation, and urinary retention.

5. Extrapyramidal symptoms (EPS) resulting from typical antipsychotic medications include which of the following? (Select all that apply.)

_____ Cardiac dysrhythmias

__X__ **Parkinson-like symptoms**

__X__ **Involuntary pelvic and hip movements**

_____ GI pain with nausea, vomiting, and diarrhea

__X__ **Muscle spasm in the neck**

__X__ **Restlessness, jitteriness**

_____ Dehydration caused by polyuria

EPS always involve uncontrollable motor symptoms caused by dopamine receptor blockade and include Parkinson-like symptoms, involuntary pelvic and hip movements, muscle spasm in the neck, restlessness, and jitteriness. Cardiac dysrhythmias, GI pain with nausea, vomiting and diarrhea, and dehydration caused by polyuria are not motor symptoms and are caused by other mechanisms.

6. Which of the following client statements indicates understanding of the nurse's teaching regarding antipsychotic medications?

A. "I will be able to stop taking the drug as soon as I feel better."

B. "If I feel sleepy I will stop taking the drug and call my health provider."

C. **"My symptoms can come back if I don't take the medication exactly as ordered."**

D. "These drugs are highly addictive and must be withdrawn slowly."

Antipsychotic medications should be taken as ordered to prevent return of psychotic symptoms. Antipsychotic medications are usually taken over a long period of time to prevent symptoms of psychosis. Drowsiness is a common adverse effect of some of the antipsychotic medications; however, stopping the medication if the client feels sleepy is not appropriate. Antipsychotic medications are not considered addictive and do not cause tolerance in clients who take them.

7. A client who has been on an antipsychotic medication for several years begins to exhibit lip smacking, tongue protrusion, and facial grimaces. Which of the following should the nurse suspect?

> A. Parkinsonism
> **B. Tardive dyskinesia**
> C. Antiadrenergic effects
> D. Anticholinergic effects

Tardive dyskinesia includes abnormal movements of the lips, tongue, face, and neck. These symptoms are not characteristic of parkinsonism, antiadrenergic effects, or anticholinergic effects.

Unit 3   Psychopharmacological Therapies

Chapter 17:   Medications to Treat Cognitive Disorders: Alzheimer's Disease

Contributor: Judith A. Harris, MSN, RNC

 NCLEX-RN® Connections:

Learning Objective: Review and apply knowledge within "**Medications to Treat Cognitive Disorders: Alzheimer's Disease**" in readiness for performance of the following nursing activities as outlined by the NCLEX-RN® test plan:

Δ   Apply knowledge of mental health when caring for the client receiving psychopharmacological therapy for a mental health disorder.

Δ   Assess the client for expected and side/adverse effects of medications used to treat cognitive disorders.

Δ   Assess the client for actual/potential specific food-medication interactions.

Δ   Identify contraindications, actual/potential incompatibilities, and interactions between medications. Intervene appropriately.

Δ   Identify symptoms/evidence of an allergic reaction and respond appropriately.

Δ   Evaluate/monitor and document the therapeutic and adverse/side effects of medications used to treat cognitive disorders.

Δ   Provide client teaching on actions, therapeutic effects, potential side/adverse effects, and interactions of medications used to treat cognitive disorders.

 Key Points

Δ   Pharmacotherapeutics is based on the theory that Alzheimer's disease is a result of depleted levels of the enzyme acetyltransferase, which is necessary to produce the neurotransmitter acetylcholine.

Δ   Alzheimer's medications temporarily slow the course of the disease and do not work for all clients.

Δ   Benefits for those clients who do respond to medication include improvements in cognition, behavior, and function.

Δ   Therapeutic agents include:

- **Cholinesterase inhibitors**: donepezil (Aricept), tacrine (Cognex), rivastigmine (Exelon), and galantamine (Razadyne, formerly available as Reminyl).

- **Memantine** (Namenda), an N-methyl-D-aspartate (NMDA) receptor antagonist. NMDA is a substance that contributes to degeneration of brain cells.

Δ   Other medications for clients with dementia attempt to target behavioral and emotional problems, such as anxiety, agitation, combativeness, and depression. These medications include antipsychotics, antidepressants, and anxiolytics. Clients receiving these medications should be closely monitored for adverse effects.

Δ   Much research is being done to discover a cure for Alzheimer's disease.

- Estrogen therapy for women may prevent Alzheimer's disease, but it is not useful in decreasing the effects of preexisting dementia.

- Ginkgo biloba, an herbal product taken by millions to increase memory and blood circulation, can cause a variety of side effects and medication interactions. If a client is using ginkgo biloba or other nutritional supplements, that information should be shared with health care providers.

Therapeutic Agents

Δ   **Donepezil (Aricept):** Cholinesterase Inhibitor

- **Expected pharmacological action**

  ◊   Donepezil increases the availability of acetylcholine at neurotransmitter receptor sites.

- **Therapeutic uses**

  ◊   Improve function for self-care and slow cognitive deterioration of Alzheimer's disease by an average of 2 years.

  ◊   Donepezil is used for mild to moderate Alzheimer's dementia.

Side/Adverse Effects	Nursing Interventions/Client Education
Nausea and diarrhea, which occur in approximately 10% of clients	• Monitor for gastrointestinal side effects and for fluid volume deficits. • Assure that the client receives adequate fluids. • The primary care provider may titrate the dosage to reduce symptoms.
Bradycardia	• Teach the family to monitor pulse rate for the client who lives at home. • The client should be screened for underlying heart disease.

- **Contraindications/precautions**

  ◊ Donepezil is a Pregnancy Risk Category C medication.

  ◊ The cholinesterase inhibitors should be used with caution in clients with preexisting asthma or other obstructive pulmonary disorders. Bronchoconstriction may be caused by an increase of acetylcholine.

Medication/Food Interactions	Nursing Interventions/Client Education
Concurrent use of **NSAIDs**, such as aspirin, may cause gastrointestinal bleeding.	• Assess the use of over-the-counter NSAIDS. • Monitor for signs and symptoms of gastrointestinal bleeding.
Antihistamines, tricyclic antidepressants, and conventional antipsychotics (medications that block cholinergic receptors) can reduce the therapeutic effects of donepezil.	• Avoid the use of cholinergic receptor blocking medications for clients taking any cholinesterase inhibitor.

Δ **Other Cholinesterase Inhibitor Medications**

- Tacrine (Cognex) – There is a high risk of liver damage with this medication; therefore, it is no longer a medication of choice.

- Rivastigmine (Exelon)

- Galantamine (Razadyne)

Δ **Memantine (Namenda)**

- **Expected pharmacological action**

  ◊ Blocks the entry of calcium into nerve cells and thus slows down brain cell death.

- **Therapeutic uses**

  ◊ Memantine is the only medication approved for moderate to severe stages of Alzheimer's disease.

  ◊ It may be added to a regimen of a cholinesterase inhibitor already prescribed.

Therapeutic Nursing Interventions and Client Education for Medications to Treat Alzheimer's Disease

Δ Assess for improvement in memory and the client's quality of life.

Δ Monitor for adverse effects and educate the client and family about these effects.

Δ Monitor the client for the ability to swallow tablets. Most of the medications are available in tablets and oral solutions. Donepezil is available in an orally disintegrating tablet.

Δ   Donepezil has a long half-life and is administered once daily at bedtime. The other cholinesterase inhibitors are usually administered twice daily.

Δ   If a client fails to improve with one medication, a trial of one of the other medications is warranted.

Nursing Evaluation of Medication Effectiveness

Δ   Improvement in symptomatology (e.g., improved cognition, memory, and ability to perform self-care)

Δ   Slower progression of disease with as few side effects as possible

Primary Reference:

Varcarolis, E. M., Carson, V. B., & Shoemaker, N. C. (2006). *Foundations of psychiatric mental health nursing: A clinical approach* (5th ed.). St. Louis, MO: Saunders.

Additional Resources:

Alzheimer's Association. (n.d.). *Standard prescriptions*. Retrieved January 8, 2007, from http://www.alz.org/AboutAD/Treatment/Standard.asp#memantine

German, D., & Lee, A. (Eds.) (2006). Alzheimer's dementia. *Nurse practitioners' prescribing reference, 13*(3), 98-102.

Lehne, R. A. (2007). *Pharmacology for nursing care* (6th ed.). St. Louis, MO: Saunders.

NANDA International (2004). *NANDA nursing diagnoses: Definitions and classification 2005-2006*. Philadelphia: NANDA.

Chapter 17: Medications to Treat Cognitive Disorders: Alzheimer's Disease

Application Exercises

Scenario: A 68-year-old client has just been diagnosed with early stage Alzheimer's disease. He is experiencing short-term memory loss, and his 56-year-old wife has quit her job to stay home with him because he is depressed and is also distressed about being so forgetful. The client just began taking donepezil (Aricept) 5 mg daily at bedtime.

1. How does donepezil (Aricept) work, and what are the benefits of the medication for this client?

2. The client's wife asks the nurse about using gingko biloba to treat her husband's Alzheimer's disease. What information should the nurse give her?

3. The client's wife asks if donepezil will help treat her husband's depression, which she feels is worsening progressively as he becomes more forgetful. How should the nurse reply?

4. Which of the following statements made by a family member indicates a need for further teaching about donepezil (Aricept)?

   A. "I will be giving my father this drug twice a day with meals to prevent stomach upset."

   B. "I better not give my father an antihistamine for his allergy unless his doctor says it's okay."

   C. "I know this drug will not cure my father's disease, but hopefully the symptoms will slow down for a while."

   D. "If this drug doesn't work, maybe one of the other ones will."

5. A family member asks if her father who has just been diagnosed with Alzheimer's disease should be taking tacrine (Cognex), since her uncle was given this medication 10 years ago when he developed Alzheimer's disease. How should the nurse respond?

Chapter 17: Medications to Treat Cognitive Disorders: Alzheimer's Disease

Application Exercises Answer Key

Scenario: A 68-year-old client has just been diagnosed with early stage Alzheimer's disease. He is experiencing short-term memory loss, and his 56-year-old wife has quit her job to stay home with him because he is depressed and is also distressed about being so forgetful. The client just began taking donepezil (Aricept) 5 mg daily at bedtime.

1. How does donepezil (Aricept) work, and what are the benefits of the medication for this client?

    Cholinesterase inhibitors prevent the breakdown of acetylcholine in cerebral neurons, increasing its availability in the brain. Donepezil and the other cholinesterase inhibitors slow memory loss and improve behavior and daily function. Their use slows the progression of the disease for a few months and is effective in 30 to 60% of clients who take them.

2. The client's wife asks the nurse about using gingko biloba to treat her husband's Alzheimer's disease. What information should the nurse give her?

    Some studies have shown that gingko biloba is able to stabilize or improve cognitive function briefly in clients with Alzheimer's disease. Like the cholinesterase inhibiting medications, it does not cure the disease. It may, however, slow progression for a few months with no greater improvement in symptoms. Gingko biloba has antiplatelet activity that may increase the risk of bleeding, especially if given with aspirin or anticoagulants.

3. The client's wife asks if donepezil will help treat her husband's depression, which she feels is worsening progressively as he becomes more forgetful. How should the nurse reply?

    Cholinesterase inhibitors do not affect a client's mood. This client should be referred to his primary care provider for possible placement on an antidepressant medication.

4. Which of the following statements made by a family member indicates a need for further teaching about donepezil (Aricept)?

   A. "I will be giving my father this drug twice a day with meals to prevent stomach upset."

   B. "I better not give my father an antihistamine for his allergy unless his doctor says it's okay."

   C. "I know this drug will not cure my father's disease, but hopefully the symptoms will slow down for a while."

   D. "If this drug doesn't work, maybe one of the other ones will."

Donepezil has a long half-life and is only administered once daily at bedtime. The other options are true statements.

5. A family member asks if her father who has just been diagnosed with Alzheimer's disease should be taking tacrine (Cognex), since her uncle was given this medication 10 years ago when he developed Alzheimer's disease. How should the nurse respond?

Tacrine (Cognex), the first cholinesterase inhibitor used for Alzheimer's disease, is now seldom prescribed, because it can cause severe liver damage. There are similar drugs that can temporarily halt progress of the disease, and they have less serious adverse effects.

Unit 3   Psychopharmacological Therapies

Chapter 18:   Medications to Treat Attention Deficit Hyperactivity Disorder (ADHD)

Contributor: Judith A. Harris, MSN, RNC

 NCLEX-RN® Connections:

Learning Objective: Review and apply knowledge within "**Medications to Treat Attention Deficit Hyperactivity Disorder (ADHD)**" in readiness for performance of the following nursing activities as outlined by the NCLEX-RN® test plan:

Δ   Apply knowledge of mental health when caring for the client receiving psychopharmacological therapy for ADHD.

Δ   Assess the client for expected and side/adverse effects of medications used to treat ADHD.

Δ   Assess the client for actual/potential specific food-medication interactions.

Δ   Identify contraindications, actual/potential incompatibilities, and interactions between medications. Intervene appropriately.

Δ   Identify symptoms/evidence of an allergic reaction and respond appropriately.

Δ   Evaluate/monitor and document the therapeutic and adverse/side effects of medications used to treat ADHD.

Δ   Provide client teaching on actions, therapeutic effects, potential side/adverse effects, and interactions of medications used to treat ADHD.

 Key Points

Δ   **ADHD**, which is characterized by hyperactivity, inattention, and impulsivity, is the most common mental health disorder of childhood in the United States. (*Refer to chapter 28, Developmental and Behavioral Disorders.*)

Δ   ADHD is treated with a combination of medication therapy and cognitive-behavioral therapy.

Δ   The various stimulant medications are not identical but are all similar; clients who are unable to take one of the medications may benefit from taking a different one.

Δ   Stimulant medications reduce the **negative symptoms** of ADHD by increasing the client's ability to focus on tasks. Therapy is then used to increase the client's positive behaviors, such as studying schoolwork.

Δ   With the exception of atomoxetine (Strattera), the medications used to treat ADHD are **central nervous system (CNS) stimulants**.

- These stimulants include members of the amphetamine family (amphetamine, dextroamphetamine, and methamphetamine).

- Increases of dopamine and norepinephrine cause:

    ◊   Therapeutic effects in both the CNS and the periphery.

    ◊   Cardiac stimulation (e.g., tachycardia and dysrhythmias).

    ◊   Vasoconstriction (hypertension) in the periphery.

- These medications cause tolerance, physical dependence, and have a high risk for abuse (Schedule II Controlled Substance).

- The initial response to stimulant medications is seen with the first dose taken.

- Adults who took stimulants for childhood ADHD may still benefit from these medications in adulthood. One third of adults either no longer tolerate the adverse effects of the stimulants or may no longer benefit from stimulant therapy.

Medications Used to Treat ADHD	
Type	Medication
CNS stimulants	• Methylphenidate (Ritalin, Ritalin SR, Concerta) • Dextroamphetamine in various salts and other forms (Dexedrine, DextroStat) • Dexmethylphenidate (Focalin)
Nonstimulant	• Atomoxetine (Strattera)

Therapeutic Agents

Δ   **Methylphenidate (Ritalin, Ritalin SR, Concerta)**: CNS Stimulant

- **Expected pharmacological action**

    ◊   All stimulant medications release norepinephrine and dopamine into the CNS and inhibit the reuptake of norepinephrine and dopamine.

- **Therapeutic uses**

    ◊   ADHD – increase in attention span and goal-directed behavior

    ◊   Narcolepsy – alleviation of symptoms of extreme drowsiness and prevention of uncontrollable urges to sleep during the daytime

Side/Adverse Effects	Nursing Interventions/Client Education
CNS stimulation (e.g., insomnia, restlessness)	• Advise the client to observe for symptoms and notify the primary care provider if they occur. • Dosage may need to be reduced.
Unwanted weight loss/growth retardation	• Monitor the client's weight. • Promote good nutrition in children. • Encourage children to eat at regular meal times and avoid unhealthy foods for snacks. • Administer the medication with or after meals.
Cardiovascular effects (e.g., dysrhythmias, chest pain, high blood pressure) – may increase the risk of sudden death in clients with heart abnormalities.	• Monitor the client's vital signs and ECG. • Advise the client to observe for symptoms and notify the primary care provider if they occur.

- **Contraindications/precautions**

  ◊ Methylphenidate is a Pregnancy Risk Category C medication.

  ◊ Use methylphenidate cautiously in clients with hyperthyroidism, heart disease, glaucoma, history of drug abuse, and in those taking MAOIs.

  ◊ Overdoses can lead to seizures and psychotic behavior.

  ◊ Methylphenidate can produce tolerance (to mood elevation, appetite suppression, stimulation of heart and blood vessels) and psychological dependence.

  ◊ Abrupt withdrawal of methylphenidate after long-term use will result in **abstinence syndrome** (exhaustion, prolonged sleep, excessive eating, depression, craving for more of the drug).

Medication/Food Interactions	Nursing Interventions/Client Education
MAOIs – Concurrent use may cause hypertensive crisis.	• Avoid concurrent use.
Caffeine – Concurrent use may cause an increase in CNS stimulant effects.	• Instruct the client to avoid foods that contain caffeine, such as tea, chocolate, and coffee.
Phenytoin (Dilantin), warfarin (Coumadin) and phenobarbital – Methylphenidate inhibits metabolism of these medications, leading to increased serum levels.	• Monitor the client for adverse effects, such as signs of bleeding for clients taking warfarin or CNS depression for those taking phenobarbital. • Concurrent use of these medications should be cautious.
Over-the-counter (OTC) cold and decongestant medications – OTC decongestants and cold remedies may contain medications with sympathomimetic action, which can lead to an increase in CNS stimulant effects.	• Instruct the client to avoid the use of OTC medications.

- **Therapeutic nursing interventions and client education**

  ◊ Obtain a thorough medical and medication history (including substance abuse), paying particular attention to the use of prescription and OTC medications that may interact with amphetamines.

  ◊ **Children**: Obtain baseline height and weight, and monitor for appropriate growth at specified intervals. Assess behavior and record as baseline for comparison.

  ◊ Standards of practice may no longer include providing for periodic "medication-free" holidays that allow for normal growth and development. Administering the medication during or after meals can minimize appetite suppression, which may lead to growth suppression.

  ◊ Monitor for medication tolerance, which develops within a few weeks. The medication may be discontinued if higher doses cannot be given safely.

  ◊ Stimulants are made in preparations designed for either short-, intermediate-, or long-duration dosing.

    ° Short-duration medications, such as Ritalin, are administered two to three times daily, often at 0800, 1200, and 1600.

    ° Intermediate-duration medications, such as Ritalin SR, have a delayed release and last 4 to 8 hr. They are usually taken twice daily: once in the morning with an early afternoon supplement.

    ° Long-duration medications, such as Concerta, are taken once daily. Concerta is made with an intermediate-duration outer coat and an inner core that releases medication slowly. It is important not to chew or crush this medication.

    ° A methylphenidate transdermal patch (Daytrana) is now available in several strengths. The patch should be applied 2 hr before the desired effect is needed and must be removed after 9 hr. The patch may be removed earlier if an effect is no longer needed or if late-day side effects, such a loss of appetite, are a problem. Clients using the patch may have the same adverse effects as those taking oral stimulants. It is important to assess the skin for redness or irritation.

  ◊ Client education includes:

    ° Advising the client to swallow sustained-release tablets whole and to avoid chewing or crushing tablets.

    ° Teaching the client the importance of administering the medication on a regular schedule and taking each medication exactly as prescribed.

    ° Instructing the client to be alert for signs of mild overdose, such as restlessness, insomnia, and nervousness. Signs of severe overdose include panic, hallucinations, circulatory collapse, and seizures.

- ° Suggesting to parents to initiate a periodic pill count if they doubt the client's medication compliance.

- ° Advising the client to avoid other CNS stimulants, such as coffee, cola, tea, and chocolate.

- ° Instructing the client to avoid alcohol or OTC medications unless approved by the primary care provider. Many OTC medications contain CNS-stimulating properties.

- ° Educating the client about the side effects of abruptly stopping the medication (potential for abstinence syndrome).

- ° Instructing the client to take the morning (or daily) dose after breakfast and the last dose in early afternoon to minimize weight loss and insomnia. The medication should be taken as least 6 hr before bedtime.

- ° Advising the client that sucking hard candy, chewing gum, and taking sips of water may help minimize dry mouth.

Δ **Atomoxetine (Strattera)**: Nonstimulant

- **Expected pharmacological action**

   ◊ Atomoxetine controls ADHD symptoms through selective inhibition of presynaptic norepinephrine transport.

   ◊ **Initial** response develops within a **few days**, with **maximum response** in **1 to 3 weeks**.

- **Therapeutic uses**

   ◊ ADHD – increase in attention span and goal-directed behavior

- **Contraindications/precautions**

   ◊ Atomoxetine has no abuse potential and is therefore not regulated as a controlled substance.

   ◊ It is not recommended for use in clients who are well controlled with stimulants.

- **Side/adverse effects**

   ◊ Gastrointestinal upset, anorexia, mood swings, insomnia, weight loss, and growth retardation

   ◊ Severe allergic reaction (rare)

   ◊ Adult use: possible occurrence of sexual dysfunction and urinary retention, along with a slight rise in heart rate and blood pressure

- **Therapeutic nursing interventions and client education**
  - ◊ Obtain a thorough medical and medication history (including substance abuse), paying particular attention to the use of prescription and OTC medications that may interact with atomoxetine.

  - ◊ Children: Obtain baseline height and weight and monitor for appropriate growth at specified intervals. Assess behavior and record as baseline for comparison.

  - ◊ Dosing schedules include once a day in the morning or twice a day, dividing the dose between a dose at breakfast and a second dose in late afternoon or early evening.

  - ◊ Standards of practice may no longer include providing for periodic "medication-free" holidays that allow for normal growth and development. Administering the medication during or after meals can minimize appetite suppression, which may lead to growth suppression.

  - ◊ Client education includes:
    - ° Teaching the client the importance of administering the medication on a regular schedule. Reinforce to the client the importance of taking the medication exactly as prescribed.

    - ° Instructing the client to avoid CNS stimulants (e.g., coffee, tea, cola) and alcohol.

    - ° Telling the client to swallow the capsule whole and that the medication may be taken with or without food.

Nursing Evaluation of Medication Effectiveness

Δ Depending on therapeutic intent, effectiveness may be evidenced by improvement of symptoms of ADHD in children and adults (e.g., increased ability to focus, complete tasks, and interact with peers).

Primary Reference:

Varcarolis, E. M., Carson, V. B., & Shoemaker, N. C. (2006). *Foundations of psychiatric mental health nursing: A clinical approach* (5th ed.). St. Louis, MO: Saunders.

Additional Resources:

German, D., & Lee, A. (Eds.) (2006). ADHD/Narcolepsy. *Nurse practitioners' prescribing reference*, *13*(3), 102-106.

Lehne, R. A. (2007). *Pharmacology for nursing care* (6th ed.). St. Louis, MO: Saunders.

NANDA International (2004). *NANDA nursing diagnoses: Definitions and classification 2005-2006*. Philadelphia: NANDA.

Chapter 18: Medications to Treat Attention Deficit Hyperactivity Disorder (ADHD)

Application Exercises

1. Which of the following is an expected outcome after administration of methylphenidate (either by transdermal patch or through oral dose)?

        A. Increased intellectual capacity

        B. Increased attention span

        C. Elimination of behavior problems

        D. Improvement in fine motor skills

2. An adult is being treated for ADHD with methylphenidate. Which of the following statements indicates that he has understood the nurse's teaching regarding the medication?

        A. "I can still take any over-the-counter drug along with this medication."

        B. "I can still continue to drink my colas without any problem."

        C. "There are no side effects to worry about with this drug."

        D. "I should take my second drug dose in the afternoon and not at bedtime."

3. A client who has taken methylphenidate (Ritalin) daily for 5 years decides to stop taking it altogether. Which of the following symptoms should the nurse expect to see a few days after the client discontinues the medication?

        A. Insomnia, irritability

        B. Increased ability to concentrate

        C. Depression and exhaustion

        D. Generalized anxiety and possible panic attacks

4. A 10-year-old boy with ADHD has been treated with methylphenidate (Ritalin) for 18 months. His symptoms have returned, and his medication is changed to atomoxetine (Strattera). His mother calls the nurse the next week to say that the new medication is "not working; he is still hyperactive and restless." What information should the nurse give this mother?

5. A 7-year-old boy has begun to have severe problems at school. His teacher says he is unable to sit still or concentrate on his schoolwork. He continually talks to other children and disrupts the entire class. However, the parents say his behavior at home is no problem at all. The mother says her son has difficulty swallowing pills. The primary care provider has placed this child on methylphenidate transdermal patches (Daytrana), 10 mg daily on school days, to be applied 2 hr before getting on the school bus. What is the rationale for putting this client on methylphenidate transdermal patches?

6. A nurse is explaining interactions between methylphenidate and food to a client's mother. The client's mother breaks in and says, "That doesn't matter because my son will be taking the medication by patch rather than swallowing a pill." How should the nurse respond?

Chapter 18: Medications to Treat Attention Deficit Hyperactivity Disorder (ADHD)

Application Exercises Answer Key

1. Which of the following is an expected outcome after administration of methylphenidate (either by transdermal patch or through oral dose)?

      A. Increased intellectual capacity

      B. Increased attention span

      C. Elimination of behavior problems

      D. Improvement in fine motor skills

Increased ability to focus is the expected outcome of methylphenidate use. Intellectual capacity is an innate quality not affected by the medication. The medication will not eliminate behavior problems; however, allowing the client to focus better may also improve his behavior. Any improvement in fine motor skills would be the result of the client being better able to focus on the fine motor task.

2. An adult is being treated for ADHD with methylphenidate. Which of the following statements indicates that he has understood the nurse's teaching regarding the medication?

      A. "I can still take any over-the-counter drug along with this medication."

      B. "I can still continue to drink my colas without any problem."

      C. "There are no side effects to worry about with this drug."

      D. "I should take my second drug dose in the afternoon and not at bedtime."

The medication should be taken at least 6 hr before bedtime to prevent insomnia. Some over-the-counter cold remedies may stimulate the sympathetic nervous system and cause increased side effects, such as irritability and tachycardia. Cola contains caffeine, which also causes increased effects of methylphenidate. This medication does have side effects that the client should know about.

3. A client who has taken methylphenidate (Ritalin) daily for 5 years decides to stop taking it altogether. Which of the following symptoms should the nurse expect to see a few days after the client discontinues the medication?

> A. Insomnia, irritability
> B. Increased ability to concentrate
> **C. Depression and exhaustion**
> D. Generalized anxiety and possible panic attacks

Abstinence syndrome could develop if one of the stimulant medications is abruptly discontinued. Symptoms are opposite of those one would expect to see if the client takes an overdose of the medication. The symptoms include: exhaustion, depression, prolonged sleeping, increased appetite, and craving for the medication.

4. A 10-year-old boy with ADHD has been treated with methylphenidate (Ritalin) for 18 months. His symptoms have returned, and his medication is changed to atomoxetine (Strattera). His mother calls the nurse the next week to say that the new medication is "not working; he is still hyperactive and restless." What information should the nurse give this mother?

With methylphenidate, near maximum effects are seen after the first dose; with atomoxetine, initial response takes a few days to develop, with maximum response in 1 to 3 weeks.

5. A 7-year-old boy has begun to have severe problems at school. His teacher says he is unable to sit still or concentrate on his schoolwork. He continually talks to other children and disrupts the entire class. However, the parents say his behavior at home is no problem at all. The mother says her son has difficulty swallowing pills. The primary care provider has placed this child on methylphenidate transdermal patches (Daytrana), 10 mg daily on school days, to be applied 2 hr before getting on the school bus. What is the rationale for putting this client on methylphenidate transdermal patches?

This child has behavioral problems and difficulty concentrating, which are only manifested at school. Use of the methylphenidate patch only during the hours that this client needs it may allow him to focus at school without any late-day adverse reactions, such as loss of appetite. In addition, there are no pills for the child to swallow.

6. A nurse is explaining interactions between methylphenidate and food to a client's mother. The client's mother breaks in and says, "That doesn't matter because my son will be taking the medication by patch rather than swallowing a pill." How should the nurse respond?

The client should still avoid foods containing caffeine, such as cola, because the interaction is in the bloodstream rather than in the stomach. Caffeine and methylphenidate cause similar effects in the CNS, and the effect of one may increase the effects, such as insomnia and restlessness, of the other.

Unit 4   Psychobiologic Disorders, Psychiatric Emergencies, and Mental Health Nursing Care of Special Populations

Section: Psychobiologic Disorders

Chapter 19:   Anxiety Disorders
Contributor: Susan Dawson, EdD, RN, APRN-BC

 NCLEX-RN® Connections:

> **Learning Objective**: Review and apply knowledge within "**Anxiety Disorders**" in readiness for performance of the following nursing activities as outlined by the NCLEX-RN® test plan:
>
> Δ   Apply knowledge of psychobiologic disorders to the nursing process when caring for clients with acute or chronic anxiety disorders.
>
> Δ   Identify the client/family's responses to the diagnosis of an anxiety disorder.
>
> Δ   Plan/provide care for the client with an anxiety disorder.
>
> Δ   Support the client's efforts in the use of strategies to decrease anxiety.
>
> Δ   Evaluate and document the client's response to treatment of an anxiety disorder.
>
> Δ   Evaluate the client's ability to follow the treatment plan for an anxiety disorder.
>
> Δ   Teach the client/family signs and symptoms of relapse of the anxiety disorder.

 Key Points

Δ   Anxiety is a response to stress.

Δ   Higher levels of anxiety result in behavior changes.

Δ   Defense mechanisms are used by people with anxiety disorders.

Δ   Except for obsessive-compulsive disorder, which has equal prevalence in men and women, anxiety disorders are much more likely to occur in women than in men.

Δ   The various anxiety disorders recognized and defined by the DSM-IV-TR include: panic disorder, phobias, obsessive-compulsive disorder, generalized anxiety disorder, and stress-related disorders, including acute stress disorder and posttraumatic stress disorder.

Key Factors

Δ   Anxiety levels can be **mild** (restlessness, increased motivation, irritability), **moderate** (agitation, muscle tightness), **severe** (inability to function, ritualistic behavior, unresponsive), or **panic** (distorted perception, loss of rational thought, immobility).

Δ   **Specific anxiety disorders** include:

- **Panic disorder** – The client experiences recurrent panic attacks.

  ◊   Episodes typically last 15 to 30 min.

  ◊   Four or more of the following symptoms are present.

  - °   Palpitations

  - °   Shortness of breath

  - °   Choking or smothering sensation

  - °   Chest pain

  - °   Nausea

  - °   Feelings of depersonalization

  - °   Fear of dying or insanity

  - °   Chills or hot flashes

  ◊   The client may experience behavior changes and/or persistent worries about when the next attack will occur.

  ◊   The client may begin to experience agoraphobia due to a fear of being in places where previous panic attacks occurred. For example, if previous attacks occurred while driving, the client may stop driving. If attacks continue while walking or taking alternative transportation, client may stay home.

- **Phobias** – The client fears a specific object or situation to an unreasonable level. Phobias include:

  ◊   Social phobia – The client has a fear of embarrassment, is unable to perform in front of others, has a dread of social situations, believes that others are judging him negatively, and has impaired relationships.

  ◊   Agoraphobia – The client avoids being outside and has an impaired ability to work or perform duties.

  ◊   Specific phobias

  - °   The client has a fear of specific objects (e.g., spiders, snakes, or strangers).

  - °   The client has a fear of specific experiences (e.g., flying, being in the dark, riding in an elevator, being in an enclosed space).

- **Obsessive-compulsive disorder (OCD)** – The client has intrusive thoughts of unrealistic obsessions and tries to control these thoughts with compulsive behaviors (e.g., repetitive cleaning of a particular object or washing of hands).

  ◊ Clients who engage in constant ritualistic behaviors may have difficulty meeting self-care needs (e.g., personal hygiene, grooming, nutrition, fluid intake, elimination, sleep).

  ◊ If rituals include constant handwashing or cleaning, skin damage and infection may occur.

- **Generalized anxiety disorder (GAD)** – More than 6 months of uncontrollable, excessive worry.

  ◊ GAD causes significant impairment in one or more areas of functioning, such as work-related duties.

  ◊ At least three of the following physical symptoms are present.

    ° Fatigue

    ° Restlessness

    ° Problems with concentration

    ° Irritability

    ° Increased muscle tension

    ° Sleep disturbances

- **Stress-related disorders** include:

  ◊ **Acute stress disorder** – Exposure to a traumatic event causes numbing, detachment, and amnesia about the event for not more than 4 weeks following the event.

  ◊ **Posttraumatic stress disorder (PTSD)** – Exposure to a traumatic event causes intense fear, horror, flashbacks, feelings of detachment and foreboding, restricted affect, and impairment for longer than 1 month after the event. Symptoms may last for years.

	Acute Stress Disorder	PTSD
Precipitating event	• In both disorders, the client witnessed or experienced an actual event that threatened death to the client or others. • The client responded with fear, helplessness, or horror to the event.	
First symptoms	Symptoms occur within 4 weeks of the traumatic event.	**The onset of symptoms is delayed at least 3 months** from the precipitating event, and onset may not occur until years afterward.

	Acute Stress Disorder	PTSD
Duration	Symptoms last from 2 days to 4 weeks.	**Symptoms last more than 1 month**. • Acute PTSD – duration less than 3 months • Chronic PTSD – duration more than 3 months
Re-experience of event	Persistent re-experience in: • Distress when reminded of event • Dreams or images • Reliving through flashbacks	Persistent re-experience in: • Recurrent, intrusive recollection of event • Dreams or images • Reliving through flashbacks, illusions, or hallucinations
Symptoms	• Dissociative symptoms, such as amnesia of the trauma event, absent emotional response, decreased awareness of surroundings, depersonalization • Symptoms of severe anxiety, such as irritability, sleep disturbance	• Symptoms of increased arousal, such as irritability, difficulty with concentration, sleep disturbance • Avoidance of stimuli associated with trauma, such as avoiding people, inability to show feelings

Δ   Related Disorders

• Anxiety can be due to an **acute medical condition**, such as pulmonary embolism. It is important that symptoms be assessed in the appropriate medical facility to rule out a physical cause.

• **Substance-induced** anxiety can be related to current use of a chemical substance or to withdrawal symptoms from a substance such as alcohol.

• Anxiety may also be classified as "**not otherwise specified**" when symptoms of anxiety or panic do not meet the DSM-IV-TR classification for anxiety disorders.

Δ   Defense mechanisms are cognitive distortions used to deal with stress and are prevalent in individuals with anxiety disorders.

Assessment

Δ   Perform a psychosocial assessment for anxiety.

• Use a standardized assessment scale, such as the Hamilton Rating Scale for Anxiety.

• Open-ended questions help to assess the client's feelings.

• The nurse may need to provide a structured interview if the client clarifies and corrects statements repeatedly.

NANDA Nursing Diagnoses

Δ   Anxiety

Δ   Ineffective coping

Δ   Post-trauma syndrome

Δ   Powerlessness

Δ   Ineffective role performance

Δ   Bathing/hygiene or toileting self-care deficit

Δ   Chronic or situational low self-esteem

Δ   Disturbed sleep pattern

Nursing Interventions

Δ   Provide safety and comfort to the client during the crisis period of these disorders.

Δ   Remain with the client during the worst of the anxiety to provide reassurance.

Δ   Sit and talk to the client using therapeutic communication skills to help the client express the feelings of anxiety.

Δ   Use relaxation techniques with the client as needed for symptoms of pain, muscle tension, and feelings of anxiety.

Δ   Teach the client about prescribed medications for anxiety as needed.

Δ   Medications used for the various types of anxiety disorders generally include:

•   Selective serotonin reuptake inhibitors (SSRIs).

•   Tricyclic antidepressants.

•   Monoamine oxidase inhibitors (MAOIs).

•   Benzodiazepines.

•   Beta blockers.

•   Anti-epileptic medications, including carbamazepine (Tegretol), gabapentin (Neurontin), and valproic acid (Depakote). These medications are used as mood stabilizers for the client who is anxious.

Δ   When the anxiety has passed, help the client to evaluate the coping mechanisms that work and do not work for controlling the anxiety.

Δ   Instill hope for positive outcomes (but avoid false reassurance).

Δ   Enhance self-esteem by encouraging positive statements and discussion of past achievements.

Δ   Postpone health teaching until after acute anxiety subsides. Clients with panic attack or severe anxiety are unable to concentrate or learn.

Δ   Advanced practice nurses may be trained in other therapies to treat anxiety disorder, including:

- Cognitive-behavioral therapy, such as cognitive reframing.

- Behavioral therapy, such as systemic desensitization and thought stopping (distraction used by client to interrupt negative or ritualistic thoughts).

- Group and family therapy, for clients with PTSD.

Primary Reference:

Varcarolis, E. M., Carson, V. B., & Shoemaker, N. C. (2006). *Foundations of psychiatric mental health nursing: A clinical approach* (5th ed.). St. Louis, MO: Saunders.

Additional Resources:

NANDA International (2004). *NANDA nursing diagnoses: Definitions and classification 2005-2006*. Philadelphia: NANDA.

Chapter 19: Anxiety Disorders

Application Exercises

1. When assessing a client who states she has been dealing with constant anxiety for the past few weeks, the nurse's questions should

   A. be open-ended.

   B. be reassuring.

   C. minimize the client's anxiety.

   D. be postponed until the anxiety has subsided.

2. During an assessment, a client tells the nurse that she removes her old makeup and reapplies new makeup every hour or so, because she is sure she looks horrible. This behavior is consistent with

   A. generalized anxiety disorder.

   B. panic disorder.

   C. obsessive-compulsive disorder.

   D. posttraumatic stress disorder.

3. An appropriate nursing intervention for a client having a panic attack is to

   A. teach the client relaxation techniques.

   B. show the client how to change his behavior.

   C. distract the client with a television show.

   D. stay with the client and speak quietly.

4. A nurse observes a client who is pacing and wringing his hands. He says that he is sure that he and his son will die a terrible death. He has been worried about this since last year. He is displaying the symptoms of

   A. generalized anxiety disorder.

   B. a specific phobia.

   C. posttraumatic stress disorder.

   D. obsessive-compulsive disorder.

5. A client hospitalized in an acute care mental health facility ritualistically cleans the sink in her bathroom multiple times daily. The outcome identified by the treatment team is that the client should use more effective coping measures. To achieve the desired outcome the nurse should

       A. encourage the client to work with the maintenance staff in cleaning unit bathrooms.

       B. focus on the client's symptoms rather than on the client's feelings.

       C. encourage the client to participate in a variety of unit activities.

       D. encourage the client to examine negative self-perceptions.

6. Match the specific anxiety disorder with its characteristics.

_____	Obsessive-compulsive disorder	A. Traumatic event causing symptoms months after the event takes place
_____	Panic disorder	B. Excessive worries for more than 6 months
_____	Generalized anxiety disorder	C. Fear of speaking or interacting in public
_____	Agoraphobia	D. Symptoms including chest pain, palpitations, feeling that one is about to die
_____	Social phobia	E. Fear of being out in open spaces
_____	Posttraumatic stress disorder	F. Ritualistic compulsions and recurrent thoughts

Chapter 19: Anxiety Disorders

Application Exercises Answer Key

1. When assessing a client who states she has been dealing with constant anxiety for the past few weeks, the nurse's questions should

   A. be open-ended.

   B. be reassuring.

   C. minimize the client's anxiety.

   D. be postponed until the anxiety has subsided.

   Open-ended questions allow the client to tell the nurse about her anxiety. Reassurance during an assessment or minimizing the symptoms may make the client feel that her concerns are being belittled. The assessment must not be postponed until anxiety has subsided, especially since the anxiety is constant and has been present for weeks.

2. During an assessment, a client tells the nurse that she removes her old makeup and reapplies new makeup every hour or so, because she is sure she looks horrible. This behavior is consistent with

   A. generalized anxiety disorder.

   B. panic disorder.

   C. obsessive-compulsive disorder.

   D. posttraumatic stress disorder.

   OCD is characterized by repetitive, unreasonable behaviors used to reduce anxiety, such as the hourly reapplication of makeup. GAD is characterized by excessive worry over multiple concerns for more than 6 months. In panic disorder, the client has recurrent panic attacks. PTSD causes repeated re-experiencing of a traumatic event.

3. An appropriate nursing intervention for a client having a panic attack is to

   A. teach the client relaxation techniques.

   B. show the client how to change his behavior.

   C. distract the client with a television show.

   D. stay with the client and speak quietly.

   During a panic attack, the individual is unable to think about anything except the symptoms being experienced. The nurse should stay with the client. The client will not be able to be distracted and will not be able to concentrate in order to learn new material. Other interventions should be postponed until after the attack.

4. A nurse observes a client who is pacing and wringing his hands. He says that he is sure that he and his son will die a terrible death. He has been worried about this since last year. He is displaying the symptoms of

    A. generalized anxiety disorder.

    B. a specific phobia.

    C. posttraumatic stress disorder.

    D. obsessive-compulsive disorder.

GAD is characterized by worry of long duration and without cause. The symptoms described are not those of a specific phobia. PTSD causes repeated re-experiencing of a traumatic event. OCD is characterized by repetitive unreasonable behaviors, such as handwashing, to reduce anxiety.

5. A client hospitalized in an acute care mental health facility ritualistically cleans the sink in her bathroom multiple times daily. The outcome identified by the treatment team is that the client should use more effective coping measures. To achieve the desired outcome the nurse should

    A. encourage the client to work with the maintenance staff in cleaning unit bathrooms.

    B. focus on the client's symptoms rather than on the client's feelings.

    C. encourage the client to participate in a variety of unit activities.

    D. encourage the client to examine negative self-perceptions.

Encouraging the client to participate in unit activities and become involved with other people helps to decrease involvement in the ritualistic behavior and encourages coping skills. Encouraging the client to clean focuses on the ritual. The nurse should focus on client feelings rather than on symptoms. Having the client examine negative self-perceptions enhances self-esteem rather than coping skills.

6. Match the specific anxiety disorder with its characteristics.

F	Obsessive-compulsive disorder	A. Traumatic event causing symptoms months after the event takes place
D	Panic disorder	B. Excessive worries for more than 6 months
B	Generalized anxiety disorder	C. Fear of speaking or interacting in public
E	Agoraphobia	D. Symptoms including chest pain, palpitations, feeling that one is about to die
C	Social phobia	E. Fear of being out in open spaces
A	Posttraumatic stress disorder	F. Ritualistic compulsions and recurrent thoughts

Unit 4   Psychobiologic Disorders, Psychiatric Emergencies, and Mental Health Nursing Care of Special Populations

Section: Psychobiologic Disorders

Chapter 20:   Somatoform Disorders

Contributor: Tanya Longabach, BSN, RNC

 NCLEX-RN® Connections:

Learning Objective: Review and apply knowledge within "**Somatoform Disorders**" in readiness for performance of the following nursing activities as outlined by the NCLEX-RN® test plan:

Δ   Assess the mental status of the client with a somatoform disorder, identifying changes in mood, judgment, cognition, and reasoning.

Δ   Identify the client/family's responses to the diagnosis of a somatoform disorder.

Δ   Plan/provide care for the client with a somatoform disorder.

Δ   Support the client's efforts in the use of strategies to decrease anxiety.

Δ   Evaluate and document the client's response to treatment of a somatoform disorder.

Δ   Evaluate the client's ability to follow the treatment plan for a somatoform disorder.

Δ   Teach the client/family signs and symptoms of relapse of the somatoform disorder.

 Key Points

Δ   Somatoform disorders are psychiatric conditions in which the physical symptoms the client is experiencing cannot be fully explained by a medical problem or another psychiatric disorder.

Δ   The major challenge for a clinician is differentiating a somatoform disorder from a medical condition, such as cerebrovascular accident (CVA, or stroke), encephalopathy, drug and alcohol abuse, or multiple sclerosis.

DSM-IV-TR Definitions for Somatoform Disorders	
Disorder	**Definition**
Somatization disorder	A chronic, severe psychiatric disorder characterized by many recurring clinically significant physical reports (e.g., pain with gastrointestinal, sexual, and neurologic symptoms) that cannot be explained fully by a physical disorder
Hypochondriasis	A preoccupation with bodily functions and fears of acquiring or having a serious disease based on misinterpretation of physical symptoms
Conversion disorder	A sudden loss of neurological function, usually at a time of severe stress, that cannot be explained fully by a physical disorder
Pain disorder	A disorder in which pain in one or more anatomic sites is exclusively or predominantly caused by psychologic factors, is the main focus of the client's attention, and results in significant distress and dysfunction
Body dysmorphic disorder	Preoccupation with a defect in appearance, causing significant distress or interfering with social, occupational, or other important areas of functioning

Key Factors

Δ The etiology of somatoform disorders is unknown. Theories include:

- Psychoanalytic theory (controlling repressed sexual urges).

- Behavioral theory (malingering, social learning).

- Biological theory (low serotonin levels in the brain).

- Genetic causes.

- Sexual or physical abuse in childhood.

Δ Providing aggressive treatment is thought to reinforce the client's desire to be and remain sick. This may be challenging, because the client often specifically demands certain treatment or diagnostic procedures.

Δ Somatoform disorders share comorbidity with drug and alcohol abuse, depression, and anxiety disorders.

Δ The client with a somatoform disorder may receive **secondary gains** from the illness. For example, the client may receive more attention from family when ill.

Δ **Somatization disorder** is an onset of unexplained medical symptoms in persons younger than 30 years.

- Symptoms of this disorder include:

  ◊ Multiple and chronic reports of unexplained physical symptoms.

  ◊ Multiple pain symptoms involving multiple sites (e.g., head, neck, back, stomach, limbs).

◊ At least two or more unexplained gastrointestinal symptoms (e.g., nausea and indigestion).

◊ At least one sexual complaint and/or menstrual complaint.

◊ At least one pseudoneurological symptom (e.g., blindness or inability to walk, speak, or move).

- Typically, the client is dramatic and emotional when recounting symptoms, often referring to them as "unbearable," "beyond description," or "the worst imaginable."

- The client tends to become extremely dependent in personal relationships, increasingly demanding help and emotional support.

- The client becomes enraged when she feels her needs are not being met.

- In an attempt to manipulate others, the client may threaten or attempt to kill himself.

- The client is often dissatisfied with medical care and may change health providers frequently. Medical history usually contains multiple procedures, tests, treatments, and consults.

- Comorbid diagnoses of personality disorders, particularly histrionic, borderline, and antisocial, are common.

Δ **Hypochondriasis** is a preoccupation with fear of having a serious medical illness that persists for at least 6 months despite negative medical evaluation.

- Bodily symptoms reported are not consistent with the client's perception of specific illness.

- Examination/reassurance by a provider does not relieve the concerns of the client, who tends to believe the provider has failed to find the real cause.

Δ **Conversion disorder** is one or more symptoms of loss of voluntary motor or sensory function (e.g., inability to walk, impaired coordination or balance, weakness, paralysis of an arm or a leg, loss of sensation in part of the body).

- Other symptoms include simulated convulsions and loss of one of the sensory functions (e.g., blindness, deafness).

- There is no evidence that the symptom is feigned or intentionally produced.

- The loss of function is not due to medical illness and is not a culturally expected behavioral response.

- The onset of symptoms is linked to a socially or psychologically stressful event.

- The client may display a lack of concern about the debilitating symptoms (*la belle indifférence*).

Δ **Pain disorder** (formerly known as psychogenic pain) is pain in one or more anatomical sites that is presented as the main symptom.

- The pain is not feigned or intentionally produced.

- There may be an underlying physical disorder that explains the pain, but not the severity or the degree of disability.

Δ **Body dysmorphic disorder** is a preoccupation with an imagined defect in appearance.

- The disorder may be associated with multiple, frantic, and unsuccessful attempts to correct the imagined defect by cosmetic surgery.

- The client may avoid appearing in public, including work and social activities, due to being self-conscious about appearance.

Assessment

Δ When obtaining the client history, assess for:

- Secondary gains, with questions such as, "How has this problem changed your life?"

- Distortions from reality.

  ◊ Does the client with hypochondriasis believe her backache is caused by a tumor?

  ◊ Is the client preoccupied with discussion of his illness?

  ◊ Is the client's history vague and disorganized?

- Ability to communicate feelings and needs. This client may be unable to discuss emotional needs in any terms other than physical symptoms.

- The client's ability to identify and verbalize sources of stress.

- Dependence on medication, such as antianxiety agents or pain medications.

- Alcohol or other chemical dependency.

- Unmet needs for safety and security, such as whether the client is at risk for falls due to symptoms of weakness.

- Possible suicidal ideation.

Δ Perform a physical assessment.

- Determine whether physical symptoms are under the client's control. For example, document if the client moves the "paralyzed" arm when instructed during physical assessment.

- Assess the client's ability to meet basic needs.

NANDA Nursing Diagnoses

Δ   Anxiety

Δ   Disturbed body image

Δ   Ineffective coping

Δ   Acute pain

Δ   Ineffective role performance

Δ   Chronic low self-esteem

Δ   Impaired social interaction

Nursing Interventions

Δ   Promote the highest level of self-care possible by encouraging the client to remain active and to limit the effect of symptoms on the quality of life and daily functioning. For example, encourage use of the left arm if the client is unable to move the right arm.

Δ   Provide health teaching regarding normal body functioning for the client and family.

Δ   Assertiveness training can benefit the client by teaching the client to meet needs through communication rather than somatic symptoms.

Δ   Avoid suggesting to the client that his condition is due to emotional rather than physical problems, and avoid arguing with the client that the symptoms are imaginary.

Δ   Encourage family members to spend time with and pay attention to the client when symptoms are absent. For the client, this reinforces the idea that the somatic symptoms do not bring special attention from others.

Δ   The nurse who is the client's case manager should attempt to manage health care resources by working closely with the client and the primary care provider to limit unnecessary diagnostic tests, provider visits, and other costs.

Δ   Advanced practice nurses or other health care providers may use psychotherapy, cognitive-behavioral therapy, biofeedback, hypnosis, and behavioral therapy. However, the client may resist suggestions for individual or group psychotherapy because she views the illness as a medical problem.

Δ   Pharmacologic treatment includes selective serotonin reuptake inhibitors (SSRIs), such as fluoxetine (Prozac), and tricyclic antidepressants (TCAs), such as imipramine (Tofranil).

Δ   Monitor/assess the client for medication responses and side effects.

Δ   Encourage the client to become aware of potential stressors and develop and maintain functional methods of dealing with them.

Δ   Set limits for interactions with the client and be consistent.

Δ   Teach stress management and relaxation techniques.

Δ   Examine one's own attitudes toward somatoform disorders and be aware of how those attitudes can affect interactions with the client.

Primary Reference:

Varcarolis, E. M., Carson, V. B., & Shoemaker, N. C. (2006). *Foundations of psychiatric mental health nursing: A clinical approach* (5th ed.). St. Louis, MO: Saunders.

Additional Resources:

Mohr, W. K. (2002). *Johnson's psychiatric-mental health nursing: Adaptation and growth* (5th ed.). Newark, NJ: Lippincott Williams and Wilkins.

NANDA International (2004). *NANDA nursing diagnoses: Definitions and classification 2005-2006*. Philadelphia: NANDA.

Chapter 20: Somatoform Disorders

Application Exercises

Scenario: A nurse case manager is caring for a client who is a 65-year-old widow living alone. The client's daughter lives nearby, but has young children and visits her mother less and less often. The client has stopped attending social activities or receiving visitors since her husband died 2 years ago. For the past year, the client has called her primary care provider several times weekly and has called to arrange clinic visits at least monthly with many physical reports of back and leg pain. She has insisted on seeing multiple specialists, and her daughter has just discovered that she is taking medications for pain and anxiety prescribed by several different providers. The client calls her daughter and her nurse case manager daily to request help.

1. Identify nursing diagnoses appropriate for this client.

2. What is the highest priority problem for this client at present?

3. The nurse case manager is the contact between the client, home health nurses, and the primary care provider. What nursing interventions are appropriate for the case manager at this time related to the priority nursing diagnosis?

4. A nurse is performing an assessment on a client who has many past reports of physical problems and is now reporting an inability to walk. A possible medical diagnosis is somatization disorder. Which of the following is least relevant when planning care for the client with somatization disorder?

    A. Level of involvement and support by family and friends

    B. Determination of whether the client's inability to walk has a physical cause

    C. Client's potential for violence toward others

    D. Client's ability to perform self-care activities

5. A nurse assesses a client in the emergency department who says that he is suddenly unable to move his legs. Which of the following should cause the nurse to suspect that this client might be experiencing a conversion disorder?

    A. The client is highly educated and has a high-paying job.

    B. The client has no previous history of neurologic problems.

    C. The client is distressed and reports that one leg is deformed.

    D. The client does not appear upset by the presence of symptoms.

6. Match the various somatoform disorders with their defining characteristics.

_____	Conversion disorder	A. The client misinterprets symptoms of left elbow tendonitis and is convinced he is having a myocardial infarction.
_____	Somatization disorder	B. The client is distressed by a "huge" facial scar, which is not noticeable to the examiner because it is hidden in the eyebrow.
_____	Hypochondriasis	C. The client suddenly becomes deaf with no physical cause, but is not noticeably concerned.
_____	Body dysmorphic disorder	D. The client has been reporting severe pelvic pain for months with no physical cause.
_____	Pain syndrome	E. The client has many symptoms in different body parts, as well as weakness of the legs, with no physical cause.

Chapter 20: Somatoform Disorders

Application Exercises Answer Key

Scenario: A nurse case manager is caring for a client who is a 65-year-old widow living alone. The client's daughter lives nearby, but has young children and visits her mother less and less often. The client has stopped attending social activities or receiving visitors since her husband died 2 years ago. For the past year, the client has called her primary care provider several times weekly and has called to arrange clinic visits at least monthly with many physical reports of back and leg pain. She has insisted on seeing multiple specialists, and her daughter has just discovered that she is taking medications for pain and anxiety prescribed by several different providers. The client calls her daughter and her nurse case manager daily to request help.

1. Identify nursing diagnoses appropriate for this client.

   Anxiety
   Disturbed body image
   Ineffective coping
   Risk for injury
   Acute pain
   Ineffective role performance
   Chronic low self-esteem
   Impaired social interaction

2. What is the highest priority problem for this client at present?

   The priority is this client's safety due to her risk for injury related to multiple psychotropic prescriptions and probable inappropriate use of pharmacologic therapy.

3. The nurse case manager is the contact between the client, home health nurses, and the primary care provider. What nursing interventions are appropriate for the case manager at this time related to the priority nursing diagnosis?

   Determine what medications the client is taking as well as the frequency. Assess for medication dependence, the presence of side effects, and the client's knowledge and level of understanding about the medications.
   Mediate between the client and the primary care provider regarding pharmacologic needs and information about current medication use.
   Assess for any suicidal ideation.
   Assess the client's level of stress, secondary gains from illness, past and present strengths; also assess her current level of functioning and other safety/security needs.

4. A nurse is performing an assessment on a client who has many past reports of physical problems and is now reporting an inability to walk. A possible medical diagnosis is somatization disorder. Which of the following is least relevant when planning care for the client with somatization disorder?

        A. Level of involvement and support by family and friends

        B. Determination of whether the client's inability to walk has a physical cause

        C. Client's potential for violence toward others

        D. Client's ability to perform self-care activities

Potential for violence is not a factor for the client with somatization disorder; a potential for self-directed violence might be relevant for this client, however. All other options are important for the nurse who is planning care.

5. A nurse assesses a client in the emergency department who says that he is suddenly unable to move his legs. Which of the following should cause the nurse to suspect that this client might be experiencing a conversion disorder?

        A. The client is highly educated and has a high-paying job.

        B. The client has no previous history of neurologic problems.

        C. The client is distressed and reports that one leg is deformed.

        D. The client does not appear upset by the presence of symptoms.

Conversion disorder symptoms are frequently accompanied by la belle indifférence, a lack of concern about the symptoms. Level of education and income are not factors in conversion syndrome. The fact that there is no history of neurologic problems is not relevant. The client's report that one leg is deformed could be a sign of body dysmorphic disorder, but it does not relate to conversion disorder.

6. Match the various somatoform disorders with their defining characteristics.

C	Conversion disorder	A. The client misinterprets symptoms of left elbow tendonitis and is convinced he is having a myocardial infarction.
E	Somatization disorder	B. The client is distressed by a "huge" facial scar, which is not noticeable to the examiner because it is hidden in the eyebrow.
A	Hypochondriasis	C. The client suddenly becomes deaf with no physical cause, but is not noticeably concerned.
B	Body dysmorphic disorder	D. The client has been reporting severe pelvic pain for months with no physical cause.
D	Pain syndrome	E. The client has many symptoms in different body parts, as well as weakness of the legs, with no physical cause.

Unit 4 Psychobiologic Disorders, Psychiatric Emergencies, and Mental Health Nursing Care of
Special Populations

Section: Psychobiologic Disorders

Chapter 21: **Dissociative Disorders**

Contributor: Tanya Longabach, BSN, RNC

 NCLEX-RN® Connections:

Learning Objective: Review and apply knowledge within "**Dissociative Disorders**"
in readiness for performance of the following nursing activities as outlined by the
NCLEX-RN® test plan:

Δ Apply knowledge of psychobiologic disorders to the nursing process when caring
for clients with acute or chronic mental illnesses.

Δ Use effective communication to interact with and assist the client/family to
foster trust in the nurse-client therapeutic relationship.

Δ Assess the client's mental status, identifying changes in mood, judgment,
cognition, and reasoning.

Δ Identify the client/family's responses to the diagnosis of a dissociative disorder.

Δ Plan/provide care for the client with a dissociative disorder.

Δ Support the client's efforts in the use of strategies to decrease anxiety.

Δ Evaluate and document the client's response to treatment of a dissociative
disorder.

Δ Evaluate the client's ability to follow the treatment plan for a dissociative
disorder.

Δ Teach the client/family signs and symptoms of relapse of the dissociative
disorder.

 Key Points

Δ In dissociative disorders, there is a failure to integrate one's memories, perceptions,
identity, or consciousness normally.

Δ Dissociative disorders affect an estimated 1 to 2% of the population.

Δ These disorders affect females more often than males and most often begin in late
childhood or early adolescence.

Δ Dissociative disorders should be differentiated from medical conditions (e.g.,
dementia, seizure disorders, substance abuse) and malingering.

DSM-IV-TR Definitions for Dissociative Disorders	
Disorder type	Definition
Dissociative amnesia	An inability to recall important personal information, usually of a traumatic or stressful nature, that is too extensive to be explained by normal forgetfulness
Dissociative fugue	Amnesia in which the inability to recall some or all of one's past, along with the loss of one's identity or the formation of a new identity, occurs with sudden, unexpected, purposeful travel away from home
Dissociative identity disorder	A disorder characterized by two or more identities or personalities that alternatively take over the person's behavior
Depersonalization disorder	Persistent or recurrent sense of detachment from one's body or mental processes and often a feeling of being an outside observer of one's life

Key Factors

Δ **Dissociative Amnesia**

- Etiology

  ◊ Dissociative amnesia is usually associated with overwhelming stress, which may be generated by traumatic life events, accidents, or disasters that are experienced or witnessed.

- Symptoms

  ◊ The most common symptom is memory loss for a period of time.

  ◊ The client may become confused or depressed shortly after an episode of amnesia.

  ◊ Some clients are very distressed by their amnesia; others are not.

- Treatment

  ◊ Establish a supportive environment and sense of safety.

  ◊ Recall of lost memories can be upsetting, but helpful to restore identity.

Δ **Dissociative Fugue**

- Etiology

  ◊ Dissociative fugue is often associated with overwhelming stress.

  ◊ It may be associated with the desire to escape responsibility or an embarrassing situation.

- Symptoms

  ◊ The client may assume a new identity and engage in complex social interactions for a period of time from hours to weeks or months and occasionally for even longer periods.

  ◊ A fugue in progress is asymptomatic to an outside observer.

◊ When the fugue ends, depression, discomfort, grief, shame, intense conflict, and suicidal or aggressive impulses may appear.

◊ Failure to remember events of the fugue may cause confusion, distress, or terror.

◊ Sometimes fugue cannot be diagnosed until the person abruptly returns to his previous identity and is distressed about unfamiliar circumstances.

- Treatment

◊ Efforts to restore pre-fugue memories are often unsuccessful but may be helpful to maintain identity.

◊ Most fugues are brief and self-limiting and do not require intervention.

Δ **Dissociative Identity Disorder (DID)**

- Etiology

◊ DID was formerly known as multiple personality disorder.

◊ Some possible causes are overwhelming stress, lack of nurturing, and sexual or physical abuse.

◊ The etiology is frequently unclear.

- Symptoms

◊ The client may have amnesia involving an inability to recall important personal information relating to some of the identities.

◊ DID is associated with a high incidence of suicide attempts.

◊ The array of symptoms can resemble other neurologic and psychiatric disorders, such as anxiety disorders, personality disorders, schizophrenic and mood psychoses, and seizure disorders.

◊ Most clients have symptoms of other comorbid conditions, including depression, anxiety (sweating, rapid pulse, palpitations), phobias, panic attacks, sexual dysfunction, eating disorders, suicidal preoccupation, self-mutilation, and posttraumatic stress disorder.

◊ The client hears inner conversations and the voices of other personalities, which often comment on or address the client.

◊ The client has fluctuating levels of function, from highly effective to disabled.

◊ The client experiences severe headaches or other bodily pain.

◊ Time distortions, time lapse, and amnesia are associated with DID.

◊ The client may experience depersonalization (feeling unreal, as if observing oneself from the outside) or derealization (experiencing familiar persons and surroundings as if they were unfamiliar and strange or unreal).

- Treatment
  - ◊ Options include:
    - ° Individual psychotherapy.
    - ° Hypnosis.
    - ° Cognitive-behavioral therapy enabling the client to deal with stress.
  - ◊ The client may be asked to keep a log of her emotions to analyze them rationally.
  - ◊ The client should be assisted in developing a crisis plan.
  - ◊ When personality integration is impossible or undesirable by the client, treatment aims at symptom reduction.

Δ **Depersonalization Disorder**

- Etiology
  - ◊ Depersonalization disorder is usually associated with a past exposure to overwhelming stress, such as childhood abuse.
- Symptoms
  - ◊ The client may feel unreal, estranged from oneself, or dreamlike.
  - ◊ The client may have chronic anxiety about his perception of the world.
- Treatment
  - ◊ Depersonalization disorder often resolves by itself once the stress is resolved.
  - ◊ Medications may be ordered for symptoms of anxiety and depression.
  - ◊ Cognitive-behavioral therapy is used to assist the client in dealing with stress.
  - ◊ The client and family should be educated about symptoms.

Assessment

Δ Assess the following:

- Memory for recent and remote events. (Are there gaps in the client's memory?)
- Orientation to time, place, and person.
- The client's knowledge of her identity. (If the client has assumed a new identify, she may speak of herself in the third person.)
- Mood – for anxiety, depression.
- Affect.

- Behavior – including recent history of self-destructive or aggressive, hostile behavior.

- Cognition and thought processes.

- Sleeping patterns.

- Use of alcohol or other chemicals.

- Client risk for suicide or self-mutilation.

NANDA Nursing Diagnoses

Δ   Impaired adjustment

Δ   Anxiety

Δ   Ineffective coping

Δ   Interrupted family processes

Δ   Impaired memory

Δ   Ineffective role performance

Δ   Risk for self- or other-directed violence

Nursing Interventions

Δ   Develop a therapeutic relationship with the client.

Δ   Be consistent; recognize mood and behavior changes.

Δ   Create a safe, structured environment (milieu therapy).

- A chaotic environment may trigger a dissociative episode and cause anxiety.

- Task-oriented therapy, such as occupational therapy, is often scheduled for the client with a dissociative disorder to increase self-awareness.

- Attendance at community or daily orientation meetings can decrease isolation and dissociation/depersonalization.

Δ   Educate the client and family about the disorder.

Δ   The client may be taught to keep a journal to increase self-awareness of behavior and to assist in identifying triggers that cause dissociation.

Primary Reference:

Varcarolis, E. M., Carson, V. B., & Shoemaker, N. C. (2006). *Foundations of psychiatric mental health nursing: A clinical approach* (5th ed.). St. Louis, MO: Saunders.

Additional Resources:

Mohr, W. K. (2002). *Johnson's psychiatric-mental health nursing: Adaptation and growth* (5th ed.). Newark, NJ: Lippincott Williams and Wilkins.

NANDA International (2004). *NANDA nursing diagnoses: Definitions and classification 2005-2006.* Philadelphia: NANDA.

Chapter 21: Dissociative Disorders

Application Exercises

Scenario: A 19-year-old woman arrived home from a friend's house early in the morning. She looked disheveled, but claimed she was not drinking or taking drugs. She reported pain in her shoulders and legs, but could not explain its cause. When her mother asked her about the details of the past evening, the client could remember going to her friend's house and talking to some people she previously knew. The last thing she remembers is talking to a group of men she met there. She does recall getting into her car this morning and driving home; however, she was very surprised to find that the side of her car was dented as if she had been in an accident. The client cannot explain a memory lapse between these events. She was brought to the emergency department by her mother. The client tested negative for drugs and alcohol; however, it was found that she had sexual intercourse with evidence of violent treatment in the past 12 hr. The client denies this and starts crying. This client and her mother are referred for mental health consultation.

1. What nursing diagnoses are applicable to this situation?

2. What are possible factors related to this client's amnesia?

3. The client is voluntarily admitted to an emergency mental health facility for observation. What interventions in this environment should the nurse implement to help keep the client safe and to make her feel secure?

4. What interventions can a nurse implement when working with a client who has a dissociative disorder and is at risk for self-directed violence?

5. Dissociative disorders are often caused by

   A. alcohol or drug abuse.

   B. insomnia.

   C. witnessing extreme violence.

   D. epileptic seizures.

6. A client describes himself by saying, "I feel like I'm floating in the air looking down at myself, but it's not really me." This statement describes

   A. derealization.

   B. rationalization.

   C. depersonalization.

   D. repression.

Chapter 21: Dissociative Disorders

Application Exercises Answer Key

Scenario: A 19-year-old woman arrived home from a friend's house early in the morning. She looked disheveled, but claimed she was not drinking or taking drugs. She reported pain in her shoulders and legs, but could not explain its cause. When her mother asked her about the details of the past evening, the client could remember going to her friend's house and talking to some people she previously knew. The last thing she remembers is talking to a group of men she met there. She does recall getting into her car this morning and driving home; however, she was very surprised to find that the side of her car was dented as if she had been in an accident. The client cannot explain a memory lapse between these events. She was brought to the emergency department by her mother. The client tested negative for drugs and alcohol; however, it was found that she had sexual intercourse with evidence of violent treatment in the past 12 hr. The client denies this and starts crying. This client and her mother are referred for mental health consultation.

---

1. What nursing diagnoses are applicable to this situation?

   Ineffective coping
   Impaired memory
   Rape trauma syndrome
   Acute pain

2. What are possible factors related to this client's amnesia?

   Stress related to rape caused her to erase the frightening and possibly shame-causing memory.

3. The client is voluntarily admitted to an emergency mental health facility for observation. What interventions in this environment should the nurse implement to help keep the client safe and to make her feel secure?

   Orient the client to the unit. Provide a nondemanding daily routine; encourage self-care activities. Briefly explain the roles of various care providers on the unit. Assign the client to a room near the nurse's station so that she may be closely monitored for any self-directed violence. Use clear, concise language when giving directions and avoid long explanations at first.

4. What interventions can a nurse implement when working with a client who has a dissociative disorder and is at risk for self-directed violence?

Clients with dissociative disorders are at risk for self-mutilation when they recall the situations that caused amnesia episodes, such as memories of abuse or exposure to violence. The nurse needs to anticipate the possibility of self-mutilation or even suicide. The nurse can: make a "no-harm agreement" with the client, have a crisis plan in place that identifies a safe place or person the client can go to when needed, teach the client and family about ways to anticipate condition exacerbation or potential for self-mutilation, and teach the client and family about the symptoms of dissociative disorders in general.

5. Dissociative disorders are often caused by

        A. alcohol or drug abuse.

        B. insomnia.

        C. witnessing extreme violence.

        D. epileptic seizures.

Dissociative disorders are caused by exposure to extreme stress. Witnessing extreme violence is an event that can bring about the stress. While abusing drugs and alcohol can cause memory lapses, these lapses are not considered dissociative disorders according to the DSM-IV-TR. Epileptic seizures can cause periods of amnesia concurrent with the seizure, but this type of amnesia is not considered dissociative. Insomnia usually does not cause amnesia, although it can cause memory impairment.

6. A client describes himself by saying, "I feel like I'm floating in the air looking down at myself, but it's not really me." This statement describes

        A. derealization.

        B. rationalization.

        C. depersonalization.

        D. repression.

In depersonalization, the individual describes himself as seeming unreal. Derealization includes describing a familiar situation or event as unreal or strange. Rationalization is a defense whereby the individual justifies his behavior using faulty logic. In repression, the individual keeps threatening thoughts or feelings from coming to consciousness.

Psychobiologic Disorders, Psychiatric Emergencies, and Mental Health Nursing Care of Special Populations

Section: Psychobiologic Disorders

Chapter 22:   Personality Disorders

Contributor: Meredith Flood, PhD, RN, APRN-BC

NCLEX-RN® Connections:

Learning Objective: Review and apply knowledge within "**Personality Disorders**" in readiness for performance of the following nursing activities as outlined by the NCLEX-RN® test plan:

△   Apply knowledge of psychobiologic disorders to the nursing process when caring for clients with personality disorders.

△   Use effective communication to interact with and assist the client/family to foster trust in the nurse-client therapeutic relationship.

△   Assess the client's mental status, identifying changes in mood, judgment, cognition, and reasoning.

△   Identify the client/family's responses to the diagnosis of a personality disorder.

△   Plan/provide care for the client with a personality disorder.

△   Support the client's efforts in the use of strategies to decrease anxiety.

△   Evaluate and document the client's response to treatment of a personality disorder.

△   Evaluate the client's ability to follow the treatment plan for a personality disorder.

△   Teach the client/family signs and symptoms of relapse of the personality disorder.

Key Points

△   A personality disorder is an enduring pattern of inner experience and behavior that:

   •   Deviates markedly from the expectation of one's culture.

   •   Is pervasive, maladaptive, and inflexible.

   •   Has an onset in adolescence or early adulthood.

- Is stable over time.

- Leads to distress or impairment.

Δ All personality disorders share four common characteristics.

- Inflexibility/maladaptive responses to stress

- Disability in social and professional relationships

- Tendency to provoke interpersonal conflict

- Capacity to cause irritation or distress in others

Δ Personality disorders are predisposing factors for many other psychiatric disorders and often co-occur with depression and anxiety.

Δ Personality disorders have a significant effect on the course of treatment for other psychiatric disorders.

Δ A client with a personality disorder demonstrates long-term maladaptive behavior that prevents accomplishment of desired goals in relationships and other efforts.

Δ The maladaptive behaviors of a personality disorder are not experienced as uncomfortable by the individual and some areas of personal functioning may be very adequate.

Δ The medical diagnosis of a personality disorder is found under Axis II of the DSM-IV-TR.

Δ Personality disorders are divided into three groups, called clusters.

- Cluster A – generally described as odd or eccentric

- Cluster B – generally described as dramatic, emotional, or erratic

- Cluster C – generally described as anxious or fearful

Key Factors

Δ **Defense mechanisms** used by clients with personality disorders include repression, suppression, regression, undoing, and splitting.

- Of these, splitting, the inability to incorporate positive and negative aspects of oneself or others into a whole image, is frequently seen in the inpatient setting.

- Splitting is commonly associated with borderline personality disorder.

- In splitting, the client tends to characterize people or things as all good or all bad at any particular moment. For example, the client might say, "You are the worst person in the world." Later that day she might say, "You are the best, but the nurse from the last shift is absolutely terrible."

Δ   Judgments about a client's personality functioning must take into account the client's ethnic, cultural, and social background.

Δ   Individuals with personality disorders tend to be less educated or unemployed, are single or have marital difficulties, often have comorbid substance use disorders, and may commit nonviolent and violent crimes, including sex offenses.

Δ   Environmental influences – such as child abuse, biological influences (e.g., genetic factors), and psychological factors – appear to play a role in the etiology of personality disorders.

Δ   **Biological Determinants**

•   Personality disorders may represent an extreme variation of a natural tendency resulting from genetic alterations and/or unfavorable environmental conditions.

•   Neurobiological research suggests that chronic stress (e.g., repeated sexual trauma or psychological trauma during childhood) may be relevant to personality disorders.

Δ   **Psychosocial Factors**

•   Learning theory proposes that curing childhood maladaptive coping responses is based on reinforcement by significant others.

•   Cognitive theory suggests that excessive anxiety is caused by a distortion in thinking that is amenable to correction.

•   Psychoanalytic theory focuses on the use of primitive defense mechanisms by clients with personality disorders.

•   Environmental factors related to specific parenting styles are suggested as causative factors in different personality disorders.

The 10 Personality Disorders		
Cluster A (Odd or eccentric traits)	Paranoid personality	Characterized by distrust and suspiciousness toward others based on unfounded beliefs that others want to harm, exploit, or deceive the person
	Schizoid personality	Characterized by emotional detachment, disinterest in close relationships, and indifference to praise or criticism; often uncooperative
	Schizotypal personality	Characterized by odd beliefs leading to interpersonal difficulties, an eccentric appearance, and magical thinking or perceptual distortions that are not clear delusions or hallucinations

The 10 Personality Disorders		
Cluster B (Dramatic, emotional, or erratic traits)	Antisocial personality	Characterized by disregard for others with exploitation, repeated unlawful actions, deceit, and failure to accept personal responsibility
	Borderline personality	Characterized by instability of affect, identity, and relationships; fear of abandonment, splitting behaviors, manipulation, and impulsiveness; often tries self-mutilation and may be suicidal
	Histrionic personality	Characterized by emotional attention-seeking behavior, in which the person needs to be the center of attention; often seductive and flirtatious
	Narcissistic personality	Characterized by arrogance, grandiose views of self-importance, the need for consistent admiration, and a lack of empathy for others that strains most relationships; often sensitive to criticism
Cluster C (Anxious or fearful traits; insecurity and inadequacy)	Avoidant personality	Characterized by social inhibition and avoidance of all situations that require interpersonal contact, despite wanting close relationships, due to extreme fear of rejection; often very anxious in social situations
	Dependent personality	Characterized by extreme dependency in a close relationship with an urgent search to find a replacement when one relationship ends; the most frequently-seen personality disorder in the clinical setting
	Obsessive-compulsive personality	Characterized by perfectionism with a focus on orderliness and control to the extent that the individual may not be able to accomplish a given task

Assessment

Δ   Client assessment should include:

- A full medical history to rule out medical causes.

- History of/presence of suicidal, homicidal, or aggressive ideations of actions.

- Currently used medications.

- History of and current use of alcohol and/or illicit substances.

- Legal history.

- Current or past physical, sexual, or emotional abuse.

- Family members/significant other's reports of client's presenting problem.

Δ   Self-assessment is vital for nurses caring for clients with personality disorders; clients with personality disorders may often evoke intense feelings in the nurse.

NANDA Nursing Diagnoses

Δ   Anxiety

Δ   Defensive coping

Δ   Ineffective coping

Δ   Hopelessness

Δ   Noncompliance

Δ   Risk for self- or other-directed violence

Δ   Risk for suicide

Nursing Interventions

Δ   Safety is always a priority concern, since some clients with a personality disorder are at risk for self- or other-directed violence.

Δ   Developing a therapeutic relationship is often challenging due to the client's distrust or hostility toward others.

- A firm, yet supportive approach and consistent care will help build a therapeutic nurse-client relationship.

- Limit-setting is important when working with the client who is manipulative or who acts out.

- Feelings of being threatened or having no control may cause a client to act out toward the nurse.

- Offering the client realistic choices may enhance the client's sense of control.

Δ   Communication strategies, client outcomes, and therapies should be aimed at the specific personality disorder.

Δ   **Communication Strategies**

- Limit-setting and consistency are essential with clients who are manipulative, especially those with borderline or antisocial personality disorders.

- Assertiveness training and modeling can be important for clients with dependent and histrionic personality disorders.

- For clients with histrionic personality disorder, who may be very flirtatious, it is important to maintain professional boundaries and communication.

- Clients with schizoid or schizotypal personality disorders tend to isolate themselves, and this need for social isolation should be respected.

- For very dependent clients, self-assess frequently for countertransference reactions to client's clinging and frequent requests for help.

Δ   **Client outcomes** include the client demonstrating:

- A decrease in suicidal/homicidal/self-injurious ideations.

- A decrease in anxiety and/or depression.

- Use of healthy coping skills.

- Improved ability to communicate feelings.

Δ   **Basic-Level Interventions**

- Milieu therapy is aimed at affect management in a group context and includes coping skills groups, psychoeducational groups, and socializing groups.

- Psychobiological interventions include the use of psychotropic agents that are geared toward maintaining cognitive function and relieving symptoms. Antidepressant, anxiolytic, antipsychotic, or a combination of these medications may be prescribed.

- Dialectical behavior therapy (DBT) is a cognitive-behavioral therapy used for clients with borderline personality disorder. It focuses on gradual behavior changes and provides acceptance and validation for these clients, who are very frequently (80% of cases) suicidal and have self-mutilating behaviors.

- Case management is beneficial for clients who have personality disorders and are persistently and severely impaired.

  ◊   In acute care facilities, case management focuses on obtaining pertinent history from current or previous providers, supporting reintegration with the family/significant other, and ensuring appropriate referrals to outpatient care.

  ◊   In long-term outpatient facilities, case management goals include reducing hospitalization by providing resources for crisis services and enhancing the social support system.

Δ   **Evaluation** of clients with personality disorders is often difficult, and small gains should be recognized as progress. Specific short-term outcomes may be more feasible; accomplishment of these can give the client a message of hope that quality of life can be improved.

Primary Reference:

Varcarolis, E. M., Carson, V. B., & Shoemaker, N. C. (2006). *Foundations of psychiatric mental health nursing: A clinical approach* (5th ed.). St. Louis, MO: Saunders.

Additional Resources:

NANDA International (2004). *NANDA nursing diagnoses: Definitions and classification 2005-2006*. Philadelphia: NANDA.

Chapter 22: Personality Disorders

Application Exercises

Scenario: A nurse on an inpatient psychiatric unit is asked to conduct a staff in-service about communicating with clients who have personality disorders. The nursing staff includes registered nurses, licensed practical nurses, and mental health technicians. Although some of them have previous mental health work experience, no one has worked in a mental health facility for more than 5 years, and there is disagreement among the staff about the best strategies for dealing with clients who have personality disorders.

1. Identify three components of care that are important to include in the in-service.

2. What communication strategies should the nurse suggest using with clients who have personality disorders?

3. How should the nurse describe splitting, and what guidelines should be included for dealing with this behavior?

4. Match the letter of the description with the personality disorder to which it corresponds.

_____	Borderline	A. Perfectionistic and orderly; demands control of every situation
_____	Antisocial	B. Evades all social situations and fears rejections
_____	Obsessive-compulsive	C. Emotionally detached and disinterested in others; not interested in praise or criticism
_____	Histrionic	D. Deceitful, manipulative, and unlawful; does not take responsibility for actions
_____	Avoidant	E. Emotional with unstable identity and relationships; fears abandonment but uses splitting, which angers others
_____	Schizoid	F. Needs to be the center of attention in all situations

5. A part-time staff nurse on a behavioral unit is stopped by a client whose treatment plan shows a nursing diagnosis of ineffective coping related to manipulation of others. When planning interventions for a manipulative client, the nurse should

    A. give negative reinforcement for acting-out behavior.

    B. ignore any inappropriate behavior.

    C. encourage the client to discuss her feelings of inadequacy.

    D. refer requests and questions related to care to the client's primary nurse.

6. A nurse has denied a request from a client with borderline personality disorder. The client says, "The nurse on the evening shift would never be nasty to me like you are! You are a horrible, awful person!" This is an example of

    A. regression.

    B. splitting.

    C. a conversion disorder.

    D. identification.

7. A client with antisocial personality disorder is admitted to a chemical dependency unit. The nurse should be alert for which of the following characteristic behaviors of the client with this type of personality disorder? (Select all that apply.)

    _____ Anxious

    _____ Indecisive

    _____ Exploitative

    _____ Submissive

    _____ Aggressive

    _____ Impulsive

Chapter 22: Personality Disorders

Application Exercises Answer Key

Scenario: A nurse on an inpatient psychiatric unit is asked to conduct a staff in-service about communicating with clients who have personality disorders. The nursing staff includes registered nurses, licensed practical nurses, and mental health technicians. Although some of them have previous mental health work experience, no one has worked in a mental health facility for more than 5 years, and there is disagreement among the staff about the best strategies for dealing with clients who have personality disorders.

1. Identify three components of care that are important to include in the in-service.

   Clients with personality disorders have a tendency to cause frustration and stress in those caring for them. Self-awareness is important when providing care for these clients in order to maintain professionalism and promote the well-being of the client. Effective communication among staff is also important, as many clients with personality disorders use the defense mechanism splitting in an effort to get their needs met. Limit-setting is often necessary with clients who have personality disorders. Other important topics to cover could include establishing trust with these clients (who are likely to be mistrustful of health care professionals), keeping clients safe, and enhancing clients' involvement and sense of control over their care.

2. What communication strategies should the nurse suggest using with clients who have personality disorders?

   Effective communication strategies when dealing with clients who have personality disorders include utilizing direct, honest communication, limit-setting, and assertiveness.

3. How should the nurse describe splitting, and what guidelines should be included for dealing with this behavior?

   Splitting refers to alternating between idealizing and devaluation, and it is a failure to integrate positive and negative qualities of self or others. For example, a client may tell his primary nurse that she is the only one who cares about him and that the other staff members are incompetent. Later, the client complains to staff that the primary nurse has neglected him after the nurse is late administering the client's medication. Maintaining open and ongoing communication among staff is essential when caring for a client with a personality disorder, as is limit-setting. Sometimes it is necessary to appoint one staff member as a single point of contact for the client to communicate his needs.

4. Match the letter of the description with the personality disorder to which it corresponds.

__E__	Borderline	A. Perfectionistic and orderly; demands control of every situation
__D__	Antisocial	B. Evades all social situations and fears rejections
__A__	Obsessive-compulsive	C. Emotionally detached and disinterested in others; not interested in praise or criticism
__F__	Histrionic	D. Deceitful, manipulative, and unlawful; does not take responsibility for actions
__B__	Avoidant	E. Emotional with unstable identity and relationships; fears abandonment but uses splitting, which angers others
__C__	Schizoid	F. Needs to be the center of attention in all situations

5. A part-time staff nurse on a behavioral unit is stopped by a client whose treatment plan shows a nursing diagnosis of ineffective coping related to manipulation of others. When planning interventions for a manipulative client, the nurse should

      A. give negative reinforcement for acting-out behavior.

      B. ignore any inappropriate behavior.

      C. encourage the client to discuss her feelings of inadequacy.

      D. refer requests and questions related to care to the client's primary nurse.

A client who frequently manipulates others should have a consistent decision-maker in order to avoid the potential for playing one staff member against another. Positive reinforcement would be a better intervention than negative reinforcement. Depending on the treatment plan, this client's inappropriate behavior may need to be addressed by staff. Inadequacy is not a common feeling for a client with an antisocial personality disorder.

6. A nurse has denied a request from a client with borderline personality disorder. The client says, "The nurse on the evening shift would never be nasty to me like you are! You are a horrible, awful person!" This is an example of

    A. regression.

    B. splitting.

    C. a conversion disorder.

    D. identification.

Splitting occurs when a person is unable to see both positive and negative qualities at the same time. The client with borderline personality disorder tends to see a person as all bad one time and all good another time. Regression refers to resorting to an earlier way of functioning, such as having a temper tantrum. A conversion disorder is a somatoform disorder in which a person converts stress/anxiety into a physical complaint. In identification, the person imitates the behavior of someone admired or feared.

7. A client with antisocial personality disorder is admitted to a chemical dependency unit. The nurse should be alert for which of the following characteristic behaviors of the client with this type of personality disorder? (Select all that apply.)

    _____ Anxious

    _____ Indecisive

    _X_ Exploitative

    _____ Submissive

    _X_ Aggressive

    _X_ Impulsive

The antisocial client typically displays behaviors that are aggressive, manipulative, exploitative, callous, impulsive, and guilt-instilling. They rarely appear anxious, indecisive, or submissive.

Unit 4   Psychobiologic Disorders, Psychiatric Emergencies, and Mental Health Nursing Care of
                Special Populations

Section: Psychobiologic Disorders

Chapter 23:   Eating Disorders
                Contributor: Anne W. Ryan, MSN, MPH, RN-BC

 NCLEX-RN® Connections:

Learning Objective: Review and apply knowledge within "**Eating Disorders**" in readiness for performance of the following nursing activities as outlined by the NCLEX-RN® test plan:

Δ   Apply knowledge of psychobiologic disorders to the nursing process when caring for clients with an eating disorder.

Δ   Use effective communication to interact with and assist the client/family to foster trust in the nurse-client therapeutic relationship.

Δ   Assess the client's mental status, identifying changes in mood, judgment, cognition, and reasoning.

Δ   Identify the client/family's responses to the diagnosis of an eating disorder.

Δ   Plan/provide care for the client with an eating disorder.

Δ   Support the client's efforts in the use of strategies to decrease anxiety.

Δ   Evaluate and document the client's response to treatment of an eating disorder.

Δ   Evaluate the client's ability to follow the treatment plan for an eating disorder.

Δ   Teach the client/family signs and symptoms of relapse of the eating disorder.

 Key Points

Δ   **Anorexia Nervosa**

•   Characterized by:

◊   Preoccupation with food and the rituals of eating, along with a voluntary refusal to eat.

◊   A morbid fear of obesity and a refusal to maintain minimally normal body weight (body weight is less than 85% of expected normal weight for the individual) in the absence of a physical cause.

- Two types:

   ◊ Restricting type – The individual drastically restricts food intake and does not binge or purge.

   ◊ Binge-eating/purging type – The individual engages in binge eating or purging.

- This condition occurs most often in females from adolescence to young adulthood.

- In females, anorexia nervosa is accompanied by amenorrhea for at least three consecutive cycles.

Δ **Bulimia Nervosa**

- Characterized by:

   ◊ Recurrent episodes of eating large quantities of food over a short period of time (bingeing) that may be followed by inappropriate compensatory behaviors to rid the body of these excessive calories such as self-induced vomiting (purging).

- Two types:

   ◊ Purging type

   ◊ Non-purging type – The client may also compensate for bingeing through other means, such as excessive exercise and the misuse of laxatives, diuretics, or enemas.

- Most clients with bulimia maintain a weight within a normal range or slightly higher.

- The average age of onset in females is 15 to 18 years of age.

- About 10 to 15% of clients with bulimia are males. Onset generally occurs between 18 and 26 years of age, and bingeing with the use of excessive exercise (non-purging type) is most common.

Δ **Eating disorder not otherwise specified (NOS)** is a category that includes disorders of eating that do not meet the criteria for either anorexia nervosa or bulimia nervosa. For example, a female client may have all the signs and symptoms of anorexia nervosa except amenorrhea.

Key Factors

Δ Risks factors for eating disorders in females include:

- Family genetics – more commonly seen in families with sisters and mothers with eating disorders.

- Biological – hypothalamic, neurotransmitter, hormonal, or biochemical imbalance; disturbances of the serotonin neurotransmitter pathways seem to be implicated.

- Interpersonal relationships – influenced by parental pressure and the need to succeed.

- Psychological influences – rigidity, ritualism, separation and individuation conflicts; feelings of ineffectiveness, helplessness, and depression; and distorted body image.

- Environmental factors – pressure from society to have the "perfect body," culture of abundance.

- Family eating patterns and individual history of being a "picky" eater in childhood.

- Participation in athletics, especially at an elite level of competition.

Δ   Males account for about 5 to 10% of all cases of anorexia nervosa and 10 to 15% of all cases of bulimia nervosa. Possible risk factors include:

- Dieting, which seems to precede the onset of anorexia nervosa in both males and females.

- Participation in a sport where lean body build is prized (e.g., bicycling) or where a specific weight is necessary (e.g., wrestling).

- A history of obesity.

Δ   Mortality rate for eating disorders is high and suicide is also a risk.

Δ   Treatment modalities focus on normalizing eating patterns and beginning to address the issues raised by the illness.

Assessment

Δ   Take a **nursing history**, including:

- The client's perception of the problem.

- Eating habits.

- History of dieting.

- Methods of weight control (restricting, purging, exercising).

- Value attached to a specific shape and weight.

- Interpersonal and social functioning.

- Difficulty with impulsivity as well as compulsivity.

- Family and interpersonal relationships (frequently troublesome and chaotic, reflecting a lack of nurturing).

Δ **Physical Assessment**

Mental status	Cognitive distortions include:
	• Overgeneralizations – "Other girls don't like me because I'm fat."
	• All-or-nothing thinking – "If I eat any dessert, I'll gain 50 lb."
	• Catastrophizing – "My life is over if I gain weight."
	• Personalization – "When I walk through the hospital hallway, I know everyone is looking at me."
	• Emotional reasoning – "I know I look bad because I feel bloated."
Vital Signs	• Low blood pressure with possible orthostatic hypotension
	• Decreased pulse and body temperature
Weight	• Clients with anorexia have body weight that is less than 85% of expected normal weight.
	• Most clients with bulimia maintain a weight within the normal range or slightly higher.
Head, neck, mouth, and throat	• Enlargement of the parotid glands
	• Dental erosion and caries
Cardiac status	• Irregular heart rate (dysrhythmias noted on cardiac monitor)
Skin, hair, and nails	• Fine, downy hair (lanugo) on the face and back
	• Mottled, cool extremities and poor skin turgor

Δ **Laboratory Findings**

- Common laboratory **abnormalities in anorexia** include:

  ◊ Hypokalemia, especially for those who are also bulimic.

    ° There is a direct loss of potassium due to purging (vomiting).

    ° Dehydration stimulates increased aldosterone production, which leads to sodium and water retention and potassium excretion.

  ◊ Anemia and leukopenia with lymphocytosis.

  ◊ Possible impaired liver function, shown by increased enzyme levels.

  ◊ Possible elevated cholesterol.

  ◊ Abnormal thyroid function tests.

  ◊ Elevated carotene levels, which cause skin to appear yellow.

  ◊ Decreased bone density (possible osteoporosis).

- Common laboratory **abnormalities in bulimia** include:

  ◊ Hypokalemia.

  ◊ Hyponatremia.

  ◊ Hypochloremia.

  ◊ The type and extent of electrolyte imbalance may depend on method used when purging, such as laxatives or diuretics.

NANDA Nursing Diagnoses

Δ   Disturbed body image

Δ   Decreased cardiac output

Δ   Ineffective coping

Δ   Hopelessness

Δ   Risk for injury

Δ   Imbalanced nutrition: Less than body requirements

Δ   Powerlessness

Δ   Chronic low self-esteem

Nursing Interventions

Δ   Establish and maintain trust through consistency and therapeutic communication. The nurse needs to be aware that the client with an eating disorder is very sensitive to the perceptions of others regarding her illness.

Δ   Address cognitive distortions through therapeutic communication or cognitive-behavioral therapy.

Δ   Monitor food intake, exercise patterns, and attempts to purge after eating.

Δ   Teach meal planning, use of relaxation techniques, maintenance of a healthy diet and exercise, coping skills, and the physical and emotional effects of bingeing and purging.

Δ   Use behavior modification; reward the client for weight gain and positive behavior.

Δ   Offer the opportunity to participate in individual psychotherapy.

Δ   **Medications** may include an antidepressant, such as fluoxetine (Prozac), which may also treat concurrent anxiety disorders, and an antipsychotic agent, such as olanzapine (Zyprexa), to improve mood and decrease disturbed thought patterns.

Δ   Provide **a highly structured milieu** in an inpatient eating disorder unit for the client requiring intensive therapy.

- Closely monitor the client during and after meals to prevent purging and to ensure the normalization of eating patterns.

- Monitor the client for maintenance of appropriate exercise.

- Teach and encourage self-care activities from the day of admission.

- Evaluate family dynamics and encourage family members to be a part of group education and family therapy sessions.

Complications and Nursing Implications

Δ **Refeeding syndrome** is a circulatory collapse when a client's completely compromised cardiac system is overwhelmed by a replenished vascular system after normal fluid intake resumes.

- Implement refeeding over at least 7 days.
- Carefully monitor serum electrolytes and intervene as prescribed.

Δ **Cardiac dysrhythmias, severe bradycardia, and hypotension** may occur with malnutrition.

- Place the client on continuous cardiac monitoring.
- Monitor vital signs frequently.
- Report changes in status to the primary care provider.

Δ **Osteoporosis**

- Provide calcium supplements.
- Provide adequate nutrition and fluid replacement.

Primary Reference:

Varcarolis, E. M., Carson, V. B., & Shoemaker, N. C. (2006). *Foundations of psychiatric mental health nursing: A clinical approach* (5th ed.). St. Louis, MO: Saunders.

Additional Resources:

Agras, W. S. (2006, June 7). The eating disorders: Anorexia nervosa. *Medscape Today*, Article 534480. Retrieved on November 19, 2006, from http://www.medscape.com/viewarticle/534480

Braun, D. L. (1997). Eating disorders in males. *Medscape Today*, Article 431281. Retrieved on November 20, 2006, from http://www.medscape.com/viewarticle/431281

NANDA International (2004). *NANDA nursing diagnoses: Definitions and classification 2005-2006*. Philadelphia: NANDA.

Chapter 23: Eating Disorders

Application Exercises

Scenario: A nurse is working with a 16-year-old client in a community mental health facility. The client and her mother have begun exploring colleges extensively. After school, the client spends her time preparing gourmet meals for her family while her mother is working. Lately, her mother has noticed that the client is not eating the food she prepares. Instead, she busies herself serving the rest of the family and says she is dieting in order to "have friends at college." During a recent physical examination, it was discovered that the client's weight dropped from an ideal weight for her height, 115 lb, to 95 lb in the past 3 months. She has also stopped menstruating. Her primary care provider has referred her to the mental health center for counseling.

1. What assessments are important for this client?

2. What physical symptoms of anorexia nervosa does this client have and what other signs of the disorder does she display?

3. What nursing diagnoses should the nurse include in this client's care plan?

4. A client is hospitalized on an eating disorders unit. She has a history of and current diagnosis of bulimia nervosa. Along with bingeing, which of the following other symptoms are congruent with the client's diagnosis?

    A. Purging, obesity, hyperkalemia

    B. Purging, normal weight, hypokalemia

    C. Laxative abuse, amenorrhea, severe weight loss

    D. Purging, severe weight loss, hyperkalemia

5. A client with bulimia has stopped vomiting on the unit and tells the nurse he is afraid he is going to gain weight. Which of the following is the most appropriate response by the nurse?

    A. "You don't need to be concerned. The dietician will ensure you don't get too many calories in your diet."

    B. "Don't worry about your weight. We are going to work on other problems while you are in the hospital."

    C. "I understand you have concerns about your weight, but right now I want you to tell me about your recent invitation to join the National Honor Society. That's quite an accomplishment."

    D. "You are not overweight, and the staff will ensure that you do not gain weight while you are in the hospital. We know that is important to you."

6. An appropriate short-term goal for any client with an eating disorder is that the client will

    A. weigh within the norms for age and height.

    B. eat a well-balanced diet.

    C. resolve conflicts with family members.

    D. look at herself in the mirror each morning.

Chapter 23: Eating Disorders

Application Exercises Answer Key

Scenario: A nurse is working with a 16-year-old client in a community mental health facility. The client and her mother have begun exploring colleges extensively. After school, the client spends her time preparing gourmet meals for her family while her mother is working. Lately, her mother has noticed that the client is not eating the food she prepares. Instead, she busies herself serving the rest of the family and says she is dieting in order to "have friends at college." During a recent physical examination, it was discovered that the client's weight dropped from an ideal weight for her height, 115 lb, to 95 lb in the past 3 months. She has also stopped menstruating. Her primary care provider has referred her to the mental health center for counseling.

1. What assessments are important for this client?

   Explore dietary habits and history, height and weight, skin condition, other physical assessment parameters (e.g., vital signs), feelings about body image, and family dynamics.

2. What physical symptoms of anorexia nervosa does this client have and what other signs of the disorder does she display?

   This client has weight loss greater than 15% of her ideal body weight and she has amenorrhea. She also is interested in food (cooks for the family and serves the food) but does not eat it. From the data in the scenario, it appears this client has anorexia nervosa, non-purging type.

3. What nursing diagnoses should the nurse include in this client's care plan?

   **Imbalanced nutrition: Less than body requirements related to refusal to eat
   Disturbed body image related to inaccurate perception of self
   Risk for injury (presence of complications) related to extreme weight loss**

4. A client is hospitalized on an eating disorders unit. She has a history of and current diagnosis of bulimia nervosa. Along with bingeing, which of the following other symptoms are congruent with the client's diagnosis?

> A. Purging, obesity, hyperkalemia
>
> **B. Purging, normal weight, hypokalemia**
>
> C. Laxative abuse, amenorrhea, severe weight loss
>
> D. Purging, severe weight loss, hyperkalemia

A client with bulimia tends to have normal or slightly increased weight and low potassium levels due to bingeing and purging. Hyperkalemia, obesity, and severe weight loss are not consistent with bulimia.

5. A client with bulimia has stopped vomiting on the unit and tells the nurse he is afraid he is going to gain weight. Which of the following is the most appropriate response by the nurse?

> A. "You don't need to be concerned. The dietician will ensure you don't get too many calories in your diet."
>
> B. "Don't worry about your weight. We are going to work on other problems while you are in the hospital."
>
> **C. "I understand you have concerns about your weight, but right now I want you to tell me about your recent invitation to join the National Honor Society. That's quite an accomplishment."**
>
> D. "You are not overweight, and the staff will ensure that you do not gain weight while you are in the hospital. We know that is important to you."

In the correct option, the nurse acknowledges the client's concerns and then focuses the conversation on the client's accomplishment. The other options minimize the client's concerns about being overweight and/or gaining weight.

6. An appropriate short-term goal for any client with an eating disorder is that the client will

> A. weigh within the norms for age and height.
>
> **B. eat a well-balanced diet.**
>
> C. resolve conflicts with family members.
>
> D. look at herself in the mirror each morning.

A realistic short-term goal focuses on making sure the client eats a nutritious diet. Weighing within the norms for age and height and resolving family conflicts might be possible long-term goals. Looking at oneself in the mirror each morning is not an appropriate goal; the client may look at herself in the mirror but have a distorted view of what she sees.

Unit 4   Psychobiologic Disorders, Psychiatric Emergencies, and Mental Health Nursing Care of
                Special Populations

Section: Psychobiologic Disorders

Chapter 24:	Mood Disorders: Depression
	Contributors: Susan Adcock, MS, RN
	Deborah Kindy, PhD, RN

 NCLEX-RN® Connections:

Learning Objective: Review and apply knowledge within "**Mood Disorders:
Depression**" in readiness for performance of the following nursing activities as outlined
by the NCLEX-RN® test plan:

Δ   Apply knowledge of psychobiologic disorders to the nursing process when caring
    for clients with a major depressive disorder.

Δ   Use effective communication to interact with and assist the client/family to
    foster trust in the nurse-client therapeutic relationship.

Δ   Assess the client's mental status, identifying changes in mood, judgment,
    cognition, and reasoning.

Δ   Identify the client/family's responses to the diagnosis of depression.

Δ   Plan/provide care for the client with depression.

Δ   Support the client's efforts in the use of strategies to decrease anxiety.

Δ   Evaluate and document the client's response to treatment of depression.

Δ   Evaluate the client's ability to follow the treatment plan for depression.

Δ   Teach the client/family signs and symptoms of relapse of the depression.

 Key Points

Δ   Depression is a **mood (affective)** disorder and is a widespread problem, ranking
    high among causes of disability.

Δ   **Unipolar** depression means the client's present mood is "normal" or depressed, as
    opposed to bipolar disorder, which includes mood swings from major depression
    to mania. (*Refer to chapter 25, Mood Disorders: Bipolar.*)

Δ   The client with depression is at **high risk for suicide**, especially if he has a family or personal history of suicide attempts, comorbid anxiety disorder or panic attacks, comorbid substance abuse or psychosis, poor self-esteem, a lack of social support, or a chronic medical condition, such as multiple sclerosis.

Δ   Classifications of Depressive Disorders

•   **Major depressive disorder (MDD)** – a single episode or recurrent episodes of unipolar depression resulting in a significant change in the client's normal functioning (e.g., social, occupational, self-care) accompanied by at least five specific symptoms.

◊   These symptoms must happen almost every day, last most of the day, and occur continuously for a minimum of 2 weeks.

◊   Symptoms include: depressed mood, difficulty sleeping or excessive sleeping, indecisiveness or decreased ability to concentrate, suicidal ideation, increase or decrease in motor activity, inability to feel pleasure, and increase or decrease in weight of more than 5% of total body weight over 1 month.

◊   MDD may be further diagnosed in the DSM-IV-TR with a more specific classification (specifier), including:

°   Psychotic features – the presence of auditory hallucinations (e.g., voices telling the client she is sinful) or the presence of delusions (e.g., client thinks she has a fatal disease).

°   Postpartum onset – begins within 4 weeks of childbirth (known as postpartum depression) and may include delusions, putting the newborn infant at high risk of being harmed by the mother.

°   Seasonal characteristics – seasonal affective disorder (SAD), which occurs during winter and may be treated with light therapy.

°   Chronic features – depressive episode lasts over 2 years in duration.

•   **Dysthymic disorder** – a milder form of depression that usually has an early onset, such as in childhood or adolescence, and lasts at least 2 years in length for adults (1 year in length for children). Dysthymic disorder contains at least three symptoms of depression and may, later in life, become major depressive disorder.

•   **Depressive disorder (not otherwise specified)** – for depression that cannot be categorized in one of the first two classifications.

Key Factors

Δ   **Etiology** – Theories related to depressive disorders include:

- Genetics – In identical twins, if one is affected with depression, there is up to a 60% chance of the other twin also being affected.

- Neurotransmitter deficiencies.

  ◊   Serotonin (5-HT), which affects mood, sexual behavior, sleep regulation, hunger, and pain perception

  ◊   Norepinephrine, which affects mood and stress response

- Dysfunction of the hypothalamic-pituitary-gonadal axis (e.g., hypothyroidism is associated with depression).

- Sleep abnormalities, including earlier onset of rapid eye movement sleep, disturbance in the continuity of sleep, and early morning awakenings.

Δ   Depression may be comorbid with:

- Anxiety disorders – occur with 70% of major depressive disorders and make the client's prognosis poorer with a higher risk for suicide and disability.

- Schizophrenia.

- Substance abuse.

- Eating disorders.

- Personality disorders.

Δ   **Risk Factors** for Depressive Disorders

- Family history and a previous personal history of depression are the most significant risk factors.

- Depressive disorders are twice as common in females between the ages of 15 and 40 than in males.

- Depression is very common among clients over age 65, but it is more difficult to recognize in the older adult client and may go untreated.

- Other risk factors include:

  ◊   Stressful life events.

  ◊   Presence of a medical illness.

  ◊   Being a female in the postpartum period.

  ◊   Poor social support network.

  ◊   Comorbid substance abuse.

- Depression occurs throughout all groups of people. There are no specific risk factors for ethnicity, education, income, or marital status.

Δ The process of recovery from a major depressive episode has three distinct treatment phases.

- Acute phase – Hospitalization may be needed in this phase, which lasts 6 to 12 weeks. In this phase, symptoms of depression are reduced along with depressive psychosocial symptoms, such as difficulty socializing with others.

- Continuation phase – Lasting from 4 to 9 months, the purpose of this phase of treatment is to prevent relapse through education, medication therapy, and psychotherapy.

- Maintenance phase – This phase includes prevention of future depressive episodes and may last several years.

Assessment

Δ Tools used to assess for depression include:

- Hamilton Depression Scale.

- Beck Depression Inventory.

- Geriatric Depression Scale.

- Zung's Self-Rating Depression Scale.

Δ Signs and symptoms of depression include:

- Anergia (lack of energy).

- Anhedonia (lack of pleasure in normal activities).

- Affect – Client most often looks sad with blunted affect.

- Anxiety.

- Poor grooming and hygiene.

- Decreased communication – The client may seem too tired even to speak.

- Psychomotor retardation (slowed movement) is more common, but psychomotor agitation (restlessness, pacing, finger tapping, or reports of feeling unable to relax and sit still) may occur in some clients.

- **Vegetative signs**, which include fatigue, change in eating patterns (usually anorexia in MDD and possible increased intake in dysthymia), change in bowel habits (usually constipation), sleep disturbances (often early morning waking), and decreased interest in sexual activity.

- **Somatic complaints** – The client with depression may have one or more somatic problems, such as fatigue, gastrointestinal symptoms, or pain.

Δ **Assessment of suicide risk is vital in any client with depression.**

NANDA Nursing Diagnoses

Δ Ineffective coping

Δ Hopelessness

Δ Imbalanced nutrition: Less than body requirements

Δ Ineffective role performance

Δ Bathing/hygiene self-care deficit

Δ Risk for self-directed violence

Δ Chronic low self-esteem

Δ Sleep deprivation

Δ Ineffective sexuality patterns

Δ Social isolation

Δ Spiritual distress

Δ Risk for suicide

Nursing Interventions

Δ **Safety**

- Remain alert for overt and covert signs that the client is planning suicide. (*Refer to chapter 31, Suicide.*)

- Keep at-risk clients safe through manipulation of the milieu along with close observation or one-to-one supervision as indicated by assessment of risk factors and of the specific client's needs.

Δ **Milieu therapy** for the hospitalized client includes maintenance of self-care, positive group activities, pharmacologic therapy, counseling and psychotherapy, and possibly electroconvulsive therapy.

Δ **Communication**

- Relate therapeutically to the client who is unable or unwilling to communicate.

  ◊ Make time to be with the client even if he does not speak.

  ◊ Make observations rather than asking direct questions, which may increase anxiety in the client. For example, the nurse might say, "I noticed that you attended the unit group meeting today," rather than asking, "Did you enjoy the group meeting?"

◊ Give directions in simple, concrete sentences, since the depressed client may have difficulty focusing on and comprehending long sentences.

◊ Give the client sufficient time to respond when holding a conversation; response time may be greatly slowed.

Δ **Counseling** may include individual counseling to assist the client with:

- Problem solving.

- Increasing coping abilities.

- Changing negative thinking to positive.

- Increasing self-esteem.

- Assertiveness training.

- Using available community resources.

Δ **Psychotherapy** by a trained therapist may include individual cognitive-behavioral therapy, group therapy, and family therapy.

Δ The nurse must monitor and teach the client about **pharmacologic** treatment.

- **Antidepressants**

  ◊ SSRIs, such as sertraline (Zoloft), are first-line therapy for depression.

  ◊ Atypical antidepressants include bupropion (Wellbutrin), a norepinephrine and dopamine reuptake blocker.

  ◊ Tricyclic antidepressants (TCAs), such as amitriptyline (Elavil), are medications that have been used for many years, but they have many side effects and interact adversely with many other medications.

  ◊ Monoamine oxidase inhibitors (MAOIs), such as tranylcypromine (Parnate), interact adversely with many other medications as well as with foods that contain tyramine, such as fermented meats and aged fish and cheese.

- **Antianxiety agents**, such as the benzodiazepine alprazolam (Xanax)

Δ **Electroconvulsive therapy (ECT)** can be useful for some clients with depression. (*Refer to chapter 12, Electroconvulsive Therapy.*)

- The nurse is responsible for monitoring the client before and after this therapy.

- Specially trained nurses assist with the treatment.

Δ **Transcranial magnetic stimulation (TMS)** is a new therapy using electromagnetic stimulation to the brain; it may be helpful for depression resistant to other forms of treatment.

Δ **Self-care** – Monitor the client's ability to perform activities of daily living and encourage independence as much as possible.

Δ Other therapies for depression include:

- Exercise – Studies have shown that 30 min of exercise daily for 3 to 5 days each week improves symptoms of depression and may help to prevent relapse. Even shorter intervals of exercise are helpful. Exercise should be thought of as an adjunct to other therapies for the client with major depressive disorder.

- St. John's Wort – a plant product (*Hypericum perforatum*) ingested by some individuals to relieve symptoms of depression.

  ◊ No research has shown conclusively that St. John's Wort is actually effective in relieving symptoms of depression. Some individuals feel it is helpful for at least relief of mild symptoms.

  ◊ Adverse effects include photosensitivity, skin rash, rapid heart rate, gastrointestinal upset, and abdominal pain.

  ◊ St. John's Wort can increase or reduce levels of some medications if taken concurrently. The client should inform his primary care provider if taking St. John's Wort.

  ◊ Medication interactions – Potentially fatal serotonin syndrome can result if St. John's Wort is taken with:

    ° Any of the SSRI antidepressants.

    ° Any of the MAOI antidepressants.

    ° Either nefazodone (Serzone) or venlafaxine (Effexor), two atypical antidepressants.

    ° Some tricyclic antidepressants, including amitriptyline (Elavil) and clomipramine (Anafranil).

Primary Reference:

Varcarolis, E. M., Carson, V. B., & Shoemaker, N. C. (2006). *Foundations of psychiatric mental health nursing: A clinical approach* (5th ed.). St. Louis, MO: Saunders.

Additional Resources:

Compton, M. T., & Nemeroff, C. B. (2006, June 28). Depression and bipolar disorder. *Medscape Today*, Article 536897. Retrieved November 19, 2006, from http://www.medscape.com/viewarticle/536897_1

Lehne, R. A. (2007). *Pharmacology for nursing care.* (6th ed.). St. Louis, MO: Saunders.

Mayo Clinic Foundation for Medical Education and Research. (2005, November 9). *Depression and anxiety: Exercise eases symptoms.* Retrieved December 6, 2006, from http://www.mayoclinic.com/health/depression-and-exercise/MH00043

NANDA International (2004). *NANDA nursing diagnoses: Definitions and classification 2005-2006.* Philadelphia: NANDA.

National Center for Complementary and Alternative Medicine, National Institutes of Health. (2002, April 9). *Study shows St. John's Wort ineffective for major depression of moderate severity.* Retrieved December 6, 2006, from http://nccam.nih.gov/news/2002/stjohnswort/pressrelease.htm

Chapter 24: Mood Disorders: Depression

Application Exercises

Scenario: A 35-year-old female client is newly admitted to an acute care mental health facility for her third episode of major depressive disorder. She lives at home with her husband and two school-age children, but she has stopped cooking, doing housework, and grooming herself or the children during the past 3 weeks. She says she has a complete lack of energy to do anything, a lack of appetite with a 5-lb weight loss, constipation, abdominal pain, and an inability to sleep more than 5 hr each night (wakes up early and cannot get back to sleep). During the admission interview, she says to the nurse, "It would be better for my family if I just wasn't around ever again. I'm no good for them anymore, and I have no control over any of my life."

1. Formulate three nursing diagnoses for this client. Indicate which one is the priority diagnosis and explain why.

2. What risk factors for depression does this client have?

3. The client's husband tells the nurse, "I hope my wife will be able to take her St. John's Wort here in the hospital." Which of the client's symptoms could be related to taking St. John's Wort?

4. The client has started taking the SSRI paroxetine (Paxil). What should the client and her spouse know about taking this medication?

5. A client is displaying vegetative signs of major depressive disorder. Which of the following nursing diagnoses are appropriate for this client? (Select all that apply.)

_____ Sleep pattern disturbance

_____ Hopelessness

_____ Sexual dysfunction

_____ Constipation

_____ Disturbed thought processes

6. A nurse interviews a 25-year-old client diagnosed with dysthymia. The nurse knows that dysthymia differs from major depressive disorder in several ways. One difference is that in dysthymia

    A. there is evidence of underlying mania.

    B. the client never has suicidal ideation.

    C. the symptoms last for at least 2 years.

    D. the disorder begins after age 40.

7. A 24-year-old female client gave birth to a baby 5 weeks ago. Today, on a visit to the community health agency, she describes feelings of severe depression to the nurse. She tells the nurse, "I don't even think this baby is mine. He was dropped into my house from an alien space ship and I believe he is trying to destroy me." Which of the following is the priority nursing diagnosis at this time?

    A. Risk for impaired parent-infant attachment

    B. Risk for other-directed violence

    C. Disturbed thought processes

    D. Fear

Chapter 24: Mood Disorders: Depression

Application Exercises Answer Key

Scenario: A 35-year-old female client is newly admitted to an acute care mental health facility for her third episode of major depressive disorder. She lives at home with her husband and two school-age children, but she has stopped cooking, doing housework, and grooming herself or the children during the past 3 weeks. She says she has a complete lack of energy to do anything, a lack of appetite with a 5-lb weight loss, constipation, abdominal pain, and an inability to sleep more than 5 hr each night (wakes up early and cannot get back to sleep). During the admission interview, she says to the nurse, "It would be better for my family if I just wasn't around ever again. I'm no good for them anymore, and I have no control over any of my life."

1. Formulate three nursing diagnoses for this client. Indicate which one is the priority diagnosis and explain why.

   Risk for suicide (or self-harm) – The client's safety is the highest priority due to her statement, which could indicate a plan for suicide. Other diagnoses include:

   > **Ineffective coping**
   > **Hopelessness**
   > **Nutrition imbalanced: Less than body requirements**
   > **Ineffective role performance**
   > **Bathing/hygiene self-care deficit**
   > **Sleep deprivation**
   > **Risk for self-directed violence**
   > **Chronic low self-esteem**
   > **Social isolation**
   > **Spiritual distress**
   > **Ineffective sexuality patterns**

2. What risk factors for depression does this client have?

   She is a female between 15 and 40 years old and has a personal past history of depression.

3. The client's husband tells the nurse, "I hope my wife will be able to take her St. John's Wort here in the hospital." Which of the client's symptoms could be related to taking St. John's Wort?

   Abdominal pain is one adverse reaction from taking St. John's Wort. Others include photosensitivity, skin rash, rapid heart rate, and gastrointestinal upset.

4. The client has started taking the SSRI paroxetine (Paxil). What should the client and her spouse know about taking this medication?

Combining any SSRI antidepressant with St. John's Wort can cause serotonin syndrome, a serious condition that includes high fever, hypertension, and delirium. On discharge from the facility, the client should not restart her St. John's Wort if she is to continue taking the paroxetine.

5. A client is displaying vegetative signs of major depressive disorder. Which of the following nursing diagnoses are appropriate for this client? (Select all that apply.)

__X__ Sleep pattern disturbance
_____ Hopelessness
__X__ Sexual dysfunction
__X__ Constipation
_____ Disturbed thought processes

Vegetative signs include alterations in body functions, such as sleep, eating, sexual activity, and elimination. Hopelessness is related to an emotion or feeling. Disturbed thought processes could occur if psychotic features occurred along with the depression.

6. A nurse interviews a 25-year-old client diagnosed with dysthymia. The nurse knows that dysthymia differs from major depressive disorder in several ways. One difference is that in dysthymia

A. there is evidence of underlying mania.

B. the client never has suicidal ideation.

C. the symptoms last for at least 2 years.

D. the disorder begins after age 40.

Symptoms of dysthymia persist for at least 2 years in adults. Mania occurs in bipolar disorders but not in dysthymia. Suicidal ideation could occur in clients with both dysthymia and major depressive disorder. Onset of dysthymia tends to be early in life, such as childhood or adolescence.

7. A 24-year-old female client gave birth to a baby 5 weeks ago. Today, on a visit to the community health agency, she describes feelings of severe depression to the nurse. She tells the nurse, "I don't even think this baby is mine. He was dropped into my house from an alien space ship and I believe he is trying to destroy me." Which of the following is the priority nursing diagnosis at this time?

    A. Risk for impaired parent-infant attachment

    B. Risk for other-directed violence

    C. Disturbed thought processes

    D. Fear

This client may have postpartum onset of major depressive disorder. She has delusions that may put the infant at risk for violence. The other nursing diagnoses may also apply but have a lower priority at present.

Unit 4 Psychobiologic Disorders, Psychiatric Emergencies, and Mental Health Nursing Care of Special Populations

Section: Psychobiologic Disorders

Chapter 25: Mood Disorders: Bipolar

Contributor: Phyllis M. Jacobs, MSN, RN

NCLEX-RN® Connections:

Learning Objective: Review and apply knowledge within "**Mood Disorders: Bipolar**" in readiness for performance of the following nursing activities as outlined by the NCLEX-RN® test plan:

Δ Apply knowledge of psychobiologic disorders to the nursing process when caring for clients with a bipolar disorder.

Δ Use effective communication to interact with and assist the client/family to foster trust in the nurse-client therapeutic relationship.

Δ Assess the client's mental status, identifying changes in mood, judgment, cognition, and reasoning.

Δ Identify the client/family's responses to the diagnosis of bipolar disorder.

Δ Plan/provide care for the client with a bipolar disorder.

Δ Support the client's efforts in the use of strategies to decrease anxiety.

Δ Evaluate and document the client's response to treatment of bipolar disorder.

Δ Evaluate the client's ability to follow the treatment plan for bipolar disorder.

Δ Teach the client/family signs and symptoms of relapse of bipolar disorder.

 Key Points

Δ Bipolar disorders are mood disorders with recurrent episodes of depression and mania. Phases may vary depending on the type of bipolar disorder.

Δ Bipolar disorders usually emerge in late adolescence/early adulthood but can be diagnosed in the school-age child as well.

Δ Periods of normal functioning alternate with periods of illness, though some clients are not able to maintain full occupational and social functioning.

Δ Psychotic, paranoid, and/or bizarre behavior may be seen during periods of mania.

∆ Types of Bipolar Disorders

- **Bipolar I disorder** – The client has at least one episode of mania alternating with major depression.

- **Bipolar II disorder** – The client has repeated hypomanic episodes alternating with major depressive episodes.

- **Cyclothymia** – The client has at least 2 years of repeated hypomanic episodes alternating with minor depressive episodes.

∆ Behaviors shown with bipolar disorders include:

- **Mania** – an abnormally elevated mood, which may also be described as expansive or irritable; usually requires inpatient treatment. (See the assessment section in this chapter for specific symptoms.)

- **Hypomania** – a less severe episode of mania that lasts at least 4 days accompanied by three to four symptoms of mania. Hospitalization, however, is not required, and the client with hypomania is less impaired.

- **Mixed episode** – a manic episode and an episode of major depression experienced by the client simultaneously. The client has marked impairment in functioning and may require admission to an acute care mental health facility to prevent self-harm or other-directed violence.

- **Rapid cycling** – four or more episodes of acute mania within 1 year.

Key Factors

∆ Etiology

- Genetic component

- Biochemical imbalances involving norepinephrine, dopamine, and serotonin

- Hypothyroidism involvement with some clients, especially the client with rapid cycling

- Neuroanatomical factors in the prefrontal cortex and medial temporal lobe, including dysregulation in the neurochemical circuits

∆ Comorbidity Factors

- Substance abuse

  ◊ The client with substance abuse problems tends to experience more rapid cycling of mania than do clients without substance abuse problems.

- Anxiety disorders

- Eating disorders

- Attention deficit hyperactivity disorder (ADHD)

Δ Relapse

• Use of substances (e.g., alcohol, drugs of abuse, caffeine) can lead to an episode of mania.

• Sleep disturbances may come before, be associated with, or be brought on by an episode of mania.

Assessment

Δ Assess physical status; symptoms of mania may also be caused by:

• Physical illness, such as delirium due to a head injury.

• Substance abuse, such as cocaine or methamphetamine overdose.

Δ Use a standardized tool, such as the Mood Disorder Questionnaire, to assess the client's mood.

• Mood may progress on a continuum from hypomania (euphoria) to acute mania (extreme irritability and hyperactivity) to delirium (completely out of touch with reality).

| Bipolar Disorder Signs and Symptoms ||
Manic phase	Depressive phase
• Persistent elevated mood (euphoria) • Agitation and irritability • Dislike of interference and intolerance of criticism • Increase in talking and activities • Flight of ideas – rapid, continuous speech with sudden and frequent topic change • Grandiose view of self and abilities (grandiosity) • Impulsivity: spending money, giving away money or possessions • Distractibility • Poor judgment • Attention-seeking behavior: flashy dress and makeup, inappropriate behavior • Impairment in social and occupational functioning • Decreased sleep • Neglect of ADLs, including nutrition and hydration • May have delusions and hallucinations • Denial of illness	• Affect: flat, blunted, labile • Tearful, crying • Lack of energy • Anhedonia: loss of pleasure, lack of interest in activities, hobbies, sexual activity • Physical symptoms of discomfort/pain • Difficulty concentrating, focusing, problem solving • Self-destructive behavior • Decrease in personal hygiene • Loss or increase in appetite and/or sleep, disturbed sleep • Psychomotor retardation or agitation

NANDA Nursing Diagnoses

Δ   Ineffective coping

Δ   Interrupted family processes

Δ   Risk for injury

Δ   Self-care deficit

Δ   Disturbed sleep pattern

Δ   Disturbed thought processes

Δ   Risk for other- or self-directed violence

Nursing Interventions

Δ   Therapeutic Milieu (within acute care mental health facility)

- Provide a safe environment during the acute phase.

  ◊ Assess regularly for suicidal thoughts, intentions, and escalating behavior.

  ◊ Decrease stimulation without isolating the client if possible; however, seclusion may be the only way to safely decrease stimulation for this client.

  ◊ Provide client protection (restraints, seclusion/observation room, one-to-one supervision) if a threat of self-injury or injury to others exists.

- Be aware of noise, music, television, and other clients, all of which may lead to an escalation of the client's behavior.

- Observe closely for escalating behavior.

- Provide outlets for physical activity. Do not involve the client in activities requiring a high level of concentration, detailed instructions, or that last a long time.

- Maintenance of self-care needs includes:

  ◊ Monitoring sleep, fluid intake, and nutrition.

  ◊ Providing portable, nutritious food, since the client may not be able to sit down to eat.

  ◊ Supervising choice of clothes.

  ◊ Giving step-by-step reminders for hygiene and dress.

Δ   Communication

- Use a calm, matter-of-fact, specific approach.

- Give concise explanations.

- Provide for consistency among staff members.

- Avoid power struggles and do not react personally to the client's comments.

- Direct energy into constructive channels, such as safe unit chores.

- Hear and act on legitimate complaints.

- Reinforce nonmanipulative behaviors.

Δ   Pharmacotherapeutics

- Medications for manic phase (*Refer to chapter 15, Medications to Treat Mood Disorders: Bipolar.*)

  ◊   Mood stabilizers, such as lithium

  ◊   Anticonvulsants, such as carbamazepine (Tegretol)

  ◊   Atypical antipsychotics, such as olanzapine (Zyprexa), which are now being used to stabilize mania in clients who do not respond to lithium or anticonvulsants

  ◊   Benzodiazepines, such as lorazepam (Ativan), which may be prescribed on a short-term basis for the client with sleep impairment related to mania

- Antidepressant medications are used during the depressive phase.

- Medication education: The client and his family need to understand the importance of adhering to the medication regimen, complying with regular laboratory studies, and managing adverse effects of medications.

Δ   Electroconvulsive therapy (ECT) may be used to subdue extreme manic behavior, especially when pharmacologic therapy, such as lithium, has not worked. ECT may also be used for clients who are suicidal or those with rapid cycling. (*Refer to chapter 12, Electroconvulsive Therapy.*)

Δ   Client and family teaching includes:

- The chronic and episodic nature of the disorder.

- Signs and symptoms of impending relapse and ways to manage the crisis.

- Precipitating factors of relapse (e.g., sleep disturbance, use of alcohol, caffeine, or drugs of abuse).

- The importance of maintaining a regular sleep, meal, and activity pattern.

- The use of psychotherapy, including cognitive-behavioral therapy, family therapy, and interpersonal psychotherapy, to learn strategies to improve overall functioning.

Primary Reference:

Varcarolis, E. M., Carson, V. B., & Shoemaker, N. C. (2006). *Foundations of psychiatric mental health nursing: A clinical approach* (5th ed.). St. Louis, MO: Saunders.

Additional Resources:

Compton, M. T., & Nemeroff, C. B. (2006, June 28). Bipolar disorder. *Medscape Today*, Article 536897. Retrieved November 19, 2006, from http://www.medscape.com/viewarticle/536897_1

NANDA International (2004). *NANDA nursing diagnoses: Definitions and classification 2005-2006*. Philadelphia: NANDA.

National Institute of Mental Health. (2006, May 9). *Bipolar disorder*. Retrieved November 19, 2006, from http://www.nimh.nih.gov/publicat/bipolar.cfm

Townsend, M. C. (2006). *Psychiatric mental health nursing: Concepts of care in evidence-based practice* (5th ed.). Philadelphia: F.A. Davis.

Varcarolis, E. M. (2006). *Manual of psychiatric nursing care plans* (3rd ed.). St. Louis, MO: Saunders.

Chapter 25: Mood Disorders: Bipolar

Application Exercises

Scenario: A client in the manic phase of bipolar I disorder is being admitted to an inpatient acute care mental health unit. The mental health provider's plan is for this client to undergo a short course of electroconvulsive therapy (ECT) treatments in the first week of hospitalization. This client has been on the unit several times in the past, and the client's behavior has typically caused upheaval on the unit. The staff is complaining about the client even before the client's arrival.

1. List communication principles the nurse manager on the unit should review with the staff regarding this client.

2. Why would ECT be used for a client with bipolar I disorder?

3. After 1 week on the acute care mental health unit, the client's mania has decreased somewhat. However, he has slept very little in the past month. What nursing interventions could assist this client to rest and sleep?

4. A client with bipolar I disorder is very manic and is unable to eat or sleep. Her moods change rapidly from elated to very irritable. If this client threatens to hit a staff member or another client, which of the following verbal responses by the nurse would be most appropriate?

    A. "We will have to restrain you immediately if you try that once more!"

    B. "Do not hit him or me. If you are unable to control yourself, we will help you."

    C. "Stop that right now! No one did anything to you and you have no reason to attack us."

    D. "You know better than this. Why do you continue this behavior?"

5. A client with mania is standing with a group of clients on the mental health unit. The client is talking excitedly and at great length about a variety of topics. The nurse can see that the other clients are becoming anxious and restless but do not know what to do to stop the conversation. The most appropriate approach by the nurse is to

    A. give honest feedback. Tell the client his behavior is annoying others.

    B. try humor. Joke to the client that the other clients will collapse if he does not leave them alone.

    C. set limits. Tell the client he must leave other clients alone.

    D. use distraction. Ask the client to come to the dining room for a snack.

6. A client with bipolar I disorder is currently in an extreme manic phase. All the following nursing diagnoses apply to her situation. Which one has the highest priority?

    A. Disturbed thought process

    B. Risk for other- or self-directed violence

    C. Disturbed sleep pattern

    D. Ineffective coping

Chapter 25: Mood Disorders: Bipolar

Application Exercises Answer Key

Scenario: A client in the manic phase of bipolar I disorder is being admitted to an inpatient acute care mental health unit. The mental health provider's plan is for this client to undergo a short course of electroconvulsive therapy (ECT) treatments in the first week of hospitalization. This client has been on the unit several times in the past, and the client's behavior has typically caused upheaval on the unit. The staff is complaining about the client even before the client's arrival.

1. List communication principles the nurse manager on the unit should review with the staff regarding this client.

   Use a firm, calm approach.
   Explain things in a short, concise manner.
   Refrain from responding personally to the client's comments.
   Be consistent in approach and expectations.
   Talk with other staff members about what techniques work and do not work.
   Adhere to agreed-upon limits.
   Let the client know the consequences of inappropriate behavior.
   Hear and act on legitimate complaints.

2. Why would ECT be used for a client with bipolar I disorder?

   ECT can calm extreme mania in clients with rapid cycling or if mood stabilizers, such as lithium, failed to work for the client.

3. After 1 week on the acute care mental health unit, the client's mania has decreased somewhat. However, he has slept very little in the past month. What nursing interventions could assist this client to rest and sleep?

   Monitor the client's sleep-wake patterns during the manic phase.
   Ascertain the client's normal bedtime routine, such as reading before bedtime, and attempt to facilitate normal patterns as much as possible.
   Maintain a quiet, nonstimulating environment in the client's sleeping area.
   Limit daytime sleep, if possible, and gradually encourage return to normal cyclic wake-sleep patterns.
   Restrict use of coffee, tea, chocolate, and other stimulants, especially before bedtime.

4. A client with bipolar I disorder is very manic and is unable to eat or sleep. Her moods change rapidly from elated to very irritable. If this client threatens to hit a staff member or another client, which of the following verbal responses by the nurse would be most appropriate?

    A. "We will have to restrain you immediately if you try that once more!"

    B. "Do not hit him or me. If you are unable to control yourself, we will help you."

    C. "Stop that right now! No one did anything to you and you have no reason to attack us."

    D. "You know better than this. Why do you continue this behavior?"

The correct response is to set limits in concrete, simple sentences to de-escalate the situation. Option A threatens the client with restraint as a punishment. Option C does not assist the client to stop her behavior. Option D asks a question the client cannot answer.

5. A client with mania is standing with a group of clients on the mental health unit. The client is talking excitedly and at great length about a variety of topics. The nurse can see that the other clients are becoming anxious and restless but do not know what to do to stop the conversation. The most appropriate approach by the nurse is to

    A. give honest feedback. Tell the client his behavior is annoying others.

    B. try humor. Joke to the client that the other clients will collapse if he does not leave them alone.

    C. set limits. Tell the client he must leave other clients alone.

    D. use distraction. Ask the client to come to the dining room for a snack.

The client with mania is easily distracted and this can be a good technique for directing him to more appropriate activities without causing a power struggle. The other techniques would likely cause anger, or at least argument.

6. A client with bipolar I disorder is currently in an extreme manic phase. All the following nursing diagnoses apply to her situation. Which one has the highest priority?

    A. Disturbed thought process

    B. Risk for other- or self-directed violence

    C. Disturbed sleep pattern

    D. Ineffective coping

Although all four nursing diagnoses require intervention, risk for self- or other-directed violence is the highest priority to prevent injury to the client, staff, or other clients.

Unit 4   Psychobiologic Disorders, Psychiatric Emergencies, and Mental Health Nursing Care of Special Populations

Section: Psychobiologic Disorders

Chapter 26:   Schizophrenia

Contributor: Linda W. Edwards, MSN, RN

⟳ NCLEX-RN® Connections:

Learning Objective: Review and apply knowledge within "**Schizophrenia**" in readiness for performance of the following nursing activities as outlined by the NCLEX-RN® test plan:

- Δ   Apply knowledge of psychobiologic disorders to the nursing process when caring for clients with schizophrenia and other types of psychosis.

- Δ   Use effective communication to interact with and assist the client/family to foster trust in the nurse-client therapeutic relationship.

- Δ   Assess the client's mental status, identifying changes in mood, judgment, cognition, and reasoning.

- Δ   Identify the client/family's responses to the diagnosis of schizophrenia.

- Δ   Plan/provide care for the client with schizophrenia.

- Δ   Support the client's efforts in the use of strategies to decrease anxiety.

- Δ   Evaluate and document the client's response to treatment of schizophrenia.

- Δ   Evaluate the client's ability to follow the treatment plan for schizophrenia.

- Δ   Teach the client/family signs and symptoms of relapse of schizophrenia.

Key Points

- Δ   Schizophrenia is a group of psychotic disorders that affect thinking, behavior, emotions, and the ability to perceive reality.

- Δ   The term "psychosis" refers to the presence of hallucinations, delusions, or disorganized speech or catatonic behavior.

- Δ   The typical age at onset is late teens and early twenties, but schizophrenia has occurred in young children and may begin in later adulthood.

Δ   Comorbidities include substance abuse (40 to 50%), nicotine dependence (80%), depression and suicidal ideation (20 to 40% make at least one suicide attempt), and anxiety disorders.

Δ   **DSM-IV-TR Diagnostic Criteria**

- Two or more of the following characteristic symptoms are present for a significant portion of time during a 1-month period: hallucinations, delusions, disorganized speech, grossly disorganized or catatonic behavior, and negative symptoms.

- One or more major areas of social or occupational dysfunction exist (e.g., work, self-care, interpersonal relationships).

- Continuous signs persist for at least 6 months.

- Signs/symptoms do not result directly from a substance or a medical condition.

- Prominent delusions or hallucinations must be present if pervasive developmental disorder exists.

Δ   Diagnostic studies used to help diagnose schizophrenia include PET scans, CT scans, MRIs, and neurotransmitter studies.

Characteristic Dimensions of Schizophrenia (No single symptom is always present in all cases.)	
Characteristics	**Examples of Symptoms in Each Dimension**
Positive symptoms – These are the most easily identified symptoms.	• Hallucinations • Delusions • Disorganized speech • Bizarre behavior, such as walking backward constantly
Negative symptoms – These symptoms are more difficult to treat successfully than positive symptoms.	• Affect – usually blunted (narrow range of normal expression) or flat (facial expression never changes) • Alogia – poverty of thought or speech; the client may sit with a visitor but may only mumble or respond vaguely to questions. • Avolition – lack of motivation in activities and hygiene; for example, the client completes an assigned task, such as making his bed, but is unable to start the next common chore without prompting. • Anhedonia – lack of pleasure or joy; the client is indifferent to things that often make others happy, such as looking at beautiful scenery. • Anergia – lack of energy

Characteristic Dimensions of Schizophrenia (No single symptom is always present in all cases.)	
Characteristics	**Examples of Symptoms in Each Dimension**
Cognitive symptoms – Problems with thinking make it very difficult for the client to live independently.	• Disordered thinking • Inability to make decisions • Poor problem-solving ability • Difficulty concentrating to perform tasks • Memory deficits 　◊ Long-term memory 　◊ Working memory, such as inability to follow directions to find an address
Depressive symptoms	• Hopelessness • Suicidal ideation

Δ   Criteria used to differentiate the five recognized types of schizophrenia:

Type of Schizophrenia	Common Symptoms
Paranoid • Characterized by suspicion toward others.	• Hallucinations, such as hearing threatening voices, and delusions, such as believing oneself president of the United States • Other-directed violence may occur.
Disorganized • Characterized by withdrawal from society and very inappropriate behaviors, such as poor hygiene or muttering constantly to oneself. • Frequently seen in the homeless population.	• Loose associations • Bizarre mannerisms • Incoherent speech • Hallucinations and delusions may be present but are much less organized than those seen in the client with paranoia.
Catatonic • Characterized by abnormal motor movements. • There are two stages: the withdrawn stage and the excited stage.	Withdrawn stage • Psychomotor retardation; the client may appear comatose. • Waxy flexibility may be present. • The client often has extreme self-care needs, such as for tube feeding due to an inability to eat. Excited stage • Constant movement, unusual posturing, incoherent speech • Self-care needs may predominate. • The client may be a danger to self or others.

Type of Schizophrenia	Common Symptoms
Residual • Active symptoms are no longer present, but the client has two or more "residual" symptoms.	• Anergia, anhedonia, or avolition • Withdrawal from social activities • Impaired role function • Speech problems, such as alogia • Odd behaviors, such as walking in a strange way
Undifferentiated • The client has symptoms of schizophrenia but does not meet criteria for any of the other types.	• Any positive or negative symptoms may be present.

Δ   Other psychotic disorders include:

- **Schizoaffective disorder** – The client's disorder meets both the criteria for schizophrenia and one of the affective disorders (depression, mania, or a mixed disorder).

- **Brief psychotic disorder** – The client has psychotic symptoms that last between 1 day to 1 month in duration.

- **Schizophreniform disorder** – The client has symptoms like those of schizophrenia, but the duration is from 1 to 6 months and social/occupational dysfunction may or may not be present.

- **Shared psychotic disorder** – One person begins to share the delusional beliefs of another person with psychosis. This is also called *Folie à Deux*.

- **Secondary (induced) psychosis** – Signs of psychosis are brought on by a medical disorder, such as Alzheimer's disease, or by use of chemical substances, such as alcohol abuse.

Key Factors

Δ   **Etiology**

- Genetics

- New theories consider the roles of serotonin and glutamate.

- Structural brain abnormalities include enlargement of lateral cerebral ventricles, cerebellar atrophy, atrophy of frontal lobe, and increased size of the fissures on the surface of the brain.

- Birth and pregnancy complications include lack of oxygen, exposure to toxins, malnutrition, father > 55 years of age, and viral infections.

- Stress

Δ **Disease Progression**

- Schizophrenia is characterized by exacerbations and remissions.

Acute phase	Periods of both positive and negative symptoms
Maintenance phase	Acute symptoms decrease in severity
Stabilization phase	Symptoms in remission

- Schizophrenia becomes problematic when symptoms interfere with interpersonal relationships, self-care, and ability to work.

Assessment

Δ Self-assessment – Identify personal feelings and responses to clients with schizophrenia.

Δ Assess the client with the Global Assessment of Functioning (GAF) scale. This helps to determine the client's ability to perform activities of daily living and to function with independence.

Δ Assess the client's use of drugs, alcohol, caffeine, and other substances.

Δ Assess the client's family or other support system, their response to the client's illness, and how they deal with the client's symptoms.

Δ Assess the client's delusions, hallucinations, and behavior to determine whether self- or other-directed violence is likely.

Δ Assess for the following symptoms:

- **Alterations in thought (delusions)** – false fixed beliefs that cannot be corrected by reasoning and are usually bizarre. These include:

Ideas of reference	Misconstrues trivial events and attaches personal significance to them, such as believing that others, who are discussing the next meal, are talking about him.
Persecution	Feels singled out for harm by others (e.g., being hunted down by the FBI).
Grandeur	Believes that she is all powerful and important, like a god.
Somatic delusions	Believes that his body is changing in an unusual way, such as growing a third arm.
Jealousy	May feel that her spouse is sexually involved with another individual.
Being controlled	Believes that a force outside his body is controlling him.
Thought broadcasting	Believes that her thoughts are heard by others.
Thought insertion	Believes that others' thoughts are being inserted into his mind.
Thought withdrawal	Believes that her thoughts have been removed from her mind by an outside agency.
Religiosity	Is obsessed with religious beliefs.

- **Alterations in speech**

Flight of ideas	<ul><li>Associative looseness</li><li>The client may say sentence after sentence, but each sentence may relate to another topic, and the listener is unable to follow the client's thoughts.</li></ul>
Neologisms	<ul><li>Made up words that only have meaning to the client, such as, "I tranged and flittled."</li></ul>
Echolalia	<ul><li>The client repeats the words spoken to him.</li></ul>
Clang association	<ul><li>Meaningless rhyming of words, often forceful, such as, "Oh fox, box, and lox."</li></ul>
Word salad	<ul><li>Words jumbled together with little meaning or significance to listener, such as, "Hip hooray, the flip is cast and wide-sprinting in the forest."</li></ul>

- **Alterations in perception**
  - ◊ **Hallucinations** – sensory perceptions that do not have any apparent external stimulus. Examples include:
    - ° Auditory – hearing voices or sounds.
    - ° Visual – seeing persons or things.
    - ° Olfactory – smelling odors.
    - ° Gustatory – experiencing tastes.
    - ° Tactile – feeling bodily sensations.
  - ◊ **Personal boundary difficulties** – disenfranchisement with one's own body, identity, and perceptions. This includes:
    - ° Depersonalization – nonspecific feeling that a person has lost her identity; self is different or unreal.
    - ° Derealization – perception that environment has changed.
- **Alterations in behavior**
  - ◊ Extreme agitation, including pacing and rocking
  - ◊ Stereotyped behaviors – motor patterns that had meaning to client (sweeping the floor) but now are mechanical and lack purpose
  - ◊ Automatic obedience – responding in a robot-like manner
  - ◊ Wavy flexibility – excessive maintenance of position
  - ◊ Stupor – motionless for long periods of time; coma-like
  - ◊ Negativism – doing the opposite of what is requested
  - ◊ Echopraxia – purposeful imitation of movements made by others

NANDA Nursing Diagnoses

Δ   Ineffective coping

Δ   Dressing/grooming self-care deficit

Δ   Risk for other- or self-directed violence

Δ   Social interaction

Δ   Disturbed thought processes

Δ   Impaired verbal communication

Nursing Interventions

Δ   Provide a structured, safe environment (milieu) for the client in order to decrease anxiety and to distract the client from constant thinking about hallucinations.

•   Milieu therapy is utilized for clients with schizophrenia both in 24-hr mental health facilities and in community facilities, such as adult day care programs.

•   Individual psychotherapy, such as cognitive-behavioral therapy, family therapy, and group therapy, can also be utilized.

Δ   Promote therapeutic communication to lower anxiety, decrease defensive patterns, and encourage participation in the milieu.

Δ   Establish a trusting relationship with the client.

Δ   Encourage the development of social skills and friendships.

Δ   Encourage participation in group work and psychotherapy.

Δ   Use appropriate communication to deal with hallucinations and delusions.

•   Ask the client directly about hallucinations. The nurse should not argue or agree with client's view of the situation, but may offer a comment, such as, "I don't hear anything, but you seem to be feeling frightened."

•   Do not argue with a client's delusions, but focus on the client's feelings and possibly offer reasonable explanations, such as, "I can't imagine that the President of the United States would have a reason to kill a citizen, but it must be frightening for you to believe that."

•   Do not dwell on the symptoms after assessing them.

•   Attempt to focus conversations on reality-based subjects.

•   Identify symptom triggers, such as loud noises (may trigger auditory hallucinations in certain clients) and situations that seem to trigger conversations about the client's delusions.

•   Be genuine and empathetic in all dealings with the client.

∆ Encourage medication compliance. (*Refer to the chapters in Unit 3, Psychopharmacological Therapies.*)

Atypical antipsychotics are current medications of choice for psychotic disorders, and they generally treat both positive and negative symptoms.	Risperidone (Risperdal), olanzapine (Zyprexa), quetiapine (Seroquel), ziprasidone (Geodon), and aripiprazole (Abilify), clozapine (Clozaril)
Typical antipsychotics are used to treat mainly positive psychotic symptoms.	Haloperidol (Haldol), loxapine (Loxitane), chlorpromazine (Thorazine), and fluphenazine decanoate (Prolixin)
Antidepressants are used to treat the depression seen in many clients with schizophrenia.	Paroxetine (Paxil)
Anxiolytics/benzodiazepines are used to treat the anxiety often found in clients with schizophrenia, as well as some of the positive and negative symptoms of schizophrenia.	Lorazepam (Ativan) and clonazepam (Klonopin)

- Monitor for extrapyramidal and other side effects, which occur most often with the typical antipsychotics but may also be seen with atypical antipsychotics.

∆ Educate the client and family regarding illness and treatment modalities.

∆ Assess discharge needs, such as ability to perform activities of daily living.

∆ Promote self-care by modeling and teaching self-care activities within the mental health facility.

∆ Facilitate integration into the family and community.

∆ Relate wellness to the elements of symptom management.

∆ Collaborate with the client to use symptom management techniques to cope with depressive symptoms and anxiety. Symptom management techniques include such strategies as using music to distract from "voices," attending activities, walking, talking to a trusted person when hallucinations are most bothersome, and interacting with an auditory or visual hallucination by telling it to stop or go away.

Primary Reference:

Varcarolis, E. M., Carson, V. B., & Shoemaker, N. C. (2006). *Foundations of psychiatric mental health nursing: A clinical approach* (5th ed.). St. Louis, MO: Saunders.

Additional Resources:

Boyd, M. A. (2005). *Psychiatric nursing contemporary practice* (3rd ed.). Philadelphia: Lippincott Williams & Wilkins.

NANDA International (2004). *NANDA nursing diagnoses: Definitions and classification 2005-2006*. Philadelphia: NANDA.

Stuart, G. W., & Laraia, M. T. (2005). *Principles and practice of psychiatric nursing* (8th ed.). St. Louis, MO: Mosby.

Townsend, M. C. (2006). *Psychiatric mental health nursing: Concepts of care in evidence-based practice* (5th ed.). Philadelphia: F.A. Davis.

Weiden, P. J. (2005, September 28). Moving beyond positive symptoms: The importance of addressing cognitive and affective symptoms in the treatment of schizophrenia. *Medscape*, Article 51186. Retrieved November 21, 2006, from http://www.medscape.com/viewarticle/511186_1

Chapter 26: Schizophrenia

Application Exercises

1. A 19-year-old college student comes to a mental health emergency facility experiencing hallucinations. Describe strategies for working with this client and her hallucinations.

2. Positive symptoms of schizophrenia include which of the following? (Select all that apply.)

    _____ Auditory hallucination

    _____ Lack of motivation

    _____ Use of clang associations

    _____ Delusion of persecution

    _____ Motor agitation

    _____ Flat affect

3. A client is in the acute stages of paranoid schizophrenia. A nursing diagnosis always applicable in this stage is

    A. risk for other- or self-directed violence.

    B. noncompliance.

    C. disturbed thought processes.

    D. readiness for enhanced coping.

4. A client with schizophrenia has great difficulty with personal boundaries. Which of the following are personal boundary problems?

    A. Delusions of grandeur or persecution

    B. Depersonalization or derealization

    C. Visual or auditory hallucinations

    D. Communication difficulties or social withdrawal

5. A nurse is speaking with a client with schizophrenia when he suddenly seems to stop focusing on the nurse's questions and begins looking at the ceiling and talking to himself. The most appropriate intervention by the nurse at this time would be to

    A. stop the interview at this point and resume later when the client is better able to concentrate.

    B. ask the client, "Are you seeing something on the ceiling?"

    C. tell the client, "You seem to be looking at something on the ceiling. I see something there, too."

    D. attempt to distract the client from his hallucinations by continuing the interview without comment on the client's behavior.

6. Which of the following are associated with catatonic schizophrenia?

    A. Purposeless motor agitations

    B. Tactile hallucinations

    C. Word salad and flight of ideas

    D. Eccentric behaviors or odd beliefs

7. Match the symptoms below with the appropriate psychotic disorders.

_____ Schizophreniform disorder   A. Psychotic symptoms caused by abuse of chemical substances or physical illness

_____ Schizoaffective disorder   B. An episode of psychotic behavior lasting from 1 day to 1 month in length

_____ Shared psychotic disorder   C. Psychotic behavior lasting between 1 and 6 months that may not impair the client's ability to function at work or in social occasions

_____ Brief psychotic disorder   D. Symptoms of schizophrenia along with symptoms of mania or major depression

_____ Induced psychosis   E. One person sharing the delusional beliefs of another person with psychosis

Chapter 26: Schizophrenia

Application Exercises Answer Key

1. A 19-year-old college student comes to a mental health emergency facility experiencing hallucinations. Describe strategies for working with this client and her hallucinations.

   Establish a trusting nurse-client relationship.
   Assess for characteristics of hallucinations, including duration, intensity, frequency, and type.
   Focus on the symptom – the "feelings" – and ask the client to describe what is happening.
   Identify whether drugs or alcohol have been used.
   If asked, point out that you are not experiencing the same stimuli.
   Help the client describe and compare current and past hallucinations.
   Help the client identify needs that may be reflected in the content of the hallucinations.
   Determine the impact of the client's symptoms on ADLs.

2. Positive symptoms of schizophrenia include which of the following? (Select all that apply.)

   __X__ **Auditory hallucination**
   _____ Lack of motivation
   __X__ **Use of clang associations**
   __X__ **Delusion of persecution**
   __X__ **Motor agitation**
   _____ Flat affect

   Auditory hallucinations, use of clang associations, delusions of persecution, and motor agitation are all positive symptoms of schizophrenia. Lack of motivation (or avolition) and flat affect (facial expression) are negative symptoms.

3. A client is in the acute stages of paranoid schizophrenia. A nursing diagnosis always applicable in this stage is

   A. risk for other- or self-directed violence.

   B. noncompliance.

   C. disturbed thought processes.

   D. readiness for enhanced coping.

   The client in the acute stages of paranoid schizophrenia would have disturbed thought processes with active hallucinations and/or delusions. A risk for violence is not universally present, although the nurse should assess for it. Noncompliance and disabled family coping are not necessarily present in clients with schizophrenia.

4. A client with schizophrenia has great difficulty with personal boundaries. Which of the following are personal boundary problems?

     A. Delusions of grandeur or persecution

     B. Depersonalization or derealization

     C. Visual or auditory hallucinations

     D. Communication difficulties or social withdrawal

Depersonalization (a feeling of being separated from one's body) and derealization (a sensation of being in a strange environment) are examples of problems with personal boundaries. Delusions and hallucinations are positive symptoms of schizophrenia. Problems with communication or social withdrawal may be present in schizophrenia, but they are not personal boundary issues.

5. A nurse is speaking with a client with schizophrenia when he suddenly seems to stop focusing on the nurse's questions and begins looking at the ceiling and talking to himself. The most appropriate intervention by the nurse at this time would be to

     A. stop the interview at this point and resume later when the client is better able to concentrate.

     B. ask the client, "Are you seeing something on the ceiling?"

     C. tell the client, "You seem to be looking at something on the ceiling. I see something there, too."

     D. attempt to distract the client from his hallucinations by continuing the interview without comment on the client's behavior.

The most appropriate intervention is to ask the client directly about his hallucinations, but avoid treating hallucinations or delusions as if they were real. Stopping the interview until a later time may not be feasible since the client may experience hallucinations much of the time. Distraction can be helpful for working with a client with hallucinations; however, continuing the interview without commenting on this client's hallucinations will not be an effective distraction.

6. Which of the following are associated with catatonic schizophrenia?

    A. Purposeless motor agitations
    B. Tactile hallucinations
    C. Word salad and flight of ideas
    D. Eccentric behaviors or odd beliefs

Purposeless motor agitation or activity are characteristics of the excited phase of catatonic schizophrenia. Hallucinations are seen in clients with paranoid, disorganized, and undifferentiated types of schizophrenia. Word salad and flight of ideas are communication abnormalities seen in other types of schizophrenia. Eccentric behavior and odd beliefs are found in clients with residual schizophrenia.

7. Match the symptoms below with the appropriate psychotic disorders.

__C__ Schizophreniform disorder	A.	Psychotic symptoms caused by abuse of chemical substances or physical illness
__D__ Schizoaffective disorder	B.	An episode of psychotic behavior lasting from 1 day to 1 month in length
__E__ Shared psychotic disorder	C.	Psychotic behavior lasting between 1 and 6 months that may not impair the client's ability to function at work or in social occasions
__B__ Brief psychotic disorder	D.	Symptoms of schizophrenia along with symptoms of mania or major depression
__A__ Induced psychosis	E.	One person sharing the delusional beliefs of another person with psychosis

Unit 4   Psychobiologic Disorders, Psychiatric Emergencies, and Mental Health Nursing Care of Special Populations

Section: Psychobiologic Disorders

Chapter 27:   **Cognitive Disorders**

Contributor: Phyllis M. Jacobs, MSN, RN

 NCLEX-RN® Connections:

Learning Objective: Review and apply knowledge within "**Cognitive Disorders**" in readiness for performance of the following nursing activities as outlined by the NCLEX-RN® test plan:

Δ   Apply knowledge of psychobiologic disorders to the nursing process when caring for clients with a cognitive disorder.

Δ   Use effective communication to interact with and assist the client/family to foster trust in the nurse-client therapeutic relationship.

Δ   Assess the client's mental status, identifying changes in mood, judgment, cognition, and reasoning.

Δ   Identify the client/family's responses to the diagnosis of a cognitive disorder.

Δ   Plan/provide care for the client with impaired cognition.

Δ   Support the client's efforts in the use of strategies to decrease anxiety.

Δ   Evaluate and document the client's response to treatment of a cognitive disorder.

Δ   Evaluate the client's ability to follow the treatment plan for the cognitive disorder.

 Key Points

Δ   Cognitive disorders are a group of conditions characterized by the disruption of thinking, memory, processing, and problem solving.

Δ   General classifications of cognitive disorders are delirium, dementia, and amnestic disorders.

Δ   Delirium and dementia have some similarities and some important differences:

	Delirium	Dementia
Onset	Rapid over a short period of time (hours or days)	Gradual deterioration of function over months or years
Signs and symptoms	• Impairments in memory, judgment, ability to focus, and ability to calculate; impairments may fluctuate throughout the day. • Level of consciousness is usually altered. • Restlessness, agitation are common; sundowning (confusion during the night) may occur; behaviors may increase or decrease daily. • Personality change is rapid. • Some perceptual disturbances may be present, such as hallucinations and illusions. • Vital signs may be unstable and abnormal due to medical illness.	• Impairments in memory, judgment, ability to focus, and ability to calculate; impairments do not change throughout the day. • Level of consciousness is usually unchanged. • Restlessness, agitation are common; sundowning may occur; behaviors usually remain stable. • Personality change is gradual. • Vital signs are stable unless other illness is present.
Cause	Caused secondary to another medical condition, such as infection, or to substance abuse	• Generally caused by a chronic disease, such as Alzheimer's, or is the result of chronic alcohol abuse • May be caused by permanent trauma, such as head injury
Outcome	Reversible if diagnosis and treatment are prompt	Irreversible and progressive

Δ   **Amnestic disorder** may be secondary to substance abuse or another medical condition. Typically, there is no personality change or impairment in abstract thinking. Signs include:

- Decreased awareness of surroundings.

- Inability to learn new information despite normal attention.

- Inability to recall previously learned information.

- Possible disorientation to place and time.

- Typically there is no personality change or impairment in abstract thinking.

Key Factors

Δ   Risk factors for cognitive disorders include physiological changes, including neurological, metabolic, and cardiovascular diseases; family genetics, infections, tumors, substance abuse, drug intoxication, and drug withdrawal.

Δ   Risk factors for Alzheimer's disease include advanced age (1 in 26 people at age 65; 2 in 5 people after age 85), female gender, head trauma, and a family history of Alzheimer's disease and/or trisomy (Down syndrome).

Various Causes of Dementia	Description
Alzheimer's disease	Progressive deterioration in function due to neurotransmitter deficiency; the most prevalent form of dementia and is characterized by memory loss, deficits in thought process, and behavioral changes in four stages
Vascular disease	Due to significant cerebrovascular disease and caused by multiple infarcts in the cortex
HIV/AIDS	Related to brain infections with a range of symptoms from acute delirium to profound dementia
Head trauma	Intellectual and memory difficulties after the trauma
Parkinson's disease	Caused by a loss of nerve cells and progressive decrease in dopamine activity
Huntington's disease	Genetically transmitted disease in which a profound state of dementia and ataxia occurs within 5 to 10 years of onset
Creutzfeldt-Jakob disease	Caused by a transmissible agent known as a "slow" virus; clinical course is rapid, with progressive deterioration and death within 1 year
Korsakoff's syndrome	Progressive dementia caused by thiamine deficiency, usually occurring due to long-term alcohol abuse
Dementia due to a general medical condition	Can be due to endocrine conditions, pulmonary disease, hepatic or renal failure, cardiopulmonary insufficiency, fluid and electrolyte imbalances, nutritional deficiencies, frontal or temporal lobe lesions, central nervous system or systemic infections, uncontrolled epilepsy, and other neurological conditions, such as multiple sclerosis

Assessment

Δ   Obtain data from:

- Client history.

- Interview of family members or other caregivers to establish normal level of cognition.

- Physical assessment.

- Psychological tests.

- Diagnostic laboratory evaluations.

- Functional assessment.

Δ   Use the Functional Dementia Scale, a tool that shows the client's ability for self-care, the extent of memory loss, mood changes, and the degree of danger to self and others.

Δ   Determine safety measures needed for the client. Questions to ask include:

- Will the client wander out into the street if doors are left unlocked?

- Is the client unable to remember his address or even his name?

- Does the client harm others when allowed to wander in a long-term care facility?

Δ   Assess for defense mechanisms used by the client to preserve self-esteem when cognitive changes are progressive.

- **Denial** – Both the client and family members may refuse to believe that changes, such as loss of memory, are taking place, even when those changes are obvious to others.

- **Confabulation** – The client may make up stories when questioned about events or activities that she does not remember. This may seem like lying, but it is actually an unconscious attempt to save self-esteem and prevent admitting that she does not remember the occasion.

- **Perseveration** – The client avoids answering questions by repeating phrases or behavior. This is another unconscious attempt to maintain self-esteem when memory has failed.

Δ   **Assessment Guidelines for Signs and Symptoms of Alzheimer's Disease**

Stage	Signs and Symptoms
Stage I, Forgetfulness	• Short-term memory loss • Decreased attention span • Subtle personality changes • Mild cognitive deficits • Difficulty with depth perception
Stage II, Confusion	• Obvious memory loss • Confusion, impaired judgment, confabulation • Wandering behavior • Sundowning (more confusion in late afternoon/early evening) • Irritability and agitation • Poor spatial orientation, impaired motor skills • Intensification of symptoms when the client is stressed, fatigued, or in an unfamiliar environment • Depression related to awareness of reduced capacities
Stage III, Ambulatory dementia	• Loss of reasoning ability • Increasing loss of expressive language • Loss of ability to perform ADLs • More withdrawn
Stage IV, End stage	• Impaired or absent cognitive, communication, and/or motor skills • Bowel and bladder incontinence • Inability to recognize family members or self in mirror

Δ   Assess teaching needs for the client and, especially, for family members when the client's cognitive ability is progressively declining.

Δ   Review the resources available to the family as the client's health declines. A wide variety of home care and community resources may be available to the family in many areas of the country, and these resources may allow the client to remain at home rather than in an institution.

Δ   Perform self-assessment regarding possible feelings of frustration, anger, or fear when performing daily care for clients with progressive dementia.

NANDA Nursing Diagnoses

Δ   Risk for caregiver role strain

Δ   Acute or chronic confusion

Δ   Ineffective coping

Δ   Risk for falls

Δ   Anticipatory grieving

Δ   Ineffective health maintenance

Δ   Risk for injury

Δ   Risk for other-directed violence

Δ   Disturbed thought processes

Δ   Impaired verbal communication

Nursing Interventions

Δ   **Environment**

- Assign the client to a room close to the nurse's station for close observation.

- Provide a room with a low level of visual and auditory stimuli.

- Provide compensatory memory aids such as clocks, calendars, photographs, memorabilia, seasonal decorations, and familiar objects.

- Windows may help time orientation and help decrease the "sundowning" effect.

Δ   **Pharmacologic Treatments**

- Administer medications as prescribed.

- Medications that have been approved by the FDA that demonstrate positive effects on cognitive, behavioral, and daily activity function include:

    ◊   Tacrine (Cognex).

    ◊   Donepezil (Aricept).

    ◊   Rivastigmine (Exelon).

    ◊   Galantamine (Reminyl) .

    ◊   Memantine (Namenda).

Δ   **Communication**

- Reinforce orientation to time, place, and person.

- Establish eye contact and use short, simple sentences when speaking to the client.

- Encourage reminiscence about happy times; talk about familiar things.

- Break instructions and activities into short timeframes when instructing the client.

Δ **Safety**

- Have the client wear an identification bracelet; use monitors and bed alarm devices as needed.

- Ensure safety in the physical environment, such as lowered bed and removal of scatter rugs to prevent falls. Many aspects of the physical environment may need to be changed for the home-bound client with dementia.

- Provide eyeglasses and hearing assistive devices as needed.

Δ **Nursing Care and Caregiver Education**

- Monitor food and fluid intake, bowel and bladder function, and sleep patterns.

- Educate family/caregivers about illness, methods of care, and adaptation of the home environment.

- Provide support for caregivers; recommend local support groups for caregivers, as well as respite care.

- Establish a routine. Make sure all caregivers know/apply the routine. Attempt to have consistency in caregivers.

Primary Resource:

Varcarolis, E. M., Carson, V. B., & Shoemaker, N. C. (2006). *Foundations of psychiatric mental health nursing: A clinical approach* (5th ed.). St. Louis, MO: Saunders.

Additional Resources:

NANDA International (2004). *NANDA nursing diagnoses: Definitions and classification 2005-2006*. Philadelphia: NANDA.

Townsend, M. C. (2006). *Psychiatric mental health nursing: Concepts of care in evidence-based practice* (5th ed.). Philadelphia: F.A. Davis.

Chapter 27: Cognitive Disorders

Application Exercises

Scenario: An 85-year-old client diagnosed with stage II Alzheimer's disease lives with his wife, who is the primary caregiver. The client is often disoriented to time and place and frequently talks about wanting to go someplace other than where he is. His wife is fearful that he will wander outside or injure himself in the home. The primary care provider arranges for the home health nurse to assess the home environment and teach the wife how to make the environment safer.

1. When making a home visit, the nurse assesses the home for safety. He is pleased to see that the client's spouse has removed all small rugs that could slide and cause falls. List some other outcomes that would make the home environment physically safe for the client with dementia.

2. The client's spouse says, "I don't mind caring for my husband, but I am so tired that I just don't know what to do. I'm here at home with him constantly; it's exactly like having young children around again, but then I knew they would grow up some day." What nursing diagnosis is appropriate for this situation?

3. Identify appropriate nursing interventions for this nursing diagnosis.

4. A client is admitted to an acute care facility with delirium caused by a severe urinary tract infection. Which of the following assessment data should the nurse expect to find? (Select all that apply.)

_____ Disorientation to time, place, and person

_____ Ability to perform most self-care activities

_____ Normal and stable vital signs

_____ Wandering attention

_____ Perceptual disturbances

_____ Change in level of consciousness

5. Which of the following interventions is appropriate for the nurse to use on clients with either delirium or dementia?

A. For safety, use physical restraints with an aggressive client.

B. Approach quietly and touch the client before speaking.

C. Speak in a loud, firm voice to the client.

D. Reorient the client to the nurse with each contact.

6. A nurse is visiting a client with Alzheimer's dementia who lives at home and continually wanders about. Which of the following is an appropriate outcome for the nursing diagnosis of risk for injury?

A. The client will take part in all self-care activities.

B. The client will be oriented to time, place, and person.

C. The client will remain safe in the home environment.

D. The client will communicate in a reality-based manner with the caregiver.

Chapter 27: Cognitive Disorders

Application Exercises Answer Key

Scenario: An 85-year-old client diagnosed with stage II Alzheimer's disease lives with his wife, who is the primary caregiver. The client is often disoriented to time and place and frequently talks about wanting to go someplace other than where he is. His wife is fearful that he will wander outside or injure himself in the home. The primary care provider arranges for the home health nurse to assess the home environment and teach the wife how to make the environment safer.

1. When making a home visit, the nurse assesses the home for safety. He is pleased to see that the client's spouse has removed all small rugs that could slide and cause falls. List some other outcomes that would make the home environment physically safe for the client with dementia.

   Door locks that cannot be easily opened
   Lock on water heater thermostat and water temperature turned down to safe levels
   Good lighting, including on stairways
   Stable chairs and tables
   Aids to assist the client in rising from bed/chair
   Lowered bed to prevent falls during sleep
   Stove/oven that cannot be easily turned on
   Clear, wide pathways for walking through a room
   Lack of clutter
   Smoke alarms present in several rooms
   Cleaning products that are locked up
   Steps that are in good repair and have a handrail
   Step edges marked with colored tape
   Electrical cords that are out of the way

2. The client's spouse says, "I don't mind caring for my husband, but I am so tired that I just don't know what to do. I'm here at home with him constantly; it's exactly like having young children around again, but then I knew they would grow up some day." What nursing diagnosis is appropriate for this situation?

   Caregiver role strain related to 24-hr care responsibilities as evidenced by spouse's verbal report

3. Identify appropriate nursing interventions for this nursing diagnosis.

Interview the client's spouse and fully assess the situation in terms of safety for the client and the need for respite care for his spouse.

Determine if other family members or friends are willing and able to provide respite care so the spouse can relax or leave the home for a few hours.

Refer the client's spouse to agencies that provide caregivers or volunteer respite assistance.

Refer the client's spouse to any local Alzheimer's support groups for families.

Refer the client to adult day care or other similar agencies where the client could be transported for at least a day or two weekly.

Provide information about long-term care options as necessary.

---

4. A client is admitted to an acute care facility with delirium caused by a severe urinary tract infection. Which of the following assessment data should the nurse expect to find? (Select all that apply.)

  X   **Disorientation to time, place, and person**

  _____   Ability to perform most self-care activities

  _____   Normal and stable vital signs

  X   **Wandering attention**

  X   **Perceptual disturbances**

  X   **Change in level of consciousness**

The client with delirium is disoriented, is unable to focus attention for more than short periods, and may have perceptual disturbances, such as hallucinations and illusions. With delirium, there is also a change in level of consciousness. The client with delirium is unable to perform many/most self-care activities and often has abnormal vital signs, such as elevated temperature, tachycardia, and blood pressure fluctuations.

5. Which of the following interventions is appropriate for the nurse to use on clients with either delirium or dementia?

        A. For safety, use physical restraints with an aggressive client.

        B. Approach quietly and touch the client before speaking.

        C. Speak in a loud, firm voice to the client.

        D. Reorient the client to the nurse with each contact.

With each contact, it is important to reorient the client by saying something like, "Mr. Jones, I am Mary Smith, your nurse." This is due to the short-term memory problems often present for clients with dementia or delirium. It is important to use the least restrictive restraint possible for aggressive clients. When approaching the client, speak before touching him to avoid making the client feel threatened. Speaking loudly and firmly may be perceived by the client as anger, which could frighten him.

6. A nurse is visiting a client with Alzheimer's dementia who lives at home and continually wanders about. Which of the following is an appropriate outcome for the nursing diagnosis of risk for injury?

        A. The client will take part in all self-care activities.

        B. The client will be oriented to time, place, and person.

        C. The client will remain safe in the home environment.

        D. The client will communicate in a reality-based manner with the caregiver.

For a nursing diagnosis of risk for injury, the appropriate outcome is that the client will remain safe. The other options are either not realistic for this client or are related to other nursing diagnoses.

Unit 4   Psychobiologic Disorders, Psychiatric Emergencies, and Mental Health Nursing Care of Special Populations

Section: Psychobiologic Disorders

Chapter 28:   Developmental and Behavioral Disorders

Contributor: Linda W. Edwards, MSN, RN

 NCLEX-RN® Connections:

Learning Objective: Review and apply knowledge within "**Developmental and Behavioral Disorders**" in readiness for performance of the following nursing activities as outlined by the NCLEX-RN® test plan:

Δ   Apply knowledge of psychobiologic disorders to the nursing process when caring for the child with a chronic developmental and/or behavioral disorder.

Δ   Use effective communication to interact with and assist the child/family to foster trust in the nurse-child therapeutic relationship.

Δ   Assess the child's mental status, identifying changes in mood, judgment, cognition, and reasoning.

Δ   Identify the child/family's responses to the diagnosis of a developmental or behavioral disorder.

Δ   Plan/provide care for the child with a developmental or behavioral disorder.

Δ   Support the child's efforts in the use of strategies to decrease anxiety.

Δ   Evaluate and document the child's response to treatment of a developmental or behavioral disorder.

Δ   Evaluate the child's ability to follow the treatment plan for a developmental or behavioral disorder.

Δ   Teach the child/family signs and symptoms of relapse of the developmental or behavioral disorder.

Key Points

Δ   Children experience some of the same mental health problems as adults.

Δ   Psychiatric disorders are more difficult to diagnose in children and more likely to go untreated. Factors that contribute to this include:

- Children do not have the ability or the necessary skills to describe what is happening.

- Children demonstrate a wide variation of "normal" behaviors, especially in different developmental stages.

- It is difficult to determine if the child's behavior indicates an emotional problem.

Δ   A child's behavior is problematic when it interferes with home, school, and interactions with peers.

Δ   Behaviors become pathologic when they:

- Are not age appropriate.

- Deviate from cultural norms.

- Create deficits or impairments in adaptive functioning.

Δ   **Pervasive Developmental Disorders (PDD)**

- **General parameters**

  ◊   Severe impairment in social interaction and communication skills, stereotypical behaviors, interests, and activities

  ◊   May also be easily frustrated, impulsive, and angry

  ◊   Often diagnosed with mental retardation (IQ < 70)

- **Autism**

  ◊   Abnormal brain function affecting language, logic, and reasoning ability

  - Impairment in communication – language delay, echolalia, failure to imitate

  - Impairment in social interactions – lack of responsiveness to and interest in others, lack of eye-to-eye contact, failure to cuddle or be comforted, lack of friendships

  - Stereotypical behaviors – rigid adherence to routines, hand or finger flapping, clapping, rocking, swaying, head banging, hand biting, preoccupation with certain repetitive activities

◊ Music and visual spatial skills often enhanced

◊ Usually observed before 3 years of age

◊ More common in males than in females (3 or 4 to 1)

- **Asperger's disorder**

  ◊ Occurs later in childhood, usually when the child enters school

  ◊ Later onset than autism, with less cognitive or language delay

  ◊ Difficulty developing and maintaining peer relationships

  ◊ Restricted areas of interest

  ◊ More common in males than in females (3 or 4 to 1)

Δ **Behavior Disorders**

- **General parameters**

  ◊ Behavioral problems usually occur in school, church, home, or recreational activities.

  ◊ In children with behavior disorders, symptoms generally worsen in:

    ° Situations that require sustained attention.

    ° Unstructured group situations, such as the playground or classroom.

- **Attention deficit hyperactivity disorder (ADHD)**

  ◊ Key symptoms include:

    ° Inattention – difficulty paying attention, does not appear to listen, easily distracted.

    ° Hyperactivity – fidgeting, inability to sit still, running and climbing inappropriately, difficulty playing quietly, excessive talking, impulsivity, difficulty waiting for turns, interrupting, blurting out answers.

  ◊ Difficult to diagnose before the age of 4

  ◊ Most often diagnosed when the child has difficulty adjusting to elementary school

  ◊ Worse when situation requires sustained attention

  ◊ Frequently present along with other mental health disorders (e.g., other behavior disorders, childhood anxiety disorders, early onset bipolar disorder)

  ◊ Subtypes include:

    ° ADHD, combined type.

    ° ADHD, inattentive type.

    ° ADHD, predominantly hyperactive-impulsive type.

- **Oppositional defiant disorder**

  ◊ Recurrent pattern of antisocial behaviors: negativity, disobedience, hostility, defiant behaviors (especially toward authority figures), stubbornness, argumentativeness, limit testing, unwillingness to compromise, refusal to accept responsibility for misbehavior

  ◊ Behaviors usually seen at home and directed toward person best known

  ◊ Do not see themselves as defiant – just responding to unreasonable demands or to circumstances

  ◊ Generally do not violate the rights of others

  ◊ More frequently seen in males before puberty; equal distribution among males and females after puberty

  ◊ Low self-esteem, mood lability, low frustration threshold

  ◊ Can develop into conduct disorder

- **Conduct disorder**

  ◊ Most common reason for psychiatric referral of children

  ◊ Incidence: males > females, urban areas > rural areas

Contributing Factors	Manifestations
• Parental rejection and neglect • Difficult infant temperament • Inconsistent child rearing practices with harsh discipline • Physical or sexual abuse • Lack of supervision • Early institutionalization • Frequent changing of caregivers • Large family size • Association with delinquent peer groups • Parent with a history of psychological illness	• Lack of remorse or care for the feelings of others • Bullies, threatens, and intimidates others • Belief that aggression is justified • Low self-esteem, irritability, temper outbursts, reckless behavior • Suicidal ideation • Learning disorders or impairments in cognitive functioning • Physically cruel to others and/or animals • Has used a weapon that could cause serious injuries • Destroys property of others • Has run away from home • Often lies, shoplifts, and is truant from school

Δ **Anxiety Disorders**

- **General parameters**

  ◊ Anxiety and worry are part of normal life, but they become an anxiety disorder when:

    ° The child has difficulty moving to a higher developmental stage due to anxiety.

    ° The anxiety is so serious that the child is unable to function normally in the home, school, and other areas of life.

- **Separation anxiety disorder**
  - ◊ Excessive anxiety when separated from or anticipating separation from home or parents
  - ◊ May develop after a specific stress (death of a relative or pet, illness, move, assault)
  - ◊ Occurs more often in females than in males
  - ◊ May progress to panic disorders
- **Posttraumatic stress disorder**
  - ◊ Can occur at any age
  - ◊ Internalization of the anxiety by children
    - ° Preschool children – sleep difficulties, nightmares, reliving the event through repetitive play of the event, increase in specific fears, irritability, whining, temper tantrums, regression, somatic reports, withdrawal from activities
    - ° School-age children – sleep difficulties, increased fighting with friends, increased startle impulse, belief that life will be short, somatic reports, difficulty concentrating, repetitive playing out of the event

Δ **Other disorders** seen in children include:

- Mental retardation.
  - ◊ Below average intellectual functioning as measured by an IQ < 70
  - ◊ Significant limitations in communication, self-care, self-direction, academic achievement, health, and safety
- Learning disorders.
  - ◊ Substandard achievement in reading, math, and writing abilities
  - ◊ Treated through special education
- Communication disorders.
  - ◊ May be expressive, receptive, or a combination of both
  - ◊ Primary manifestation is stuttering
  - ◊ Treated by speech and language therapies

Key Factors

Δ **Genetic** – the style of behavior (temperament) a child uses to cope with the demands and expectations thought to be genetically determined

Δ **Biochemical** – alterations in neurotransmitters norepinephrine and/or serotonin

Δ **Social and environmental** – severe marital discord, low socioeconomic status, large families and overcrowding, parental criminality, maternal psychiatric disorders, foster care placement, physical and sexual abuse, traumatic life events

Δ **Cultural and ethnic** – difficulty with assimilation, lack of cultural role models, lack of support from the dominant culture

Δ **Resiliency** – the ability to adapt to changes in the environment, form nurturing relationships, distance oneself from the emotional chaos of the parent or family, and use problem-solving skills

Assessment

Δ Mental status assessment in children is similar to that of adults, with a greater emphasis on developmental stages. It should include general appearance, activity level, speech, coordination, motor function, affect, thought processes, characteristics of play, and intellectual function.

Δ Assess for uneven development, spurts or lags, or loss of previous skills.

Δ Assess the child for signs of physical, emotional, or sexual abuse.

Δ Assess the relationship between the parents/caregivers and the child.

Δ Assess for the presence, proximity, and severity of stressors in children with anxiety.

Δ Assess for comorbid conditions, such as depression, suicidal ideation, and substance abuse.

Δ Consider suicide risk (third-leading cause of death in adolescents with risk increasing throughout teenage years).

NANDA Nursing Diagnoses

Δ Anxiety

Δ Readiness for enhanced family coping

Δ Ineffective coping

Δ Interrupted family processes

Δ Impaired verbal communication

Δ   Fear

Δ   Delayed growth and development

Δ   Risk for injury

Δ   Impaired parenting

Δ   Risk for other- or self-directed violence

Nursing Interventions

Δ   Teach the child and family about prescribed medications and monitor for side effects.

Δ   Collaborate with teachers to foster academic success.

Δ   Educate the family as to diagnosis, interventions, and treatment.

Δ   Use behavior modification techniques and teach techniques to family members.

Δ   For the child with a **pervasive developmental disorder,** such as autism:

• Use one-on-one interactions.

• Monitor for signs/symptoms of anxiety or distress; prognosis for more normal development is enhanced by early intervention.

• Identify desired behaviors and reward them.

• Role model social skills.

• Role play situations that involve conflict.

• Encourage verbal communication.

• Limit self-stimulating and ritualistic behaviors by providing alternative play activities.

• Determine emotional and situational triggers.

• Give plenty of notice when changing routines.

Δ   For the child with a **behavior disorder**:

• Observe interactions between the child and caregiver.

• Assess levels of anxiety, inattention, hyperactivity, anger, and hostility.

• Assess for defiant behavior and its impact on the child's life at home, at school, and with peers.

• Assess for difficulty in making friends and performing in school.

• Assess the child's moral, cognitive, and psychosocial development for lags.

- Assist with implementing a behavior modification system.

- Set clear limits on unacceptable behaviors and be consistent.

- Assess support systems.

Δ   For the child with a **severe behavior problem**, such as conduct disorder, which may require care in a mental health facility:

- Focus on the family and child's strengths, not just the problems.

- Support the parents' efforts to remain hopeful.

- Ask parents how they are doing; allow opportunities for questions.

- Provide a safe environment for the child and others.

- Provide short and clear explanations.

- Provide the child with specific positive feedback when expectations are met.

- Structure daily routines.

- Identify issues that result in power struggles.

- Assist the child in developing effective coping mechanisms.

- Encourage the child to participate in group, individual, and family therapy.

- Administer medications, such as antipsychotics, mood stabilizers, anticonvulsants, and antidepressants; monitor for side effects.

Primary Resource:

Varcarolis, E. M., Carson, V. B., & Shoemaker, N. C. (2006). *Foundations of psychiatric mental health nursing: A clinical approach* (5th ed.). St. Louis, MO: Saunders.

Additional Resources:

American Psychiatric Association (2000). *Diagnostic and statistical manual of mental disorders* (4th ed., text revision). Washington, DC: American Psychiatric Association.

Fortinash, K. M., & Holoday Worret, P. A. (2004). *Psychiatric mental health nursing* (3rd ed.). St. Louis, MO: Mosby.

NANDA International (2004). *NANDA nursing diagnoses: Definitions and classification 2005-2006*. Philadelphia: NANDA.

Townsend, M. C. (2006). *Psychiatric mental health nursing: Concepts of care in evidence-based practice* (5th ed.). Philadelphia: F.A. Davis.

Varcarolis, E. M. (2006). *Manual of psychiatric nursing care plans* (3rd ed.). St. Louis, MO: Saunders.

Videbeck, S. L. (2006). *Psychiatric mental health nursing* (3rd ed.). Philadelphia: Lippincott Williams & Wilkins.

Chapter 28: Developmental and Behavioral Disorders

Application Exercises

1. Describe therapeutic activities for a 6-year-old child with a diagnosis of impaired verbal communication.

2. Describe how behavior modification could be used in the home for a school-age child with ADHD.

3. A 5-year-old boy is brought to a mental health agency by his mother. The mother says the child is unable to sit through meals and is so easily distracted that he cannot even sit through a 30-min cartoon video. At night he gets up while the family is sleeping and wanders about the house. His kindergarten teacher is unable to handle him either and says he talks constantly during school. As the nurse assesses the child's behavior, she knows that his problems are most consistent with the DSM-IV-TR diagnosis of

    A. mental retardation.

    B. oppositional defiant disorder.

    C. Rett's disorder.

    D. attention deficit hyperactivity disorder.

4. A 12-year-old child demonstrates signs and symptoms of conduct disorder. These include which of the following manifestations? (Select all that apply.)

    _____ Hostility

    _____ Frequent lying

    _____ Breaking of objects due to impulsiveness

    _____ Law-breaking activities

    _____ Careless mistakes

    _____ Cruelty to neighborhood pets

    _____ Poor eye contact with others

5. A nurse is assessing a 4-year-old child for signs of autism. The nurse should be alert for

    A. constant talking and impulsive behavior.

    B. poor language and interpersonal skills.

    C. destructiveness and history of irritability and hostility.

    D. night terrors and reports of somatic problems.

6. A school-age child with autism continually rubs and scratches her right arm, causing bleeding and frequent infections. When planning care, the desired client outcome is that the child will develop self-control to prevent the behavior. The nurse would evaluate the plan of care as effective when the child

    A. wears padded mittens to prevent further injury.

    B. begins head-banging behaviors instead of scratching.

    C. seeks out a staff member instead of rubbing or scratching.

    D. is placed in bilateral arm restraints when she scratches.

Chapter 28: Developmental and Behavioral Disorders

Application Exercises Answer Key

1. Describe therapeutic activities for a 6-year-old child with a diagnosis of impaired verbal communication.

   Quiet one-on-one activities that build a trust relationship
   Role playing positive behaviors
   Board games that encourage talking about feelings and emotions
   Therapeutic drawing; encouraging the child to talk about what he has created
   Safe and secure environment
   Hand puppets and puppet shows
   Storytelling by the child
   Children's stories read aloud and discussed by both the child and nurse

2. Describe how behavior modification could be used in the home for a school-age child with ADHD.

   Interview the parents and child to find a reward system individualized for the child, such as short intervals playing a certain video game as reward for sitting through dinner or focusing during a homework session.
   Use a tangible system the child can actually see or hold, such as a wall chart or "tokens," which can be turned in for rewards.
   Allow the child to have some input in planning.
   Teach the parents to be consistent and patient.

3. A 5-year-old boy is brought to a mental health agency by his mother. The mother says the child is unable to sit through meals and is so easily distracted that he cannot even sit through a 30-min cartoon video. At night he gets up while the family is sleeping and wanders about the house. His kindergarten teacher is unable to handle him either and says he talks constantly during school. As the nurse assesses the child's behavior, she knows that his problems are most consistent with the DSM-IV-TR diagnosis of

   A. mental retardation.

   B. oppositional defiant disorder.

   C. Rett's disorder.

   D. attention deficit hyperactivity disorder.

   This child is constantly in motion, talks excessively, is very easily distracted, and has difficulty talking. All these problems are found with ADHD. Developmental delays would be prominent if mental retardation were the problem. Rett's disorder occurs only in females and also includes severe mental retardation. If oppositional defiant disorder were the problem, the child would be argumentative and push the limits of parental authority.

4. A 12-year-old child demonstrates signs and symptoms of conduct disorder. These include which of the following manifestations? (Select all that apply.)

  X   **Hostility**

  X   **Frequent lying**

  _____ Breaking of objects due to impulsiveness

  X   **Law-breaking activities**

  _____ Careless mistakes

  X   **Cruelty to neighborhood pets**

  _____ Poor eye contact with others

Hostility, telling lies, breaking laws, and cruelty to animals are all manifestations common in conduct disorder. Breaking objects and making careless mistakes are more likely related to ADHD. Poor eye contact is more likely a manifestation of autism or Asperger's disorder.

5. A nurse is assessing a 4-year-old child for signs of autism. The nurse should be alert for

    A. constant talking and impulsive behavior.

    B. poor language and interpersonal skills.

    C. destructiveness and history of irritability and hostility.

    D. night terrors and reports of somatic problems.

Children with autism have difficulty learning language skills, and failure to develop interpersonal relationships is also very common. Constant talking and impulsive behavior are among the signs of ADHD. Destructiveness, irritability, and hostility relate to conduct disorder. Night terrors and somatic problems relate to posttraumatic stress disorder.

6. A school-age child with autism continually rubs and scratches her right arm, causing bleeding and frequent infections. When planning care, the desired client outcome is that the child will develop self-control to prevent the behavior. The nurse would evaluate the plan of care as effective when the child

    A. wears padded mittens to prevent further injury.

    B. begins head-banging behaviors instead of scratching.

    C. seeks out a staff member instead of rubbing or scratching.

    D. is placed in bilateral arm restraints when she scratches.

If the child seeks intervention to prevent the unacceptable behavior, it shows that she is using self-control to prevent self-mutilation. Wearing padded mittens might be an intervention to prevent injury, but it does not demonstrate self-control. Head banging is not acceptable, since it substitutes one destructive behavior for another. The use of arm restraints is a form of punishment and would be an unacceptable intervention.

Unit 4   Psychobiologic Disorders, Psychiatric Emergencies, and Mental Health Nursing Care of Special Populations

Section: Psychobiologic Disorders

Chapter 29:   Substance-Related and Non-Substance-Related Dependencies
Contributor: Anne W. Ryan, MSN, MPH, RN-BC

 NCLEX-RN® Connections:

Learning Objective: Review and apply knowledge within "**Substance-Related and Non-Substance-Related Dependencies**" in readiness for performance of the following nursing activities as outlined by the NCLEX-RN® test plan:

Δ   Apply knowledge of psychobiologic disorders to the nursing process when caring for clients with a substance-related or non-substance-related dependency.

Δ   Use effective communication to interact with and assist the client/family to foster trust in the nurse-client therapeutic relationship.

Δ   Assess the client's mental status, identifying changes in mood, judgment, cognition, and reasoning.

Δ   Assess the client for signs and symptoms of substance dependency, withdrawal, or toxicity.

Δ   Counsel the client who has a substance-related or non-substance-related dependency and encourage participation in support groups.

Δ   Assess/evaluate the client/family's reactions and response to the diagnosis/treatment of a substance-related disorder.

Δ   Identify external factors that may impede the client's recovery (e.g., peer pressure).

Δ   Plan and provide psychosocial care and symptom management for the client experiencing substance-related withdrawal or toxicity.

Δ   Plan and provide psychosocial care for the client with a non-substance dependency.

Key Points

Δ   **Substance abuse** involves a repeated use of chemical substances, leading to clinically significant impairment over a 12-month period, and at least **one of the following problems**:

- Inability to perform normal duties at home, school, and work.

- Taking part in hazardous situations while impaired, such as driving.

- Repeated legal or other personal problems caused by the substance use, such as losing one's job due to missed work time.

- Continued use of the substance despite the problems it has caused.

Δ   **Substance dependence** involves repeated use of chemical substances, leading to clinically significant impairment over a 12-month period, and **three or more of the following**:

- The presence of tolerance – a need for higher and higher doses of a substance to achieve the desired effect, such as requiring larger amounts of alcohol to feel euphoric.

- The phenomenon of withdrawal – the stopping or reduction of intake that results in specific physical and psychological signs and symptoms, such as tremors, headaches, and other symptoms when alcohol is not available.

- The substance taken in larger amounts or for longer periods than intended, such as continuing to take a prescribed opioid after surgical pain has ceased.

- A persistent (but unsuccessful) desire to control use of the substance.

- Progressively more time spent in obtaining, using, and recovering from use of the substance.

- Reduction in normal social or occupational activities.

- Continued use of the substance despite the problems it has caused.

Δ   Other phenomena frequently encountered in substance abuse are flashbacks and synergistic effects or antagonistic effects of the chemicals used. These are seen in many situations, not just in dependency situations.

Δ   **Substances of Abuse and Dependency**

- Central nervous system (CNS) depressants

    ◊   Alcohol (most common drug of abuse in the United States; poses the greatest withdrawal dangers)

    ◊   Barbiturates, such as phenobarbital

    ◊   Benzodiazepines, such as alprazolam (Xanax)

    ◊   Opioids, such as heroin or morphine

- CNS stimulants
  - ◊ Methamphetamine
  - ◊ Cocaine
  - ◊ Caffeine
- Hallucinogens, such as LSD
- Inhalants
  - ◊ Anesthetics, such as nitrous oxide
  - ◊ Volatile nitrates, such as amyl nitrite
  - ◊ Organic solvents (e.g., lighter fluid, several types of glue)
- Cannabis (marijuana and hashish)
- Nicotine

Δ **Non-Substance Related Dependency (Process Addictions)** – dependency to a behavior. While substance-related dependencies are better known and better researched, process addictions can be equally as problematic for these clients and must be addressed with similar treatment modalities. Abused processes include:

- Gambling.
- Sexual behaviors.
- Shopping/spending.
- Internet use.

Δ **Addiction** is characterized by:

- Loss of control due to participation in the dependency, whether that dependency is to a substance or to a process.
- Participation in this dependency continuing despite associated problems.
- A tendency to relapse back into the dependency.

Δ Although relapse with any form of dependency is common and should be expected, ideally, complete abstinence is the goal for each client.

Δ The defense mechanism "denial" is commonly used by clients who have problems with drug abuse or dependency. For example, a person with long-term nicotine abuse might say, "I can quit whenever I want to, but smoking really doesn't cause me any problems." Frequently, denial prevents a client from obtaining help with substance or process abuse or dependency.

Key Factors

Δ Biological Theories

- Effect on neurotransmitters – The GABA (gamma-aminobutyric acid) system, the dopamine system, and the opioid system have been used to explain biologic theories.

  ◊ When drugs that cause dependency are ingested, molecules in the brain begin to change over time.

  ◊ The reward circuitry of the brain, which utilizes dopamine as a neurotransmitter, reinforces the pleasurable activity of ingesting the drug and makes the individual more likely to keep using it.

- Genetics – A person who is alcohol dependent is three to four times as likely to come from parents who abused alcohol than a person with parents who did not abuse alcohol.

Δ Psychological Theories – The person who abuses substances/processes may have certain personal tendencies, including:

- Lowered self-esteem.

- Lowered tolerance for pain and frustration.

- Few meaningful personal relationships.

- Few life successes.

- Risk-taking tendencies.

Δ Sociocultural Theories

- Certain cultures within the United States, such as Native American groups, have a high percentage of members with alcohol dependence. Other cultures, such as Asian groups, have a low percentage of alcohol dependence.

- Peer pressure and other sociologic factors can increase the likelihood of substance use.

Δ   Selected Substances of Abuse

• **Alcohol (Ethanol)**

◊   A laboratory blood alcohol concentration (BAC) of 0.08% (80 g/dL) is considered legally intoxicated for adults operating automobiles in every U.S. state. Death could occur from acute toxicity in levels greater than about 0.35% (350 g/dL).

◊   Blood alcohol concentration depends on many factors, including body weight, gender, concentration of alcohol in drinks, number of drinks, gastric absorption rate, and the individual's tolerance level.

Intended Effects	Toxic Effects	Withdrawal Signs/Symptoms
• Relaxation, decreased social anxiety, maintaining calm	• Effects of excess – altered judgment, decreased motor skills, decreased level of consciousness (which can include stupor or coma), respiratory arrest, peripheral collapse, and death (can occur with large doses) • Chronic use – direct cardiovascular damage, liver damage (ranging from fatty liver to cirrhosis), erosive gastritis and GI bleeding, acute pancreatitis, sexual dysfunction	• The degree of symptoms is based on the degree of physical dependence. Withdrawal from a low degree of alcohol dependence will result in a mild reaction including nausea, anxiety, and tremors. Withdrawal from a high degree of alcohol dependence can be life-threatening and require hospitalization. Effects usually start within 12 to 72 hr of the last intake of alcohol and continue for 5 to 7 days. • Symptoms include abdominal cramping, vomiting, tremors, restlessness and inability to sleep, increased heart rate, blood pressure, respiratory rate, and temperature; and tonic-clonic seizures. • Delirium tremens (DTs) – more serious symptoms which are less common, occur after the early symptoms, and last at least 10 days. Symptoms of DTs include severe disorientation, psychotic symptoms (e.g., hallucinations), severe hypertension, cardiac dysrhythmias, delirium; may progress to death.

• **Nicotine** – cigarettes, cigars, and smokeless tobacco

Intended Effects	Toxic Effects	Withdrawal Signs/Symptoms
• Relaxation, decreased anxiety	• Highly toxic, but acute toxicity seen only in children or when exposure is to nicotine in pesticides • Long-term effects: cardiovascular disease (e.g., hypertension, stroke) and respiratory disease (e.g., emphysema, lung cancer); with smokeless tobacco (snuff or "chew"): irritation to oral mucous membranes and cancer	• Abstinence syndrome is evidenced by irritability, craving, nervousness, restlessness, anxiety, insomnia, increased appetite, and difficulty concentrating.

• **Opioids** – such as heroin, can be injected, smoked, and inhaled

Intended Effects	Toxic Effects	Withdrawal Signs/Symptoms
• A rush of euphoria (extreme well-being), relief from pain • Other effects - constriction of the pupils (myosis) and constipation	• Decreased respirations and level of consciousness, which may cause death • An antidote, naloxone (Narcan), available for IV use to relieve symptoms of overdose	• Abstinence syndrome begins with sweating and rhinorrhea progressing to piloerection (gooseflesh), tremors, and irritability followed by severe weakness, nausea and vomiting, pain in the muscles and bones, and muscle spasms. • Withdrawal is very unpleasant but not life-threatening, and it is self-limiting in 7 to 10 days.

• **Barbiturates** – can be ingested orally and injected

Intended Effects	Toxic Effects	Withdrawal Signs/Symptoms
• Sedation, decreased anxiety	• Respiratory depression and decreased level of consciousness, which may be fatal • No antidote to reverse barbiturate toxicity	• Milder symptoms – the same as those seen in alcohol withdrawal • Severe symptoms – possibly life-threatening convulsions, delirium, and cardiovascular collapse similar to that of alcohol withdrawal

- **Benzodiazepines** – such as diazepam (Valium), can be taken orally or injected

Intended Effects	Toxic Effects	Withdrawal Signs/Symptoms
• Decreased anxiety, sedation	• Increased drowsiness and sedation • Life-threatening hypotension (rare), respiratory depression • An antidote, flumazenil (Romazicon), available for IV use for benzodiazepine toxicity • Effects less dangerous than those of barbiturates • Rapid dependence	• Milder than for barbiturates • Anxiety, insomnia, diaphoresis, hypertension, possible psychotic reactions, and sometimes convulsions

- **Amphetamines** – can be taken orally, injected intravenously, or smoked (crystal meth)

Intended Effects	Toxic Effects	Withdrawal Signs/Symptoms
• Increased energy, euphoria similar to cocaine	• Extreme irritability and psychosis, which resembles paranoid schizophrenia • Acute cardiovascular effects, which could cause death	• Craving, depression, fatigue, sleeping (similar to those of cocaine) • Not life threatening

- **Cocaine** – can be injected, smoked, or inhaled (snorted)

Intended Effects	Toxic Effects	Withdrawal Signs/Symptoms
• Rush of euphoria and pleasure, increased energy	• Mild toxicity – dizziness, irritability, tremor, blurred vision • Severe effects – convulsions, extreme fever, tachycardia, hypertension, chest pain, possible cardiovascular collapse and death	• Depression, fatigue, craving, excess sleeping • Not life threatening, although suicidal ideation may occur

- **Cannabis** – marijuana or hashish (which is more potent), can be smoked or eaten

Intended Effects	Toxic Effects	Withdrawal Signs/Symptoms
• Euphoria, sedation, hallucinations	• Chronic use – lung cancer, chronic bronchitis, and other respiratory effects • Reproductive problems, such as fetal defects, seen in animals, but not proven in humans • In high doses, occurrence of paranoia and other psychotic behavior that can linger for weeks	• Possibly some depression

- **Inhalants** –such as amyl nitrate, nitrous oxide, and solvents, are "sniffed," "huffed," or "bagged," often by young children or teenagers

Intended Effects	Toxic Effects	Withdrawal Signs/Symptoms
• Euphoria	• Depend on the drug, but generally can cause CNS depression, symptoms of psychosis (hallucinations), respiratory depression, and possible death	• None

- **Psychedelics** – such as LSD and mescaline (peyote), usually ingested orally, can be injected or smoked

Intended Effects	Toxic Effects	Withdrawal Signs/Symptoms
• Heightened sense of self and altered perceptions (e.g., colors being more vivid under the influence)	• Vary with the psychedelic drug, but generally psychologic rather than physical • Panic attacks, flashbacks (visual disturbances or hallucinations) which can occur intermittently for years • Symptoms mimicking schizophrenia	• None

Δ   Clients with substance abuse and dependency experience the phenomena of
tolerance and **cross tolerance** (tolerance to one drug causes tolerance to
another drug or class of drugs.).

Substance	Tolerance and Cross Tolerance
Alcohol (Ethanol)	Tolerance: • Occurs with chronic use Cross tolerance: • Other CNS depressants (e.g., general anesthetics, barbiturates, and benzodiazepines) • No cross-tolerance to opioids
Opioids	Tolerance: • Develops over time to some effects (e.g., respiratory depression, nausea) • Does not develop to constipation, which can be a serious problem Cross tolerance: • Other opioids • No cross-tolerance to other classes of CNS depressants, such as benzodiazepines
Barbiturates	Tolerance: • Develops over time, but not to respiratory depression, which can be fatal
Benzodiazepines	Tolerance: • Moderate when these drugs are used as prescribed, but can be severe when the drugs are abused
Cocaine	Tolerance: • Develops with use over time
Amphetamines	Tolerance: • Develops to mood elevation, cardiovascular effects, and appetite suppression
Psychedelics	Tolerance: • Occurs after only a few uses, but fades rapidly when LSD use stops • Not as great for cardiovascular effects, but occurs more with behavioral and subjective effects Cross tolerance: • Occurs with LSD, mescaline, and psilocybin • No cross-tolerance with amphetamines
Inhalants	Tolerance: • Does not develop over time
Nicotine	Tolerance: • Develops to nausea and dizziness, but not to the cardiovascular effects, such as hypertension

Δ   **Dual diagnosis**, or comorbidity, means that an individual has both a mental illness, such as depression, as well as a problem with substance or process abuse. Clients with a serious mental illness often have a dual diagnosis of some type of substance abuse. The nurse should assess all clients for substance abuse.

Δ   **Codependency** – a common behavior by the significant other/family/friends of an individual with substance or process dependency. The codependent person reacts in over-responsible ways that actually allow the dependent individual to continue the substance (or process) abuse or dependency. For example, a spouse may call the client's employer with an excuse of illness when the client is actually intoxicated.

Assessment

Δ   The nurse must self-assess his own feelings regarding abuses, as those feelings may be transferred to the client through body language and the terminology the nurse may use in assessing the client. An objective, nonjudgmental approach by the nurse is imperative.

Δ   Use open-ended questions, such as "When was your last drink?"

Δ   Chemical Use Assessment - Ask about each substance or behavior separately.

- Type of substance

- Type of compulsive behavior

- Pattern and frequency of substance use

- Amount

- Age at onset

- Age of regular use

- Changes in use patterns

- Periods of abstinence in history

- Previous withdrawal symptoms

- Date of last substance use/compulsive behavior

Δ   Perform a family history assessment.

Δ   Standardized **screening and assessment tools** are available to screen for chemical dependency.

- Rapid, simple tools include the modified MAST (Michigan Alcohol Screening Test) and the CAGE-AID (adapted to include drugs) screening tool. The CAGE acronym involves the following questions:

  ◊   C – Has anyone ever told you that you should **cut** down on your drinking/drug use?

  ◊   A – Have people **annoyed** you by criticizing you for drinking/using drugs?

  ◊   G – Have you ever felt **guilty** for drinking/using drugs?

  ◊   E – Have you ever taken an **eye-opener** (morning drink or drug) to steady your nerves or to get rid of a hangover?

  ◊   One positive response indicates that a more in-depth assessment is needed. A problem with alcohol dependency or abuse is present in 90% of individuals who have two positive responses to the CAGE assessment.

Δ   Review of Systems

- Blackout or loss of consciousness

- Changes in bowel movements

- Weight loss or weight gain

- Experience of stressful situation

- Sleep problems

- Chronic pain

- Concern over substance abuse

- Cutting down on consumption or behavior

NANDA Nursing Diagnoses

Δ   Anxiety

Δ   Dysfunctional family processes: Alcoholism

Δ   Family processes: Interrupted

Δ   Risk for injury

Δ   Ineffective role performance

Δ   Disturbed sensory perception

Δ   Disturbed sleep pattern

Nursing Interventions

Δ   **Safety** is the primary focus of nursing care during the **acute stage** of abuse.

   •   Maintain a safe environment to prevent falls; implement seizure precautions as necessary.

   •   Provide close observation for withdrawal symptoms, possibly one-on-one supervision. Physical restraint should be a last resort.

   •   Orient the client to time, place, and person.

   •   Maintain adequate nutrition and fluid balance.

   •   Monitor for beginning of withdrawal signs and symptoms.

   •   Create a low-stimulation environment.

   •   Administer withdrawal medications as prescribed.

   •   Monitor for covert substance abuse during the detoxification period.

Δ   Provide emotional support and reassurance to the client and family.

Δ   Begin to educate the client about addiction and the initial treatment goal of abstinence.

Δ   Begin to develop motivation and commitment for abstinence and recovery (abstinence plus working a program of personal growth and self-discovery).

Δ   Encourage self-responsibility.

Δ   Help the client develop an emergency plan – a list of things the client would do and people he would contact if he felt like using or actually used.

Δ   Treatments used for Substance/Process Abuse

   •   **Individual psychotherapies**

      ◊   Advanced practice nurses may use cognitive-behavioral therapy or psychodynamic psychotherapy.

      ◊   Relapse prevention therapy teaches the client to recognize signs/ symptoms of relapse and factors that contribute to relapse and helps the client develop strategies, such as meditating or exercising, to create feelings of pleasure from activities other than using substances or from process addictions.

   •   **Group therapy**

      ◊   Groups of clients with similar diagnoses may meet in an outpatient setting or within mental health residential facilities.

- **Family therapy**

  ◊ Teaches families about abuse of specific substances

  ◊ Educates the client/family regarding such issues as family coping, problem solving, relapse signs, and availability of support groups

- **Self-help groups**

  ◊ 12-step programs, including Alcoholics Anonymous (AA), Narcotics Anonymous, Gambler's Anonymous, and family groups like Al-Anon or Ala-Teen, teach that abstinence is necessary for recovery and use the belief in a higher power to assist recovery.

Δ **Psychopharmacology**

- **Alcohol withdrawal**

  ◊ **Benzodiazepines**, including chlordiazepoxide (Librium), diazepam (Valium), lorazepam (Ativan)

Intended Effects	Nursing Interventions and Client Education
• Maintenance of the client's vital signs within normal limits • Decrease in the risk of seizures • Decrease in the intensity of symptoms	• May be administered when necessary or around the clock. • Obtain the client's baseline vital signs. • Monitor the client's vital signs on an ongoing basis. • Provide for seizure precautions (e.g., padded side rails, suction equipment at bedside).

  ◊ Adjunct medications: carbamazepine (Tegretol), clonidine (Catapres), propranolol (Inderal)

Intended Effects	Nursing Interventions and Client Education
• Decrease in seizures • Decrease in craving • Depression of autonomic response – decrease in blood pressure, heart rate, and temperature	• Obtain the client's baseline vital signs. • Monitor the client's vital signs on an ongoing basis. • Provide for seizure precautions (e.g., padded side rails, suction equipment at bedside).

- **Alcohol abstinence maintenance (following detoxification)**
  ◊ Disulfiram (Antabuse)

Intended Effects	Nursing Interventions and Client Education
• Disulfiram is a daily oral medication that is a type of aversion (behavioral) therapy. • Disulfiram used concurrently with alcohol will cause acetaldehyde syndrome to occur. • Effects can be mild (e.g., nausea) or extreme (e.g., vomiting, weakness, and hypotension). • Acetaldehyde syndrome can progress to respiratory depression, cardiovascular suppression, seizures, and death.	• Inform the client of the potential dangers of drinking any alcohol. • Advise the client to avoid any products that contain alcohol (e.g., cough syrups, aftershave lotion). • Encourage the client to wear a Medic Alert bracelet.

◊ Naltrexone (ReVia)

Intended Effects	Nursing Interventions and Client Education
• Naltrexone is a pure opioid antagonist that suppresses the craving and pleasurable effects of alcohol (also used for opioid withdrawal).	• Take the client's accurate history to determine if the client is also dependent on opioids. Use of naltrexone will initiate withdrawal syndrome. • Advise the client to take with meals to decrease gastrointestinal distress. If the client has difficulty with compliance, recommend monthly IM injections.

◊ Acamprosate (Campral)

Intended Effects	Nursing Interventions and Client Education
• Acamprosate decreases unpleasant effects resulting from abstinence (e.g., anxiety, restlessness).	• Inform the client that diarrhea may result. • Advise the client to maintain adequate fluid intake and to receive adequate rest. • Advise the client to avoid use in pregnancy.

- **Opioid withdrawal**
    - ◊ Methadone (Dolophine) substitution

Intended Effects	Nursing Interventions and Client Education
• Methadone substitution is an oral opioid that replaces the opioid to which the client is addicted. • This will prevent abstinence syndrome from occurring and remove the need for the client to obtain illegal drugs. • It is used for withdrawal and long-term maintenance. • Dependence will be transferred from the illegal opioid to methadone.	• Inform the client that the methadone dose must be slowly tapered to produce detoxification.

◊ Levomethadyl (ORLAAM) – a newer analog of methadone

Intended Effects	Nursing Interventions and Client Education
• Levomethadyl is a narcotic similar in effects and side effects to morphine. • It is highly addictive. • Use is similar to that of methadone substitution.	• Duration of action is up to 3 days. • Administer three times/week.

◊ Clonidine (Catapres)

Intended Effects	Nursing Interventions and Client Education
• Clonidine assists with the control of symptoms related to autonomic hyperactivity (e.g., nausea, vomiting).	• Obtain baseline vital signs. • If the client experiences drowsiness, advise the client to avoid activities that require mental alertness until symptoms subside. • To treat dry mouth, encourage the client to chew on gum or hard candy and to take small amounts of water or ice chips.

◊ Buprenorphine (Subutex), buprenorphine combined with naloxone (Suboxone)

Intended Effects	Nursing Interventions and Client Education
• These medications are agonist-antagonist opioids used for both detoxification and maintenance.	• The client must receive the medication from an approved treatment center.

- **Nicotine** withdrawal
  ◊ Bupropion (Zyban)

Intended Effects	Nursing Interventions and Client Education
• Bupropion decreases nicotine craving and symptoms of withdrawal.	• To treat dry mouth, encourage the client to chew on gum or hard candy and to take small amounts of water or ice chips. • Advise the client to avoid caffeine and other CNS stimulants to control insomnia.

  ◊ Nicotine replacement therapy, including nicotine gum (Nicorette) and nicotine patch (Nicotrol)

Intended Effects	Nursing Interventions and Client Education
• These nicotine replacements are pharmaceutical product substitutes for the nicotine in cigarettes or chewing tobacco.	• Advise the client to chew gum slowly and intermittently over 30 min. • Advise the client to avoid eating or drinking 15 min prior to and while chewing the gum. • Use of chewing gum is not recommended for longer than 6 months. • Advise the client to apply a nicotine patch to an area of clean, dry skin each day. • Advise the client to follow product directions for dosage times. • Advise the client to stop using patches and to notify the primary care provider if local skin reactions occur. • Advise the client to avoid using any nicotine products while pregnant or breastfeeding.

Primary Reference:

Varcarolis, E. M., Carson, V. B., & Shoemaker, N. C. (2006). *Foundations of psychiatric mental health nursing: A clinical approach* (5th ed.). St. Louis, MO: Saunders.

Additional Resources:

Cohagan, A., Plewa, M. C., & Worthington, R. (2005, March 16). Alcohol and substance abuse evaluation. *eMedicine*, Topic 20. Retrieved November 28, 2006, from http://www.emedicine.com/EMERG/topic20.htm

Lehne, R. A. (2007). *Pharmacology for nursing care* (6th ed.). St. Louis, MO: Saunders.

NANDA International (2004). *NANDA nursing diagnoses: Definitions and classification 2005-2006.* Philadelphia: NANDA.

Chapter 29: Substance-Related and Non-Substance-Related Dependencies

Application Exercises

Scenario: A 45-year-old client was admitted to the acute care facility for medically supervised detoxification 8 hr ago. Earlier today, he ran head-on into a tree while driving drunk. He was not physically injured. His blood alcohol concentration (BAC) was 200 g/dL (0.20%) in the emergency department. The client has a 30-year history of alcohol abuse; he says he began to drink alcohol at age 15 because several friends talked him into it. Both parents were alcoholics and his mother died of liver failure. He has been in rehabilitation facilities several times but has always relapsed. He is currently living alone after a separation from his second wife and three teenage children; he has not seen any of them in a year. He lost his last four jobs due to poor attendance at work, and he has been out of work for the past 6 months. He has had several driving-under-the-influence (DUI) citations. The nurse checks on the client and finds that he has fine tremors of both hands and is restless and anxious. The client's blood pressure is 160/94 mm Hg, pulse is 100/min, respirations are 24/min, and oral temperature is 37.7° C (99.8° F). He says he sees "bugs crawling on the ceiling."

1. Identify the predisposing genetic factors, current circumstances, and past experiences that influence this client's behavior.

2. According to the DSM-IV-TR, what signs of substance dependence does this client have?

3. List at least two nursing diagnoses with related information for the client at this time.

4. Describe interventions the nurse should implement at this time in response to the client's withdrawal symptoms.

5. Match the drugs below with some of their most common withdrawal signs/symptoms.

_____ Alcohol

_____ Crystal meth

_____ Cigarettes

_____ Heroin

_____ LSD

A. Yawning, piloerection, abdominal cramps, muscle pain

B. Craving, nervousness, anxiety, irritability, increased appetite

C. Possible life-threatening increase in vital signs, psychotic behavior, seizures

D. Depression, prolonged sleeping

E. No withdrawal symptoms

6. True or False: A client with acute opioid overdose would be given the specific opioid antidote flumazenil (Romazicon) intravenously.

7. True or False: A client in a rehabilitation facility due to chronic heroin abuse tells the nurse, "I have used heroin, but it doesn't affect me and I could stop any time I really wanted." This is an example of the defense mechanism projection.

8. True or False: A client who has developed tolerance for alcohol would likely need a larger than usual dose of benzodiazepine to obtain a therapeutic effect.

Chapter 29: Substance-Related and Non-Substance-Related Dependencies

Application Exercises Answer Key

Scenario: A 45-year-old client was admitted to the acute care facility for medically supervised detoxification 8 hr ago. Earlier today, he ran head-on into a tree while driving drunk. He was not physically injured. His blood alcohol concentration (BAC) was 200 g/dL (0.20%) in the emergency department. The client has a 30-year history of alcohol abuse; he says he began to drink alcohol at age 15 because several friends talked him into it. Both parents were alcoholics and his mother died of liver failure. He has been in rehabilitation facilities several times but has always relapsed. He is currently living alone after a separation from his second wife and three teenage children; he has not seen any of them in a year. He lost his last four jobs due to poor attendance at work, and he has been out of work for the past 6 months. He has had several driving-under-the-influence (DUI) citations. The nurse checks on the client and finds that he has fine tremors of both hands and is restless and anxious. The client's blood pressure is 160/94 mm Hg, pulse is 100/min, respirations are 24/min, and oral temperature is 37.7° C (99.8° F). He says he sees "bugs crawling on the ceiling."

1. Identify the predisposing genetic factors, current circumstances, and past experiences that influence this client's behavior.

   Began to drink due to peer pressure
   Both parents being alcoholic – genetic predisposition
   Failed work history due to poor attendance practices
   History of DUI and auto accidents due to alcohol
   Family separation and probable role-relationship difficulties

2. According to the DSM-IV-TR, what signs of substance dependence does this client have?

   Beginning to experience withdrawal symptoms – tremor, anxiety, increased vital signs
   Has tried to stop drinking several times, but always relapses
   Reduction in normal social or occupational activities – has lost his family and his job
   Continued use of the substance despite the problems it has caused

3. List at least two nursing diagnoses with related information for the client at this time.

   Risk for injury related to presence of withdrawal symptoms
   Disturbed sensory perception related to alcohol withdrawal (having visual hallucination or illusion about "bugs on the ceiling")
   Dysfunctional family processes: alcoholism, related to deterioration in family relationships due to alcohol use
   Family processes interrupted related to separation from family
   Anxiety, related to alcohol withdrawal and/or to hospitalization, car accident, and more

4. Describe interventions the nurse should implement at this time in response to the client's withdrawal symptoms.

Provide a low-stimulation environment – should be quiet, without dark shadows (could increase delusions/hallucinations).
Provide close observation to prevent falls due to restlessness, confusion.
Encourage fluids and nourishing diet as tolerated; the nurse should contact the primary care provider if the client is unable to eat or drink adequately or is nauseated.
Orient the client to time, place, and person as needed.
Continue assessment of symptoms and assess what level of care this client requires, such as one-on-one care.
Administer medications as ordered to treat withdrawal symptoms.
Monitor effectiveness of medications and watch for complications.

---

5. Match the drugs below with some of their most common withdrawal signs/symptoms.

C	Alcohol	A. Yawning, piloerection, abdominal cramps, muscle pain
D	Crystal meth	B. Craving, nervousness, anxiety, irritability, increased appetite
B	Cigarettes	C. Possible life-threatening increase in vital signs, psychotic behavior, seizures
A	Heroin	D. Depression, prolonged sleeping
E	LSD	E. No withdrawal symptoms

6. True or False: A client with acute opioid overdose would be given the specific opioid antidote flumazenil (Romazicon) intravenously.

False: Flumazenil (Romazicon) is a specific antidote for benzodiazepine toxicity. An antidote for opioid toxicity is intravenous naloxone (Narcan).

7. True or False: A client in a rehabilitation facility due to chronic heroin abuse tells the nurse, "I have used heroin, but it doesn't affect me and I could stop any time I really wanted." This is an example of the defense mechanism projection.

False: The statement is an example of denial. Projection would occur if the client blamed someone else for her own unacceptable mistakes or shortcomings.

8. True or False: A client who has developed tolerance for alcohol would likely need a larger than usual dose of benzodiazepine to obtain a therapeutic effect.

True: Alcohol and benzodiazepines are cross-tolerant. Therefore, tolerance to one would mean that the client also has tolerance to the other.

Unit 4   Psychobiologic Disorders, Psychiatric Emergencies, and Mental Health Nursing Care of
              Special Populations

Section: Psychiatric Emergencies

Chapter 30:   Crisis Management
              Contributor: Deborah Kindy, PhD, RN

 NCLEX-RN® Connections:

Learning Objective: Review and apply knowledge within **"Crisis Management"** in
readiness for performance of the following nursing activities as outlined by the
NCLEX-RN® test plan:

Δ   Assess the client's risk for self-injury and monitor the client.

Δ   Plan and provide care to protect the client from self-injury.

Δ   Assist the client to cope by using crisis intervention techniques.

Δ   Support the client's efforts to explore options to cope with crisis.

Δ   Teach the client management strategies to cope with crisis.

Δ   Evaluate and document the client's response to crisis intervention techniques.

 Key Points

Δ   A **crisis** is an **acute, time-limited** (usually lasting 4 to 6 weeks) event in which
     the client experiences an emotional response that cannot be managed with the
     client's **normal coping mechanisms**.

Δ   Common characteristics include:

     •   Experience of a sudden event with little or no time to prepare.

     •   Perception of the crisis as life threatening.

     •   Loss or decrease in communication with significant others.

     •   Sense of displacement from the familiar.

     •   An actual or perceived loss.

Δ   The steps of crisis intervention are consistent with the steps of the nursing process:
     assessment, diagnosis, planning, intervention, and evaluation.

Δ   The basis of crisis intervention includes:

- Timely interventions.

- Identifying the current problem and directing interventions to its resolution.

- Establishing a trusting nurse-client relationship.

- Assisting the client to regain a normal level of functioning.

- Awareness that the client in crisis usually is mentally healthy.

- Recognizing that during a crisis the client will often be amenable to outside interventions.

- Taking an active, directive role with the client.

- Helping the client to set realistic, attainable goals.

Δ   Short-term pharmacological intervention may include antidepressants, benzodiazepines, and sedative/hypnotics.

Key Factors

Δ   Types of crises include:

- Situational/external – loss or change experienced in everyday, often unanticipated, life events.

- Maturational/internal – achieving new developmental stages, which requires learning additional coping mechanisms.

- Adventitious – the occurrence of natural disasters, crimes, or national disasters.

Δ   Factors affecting an individual's ability to cope with stress and crisis include:

- Accumulation of unresolved losses.

- Current life stressors.

- Concurrent mental and physical health.

- Excessive fatigue or pain.

- Age and developmental stage.

- Support system.

- Prior experience with stress/crisis.

Δ   **Phases of a Crisis**

Phase	Manifestations
Phase 1	Escalating anxiety from a threat activates increased defense responses.
Phase 2	Anxiety continues escalating as defense responses fail, and the client resorts to trial-and-error attempts to resolve anxiety.
Phase 3	Trial-and-error methods of resolution fail, and the client's anxiety escalates to severe or panic levels, leading to flight or withdrawal behaviors.
Phase 4	The client experiences overwhelming anxiety that can lead to anguish and apprehension, dissociative symptoms, depression, confusion, and/or violence against others or self.

Assessment

Δ   Assess for suicidal or homicidal ideation requiring hospitalization.

Δ   Assess for feelings of depression, powerlessness, being overwhelmed, or anger.

Δ   Determine if the client can recognize the precipitating event.

Δ   Identify cultural or religious needs of the client.

Δ   Assess the client's support system.

Δ   Assess the client's coping skills.

NANDA Nursing Diagnoses

Δ   Anxiety

Δ   Acute confusion

Δ   Ineffective coping

Δ   Hopelessness

Δ   Risk for post-trauma syndrome

Δ   Powerlessness

Δ   Spiritual distress

Δ   Disturbed thought processes

Δ   Risk for other- or self-directed violence

Nursing Interventions

Δ   Provide for client **safety**.

- Ensure that external controls, such as hospitalization, are applied for protection of the person in crisis if the individual has suicidal or homicidal thoughts.

- Organize interventions so tangible threats are addressed first.

Δ   Use strategies to **decrease anxiety**.

- Develop a therapeutic nurse-client relationship.

  ◊   Listen, observe, and ask questions.

  ◊   Make eye contact.

  ◊   Ask questions related to the client's feelings.

  ◊   Ask questions related to the event.

- Demonstrate genuineness and caring.

- Communicate clearly and, if needed, with clear directives.

- Avoid false reassurance and other nontherapeutic responses.

- Teach relaxation techniques, such as meditation.

- Use problem solving to anticipate the client's needs (anticipatory guidance).

Δ   Identify and teach coping skills (e.g., assertiveness training, parenting skills, occupational training).

Δ   Assist the client with the development of an action plan.

- Short-term, no longer than 24 to 72 hr

- Focused on the crisis

- Realistic and manageable

Δ   Identify and coordinate with support agencies and other resources.

Δ   Plan and provide for follow-up care.

Primary Reference:

Varcarolis, E. M., Carson, V. B., & Shoemaker, N. C. (2006). *Foundations of psychiatric mental health nursing: A clinical approach* (5th ed.). St. Louis, MO: Saunders.

Additional Resources:

Crisis Intervention and Domestic Violence National Resource. (n.d.). *Four steps to effective crisis intervention.* Retrieved on December 12, 2006, from http://www.crisisinterventionnetwork.com/intervention_foursteps.html

Fortinash, K. M., & Holoday Worret, P. A. (2004). *Psychiatric mental health nursing* (3rd ed.). St. Louis, MO: Mosby.

Kneisl, C. R., Wilson, H. S., Trigoboff, E. (2004). *Contemporary psychiatric-mental health nursing.* Upper Saddle River, NJ: Pearson/Prentice Hall.

NANDA International (2004). *NANDA nursing diagnoses: Definitions and classification 2005-2006.* Philadelphia: NANDA.

Chapter 30: Crisis Management

Application Exercises

Scenario: A client is being seen in the emergency department after a motor vehicle accident in which a drunk driver crashed into the passenger's side of the client's car. The client was trapped in the wreckage next to his adolescent son, who did not survive the impact. The client has lacerations requiring sutures, moderate blood loss, and a broken arm, but he was not seriously injured. The nurse notices that, despite being informed that his son has died, the client continues to ask about the son's well-being, seems confused when attempting to answer simple questions, and appears "empty."

1. What is the priority nursing intervention for this client?

2. Which phase of crisis is this client experiencing? What assessment data confirm this?

3. Identify initial nursing interventions appropriate for this client.

4. What type of crisis did this client experience?

5. The nurse assesses that the client is experiencing confusion and disorganized personality behaviors. Which of the following nursing diagnoses is most appropriate for these symptoms?

      A. Impaired social interactions

      B. Disturbed thought processes

      C. Chronic sorrow

      D. Chronic low self-esteem

6. Which of the following medications might be prescribed short term for a client experiencing a crisis?

      A. Mood stabilizers

      B. Antidepressants

      C. Antipsychotics

      D. Opioids

Chapter 30: Crisis Management

Application Exercises Answer Key

Scenario: A client is being seen in the emergency department after a motor vehicle accident in which a drunk driver crashed into the passenger's side of the client's car. The client was trapped in the wreckage next to his adolescent son, who did not survive the impact. The client has lacerations requiring sutures, moderate blood loss, and a broken arm, but he was not seriously injured. The nurse notices that, despite being informed that his son has died, the client continues to ask about the son's well-being, seems confused when attempting to answer simple questions, and appears "empty."

1. What is the priority nursing intervention for this client?

The priority nursing intervention for this client is safety. He should be assessed for suicidal or homicidal ideation.

2. Which phase of crisis is this client experiencing? What assessment data confirm this?

Phase 4: The individual experiences overwhelming anxiety that can lead to anguish, apprehension, depression, confusion and/or violence against others or self. This client is unable to answer simple questions and appears "empty," which implies dissociative behaviors, including depersonalization, derealization, and detachment from reality.

3. Identify initial nursing interventions appropriate for this client.

Stay with the client; listen, observe, and ask questions based on cues from the client. Notify the appropriate support system in the facility, such as the chaplain, social workers, and/or trained volunteers. Question the client about family support and ask other members of the health care team to notify them. Prioritize care starting with the client's immediate physical needs.

4. What type of crisis did this client experience?

Situational: unanticipated loss in an external life event

5. The nurse assesses that the client is experiencing confusion and disorganized personality behaviors. Which of the following nursing diagnoses is most appropriate for these symptoms?

    A. Impaired social interactions
    B. Disturbed thought processes
    C. Chronic sorrow
    D. Chronic low self-esteem

The diagnosis of disturbed thought processes is appropriate due to the denial and dissociative behaviors this client is displaying. Social interactions have not been assessed for this client. The crisis the client is experiencing is acute, rather than a chronic problem; therefore, chronic sorrow or chronic low self-esteem are not appropriate diagnoses.

6. Which of the following medications might be prescribed short term for a client experiencing a crisis?

    A. Mood stabilizers
    B. Antidepressants
    C. Antipsychotics
    D. Opioids

Antidepressants are most likely to be prescribed for the depression that may follow a crisis situation. Mood stabilizers are used for bipolar disorder. Antipsychotic medications may be prescribed for disturbed thought processes but usually when accompanied by other psychotic symptoms (e.g., hallucinations, delusions, blunt affect). Antipsychotics are not indicated in a short-term crisis situation. Opioids are for physical pain.

Unit 4   Psychobiologic Disorders, Psychiatric Emergencies, and Mental Health Nursing Care of
                Special Populations

Section: Psychiatric Emergencies

Chapter 31:   Suicide
Contributor: Linda W. Edwards, MSN, RN

 NCLEX-RN® Connections:

Learning Objective: Review and apply knowledge within "**Suicide**" in readiness for
performance of the following nursing activities as outlined by the NCLEX-RN® test plan:

  Δ   Assess the client's risk for self-injury and monitor the client.

  Δ   Plan and provide care to protect the client from self-injury (e.g., suicide
        precautions).

  Δ   Assist the client to cope by using crisis intervention techniques.

  Δ   Support the client's efforts to explore options to cope with crisis.

  Δ   Teach the client management strategies to cope with crisis.

  Δ   Evaluate and document the client's response to crisis intervention techniques.

 Key Points

  Δ   **Suicide** is the intentional act of killing oneself.

  Δ   Those at highest risk include adolescent, young adult, and older adult males;
        Native Americans as a group, and persons with comorbid mental illness.

        •   Comorbidity: More than 90% of suicide victims meet criteria for at least one
             psychotic disorder at the time of death. These include:

             ◊   Major depression.

             ◊   Bipolar disorder.

             ◊   Schizophrenia.

             ◊   Alcohol and substance abuse.

             ◊   Borderline and antisocial personality disorders.

             ◊   Panic disorder.

Δ   Suicidal ideation is having thoughts about committing suicide.

Δ   Parasuicide is inflicting a nonlethal injury to oneself with the intent to die or commit bodily harm.

Δ   Self-injurious behavior (SIB) is the purposeful intent to inflict harm on one's body without an obvious intent to actually commit suicide. SIB is often present in clients with comorbid at-risk disorders and in adolescents. These are individuals who may not be able to resist the impulse to injure themselves.

Δ   **Myths**

◊   People who talk about suicide never commit it.

◊   People who are suicidal only want to hurt themselves, not others.

◊   There is no way to help someone who really wants to kill himself.

◊   Mention of the word suicide will cause the suicidal individual to actually commit suicide.

◊   Ignoring verbal threats of suicide or challenging a person to carry out suicide plans will reduce the individual's use of these behaviors.

Δ   The client who is suicidal may be ambivalent about death; intervention can make a difference.

Δ   The client contemplating suicide believes the act is the end to her problems. Little concern is given to the aftermath and the ramifications to those left behind. Long-term therapy is needed for the survivors.

Δ   Treatment for the client who has suicidal ideation or has made attempts includes milieu therapy within an acute care mental health facility, counseling, and individual, group, and family therapy.

Δ   Pharmacotherapy to prevent suicide includes:

• Antidepressants.

• Lithium therapy for the client with bipolar disorder.

• Antipsychotic medications for clients with schizophrenia or bipolar disorder.

• Antianxiety medications for clients with panic disorder and/or sleep deprivation.

Key Factors

Δ **Biological**

- Genetics – Studies of twins suggest a genetic factor; suicidal behavior within families is common.

- Low levels of the neurotransmitter serotonin are associated with suicidal behavior (also found in major depressive disorders).

- There is a role of physical disorders such as AIDS, cancer, cardiovascular disease, stroke, chronic renal failure on dialysis, cirrhosis, dementia, epilepsy, head injury, Huntington's disease, and multiple sclerosis.

Δ **Psychosocial**

- A sense of hopelessness – loss of love, overwhelming emotion such as rage or guilt, or identification with a suicide victim

- Motivations (e.g., revenge, reunion with a loved one, rebirth)

- Anger turned inward

- History of aggression and violence

- Developmental stressors

- In adolescents, interpersonal conflicts precipitating suicide attempts

Δ **Cultural** – religion, family values, and attitudes

Δ **Environmental** – peak times during spring and October

Δ **Comorbidities** – depression, substance abuse, schizophrenia

Δ **Protective Factors**

- Feelings of responsibility toward family

- Current pregnancy

- Religious beliefs (in certain religions, such as Roman Catholic)

- Overall satisfaction with life

- Presence of adequate social support

- Effective coping and problem-solving skills

- Intact reality testing

Risk Factors for Suicide in the United States		
Factor	Description	Incidence
Marital Status	Single	• 2 times that of married people
	Divorced, separated, or widowed	• 4 to 5 times greater
Gender	Men	• More successful • Use more lethal means, such as firearms • View seeking help as a sign of weakness • Commit suicide 4 times more often than women
	Women	• More attempts • Overdose as usual method • More likely to seek and receive help
Age	Men	• Teenagers 15 to 19 years and again after the age of 65 • White men 80 years and older at the greatest risk
	Women	• Rates fairly constant until age 65, when incidence decreases
Religion	Roman Catholics	• Believe that suicide is a sin • Rates lower than rates among Protestants
	No religious affiliation	• Higher risk
Culture and Ethnicity	European Americans	• Twice the suicide rate of minorities
	Native Americans	• Higher than the overall U.S. rates
	African Americans	• Higher rate in men than in women • Usually occurs in adolescents and young adults
	Asian Americans	• Increasing rates with age
	Latino Americans	• High percentage of Roman Catholic background
Socioeconomic Status	Highest and lowest social classes	• Higher rates • Rates higher among physicians, musicians, dentists, law enforcement agents, lawyers, and insurance agents

Assessment

Δ Assess carefully for verbal and nonverbal clues.

- Comments are usually made to someone the client perceives as supportive.

- Comments or signals may be overt or covert.

  ◊ Overt comment – "I wish I was dead."

  ◊ Covert comment – "Everything is looking pretty grim for me."

- **Asking someone if he is thinking of suicide does not give the person ideas of suicide.**

- When questioning the client about suicide, always use a follow-up question if the first answer is negative. Example: Client says, "I'm feeling completely hopeless." Nurse says, "Are you thinking of suicide?" Client, "No, I'm just sad." Nurse, "I can see you're very sad. Are you thinking about hurting yourself?" Client, "Well, I've thought about it a lot."

Δ Assess the client's skin for lacerations, scratches, and scars that could indicate previous attempts at self-harm in the client at risk for self-mutilation.

Δ Determine the lethality of the suicide plan – how quickly the person would die using the intended method.

- Is there a specific plan with details? Can the person describe exactly how the plan will be carried out?

- How lethal is the proposed method? For example, using a gun or hanging oneself are more lethal methods than slashing one's wrists or ingesting medication.

- Is there access to the planned method? Does the individual have access to a gun?

Δ **Assessment tools – SAD PERSONS** is a valuable tool that assesses 10 major risk factors for suicide by assigning scores based on an easily memorized acronym.

S	**S**ex	1 point for male gender
A	**A**ge	1 point for at-risk ages, 25-44, > 65 years
D	**D**epression	1 if depression is present
P	**P**revious attempt	1 point for previous attempt(s)
E	**E**thanol abuse (recent)	1 point for positive reply
R	**R**ational thought loss	1 point for disturbed thought
S	**S**ocial supports lacking	1 point if lacking, especially recent loss
O	**O**rganized plan	1 point for organized plan
N	**N**o spouse	1 point if divorced, widowed, single male
S	**S**ickness	1 point for severe illness or chronic illness with poor prognosis, such as cancer

Scoring: 0-2 send home with follow-up; 3-4 closely follow up, consider hospitalization; 5-6 strongly consider hospitalization; 7-10 hospitalize or commit

Δ   Self-Assessment

- The nurse must determine how he feels about suicide.

- Will the nurse's feelings affect the way he works with a client?

- The nurse must become comfortable asking personal questions about suicidal ideation and following up on client's answers.

- Suicide can cause health care professionals to experience hopelessness, helplessness, ambivalence, anger, anxiety, avoidance, and denial.

NANDA Nursing Diagnoses

Δ   Ineffective coping

Δ   Interrupted family processes

Δ   Hopelessness

Δ   Deficient knowledge

Δ   Risk for loneliness

Δ   Situational or chronic low self-esteem

Δ   Social isolation

Δ   Spiritual distress

Δ   Risk for self-directed violence

Nursing Interventions

Δ   Levels of Intervention

- **Primary** – activities that provide support, information, and education to prevent suicide, such as speaking in a high school health class

- **Secondary** – treatment of the actual suicide crisis

- **Tertiary** – interventions with the family and friends of a victim who committed suicide to reduce the traumatic aftereffects

Δ   **A no-suicide contract** is a verbal or written agreement made with the client that she will not harm herself.

- Contracts have not been proven valid with research but can be thought of as part of the client assessment for a suicide plan, as well as a behavioral tool to reinforce teaching. A no-suicide contract is not legally binding.

- An effective contract is written, signed by the client, and completed as a result of a therapeutic alliance between the client and health care professional. It should be specific and detailed regarding the agreement.

- Contracts are discouraged for clients who are: in crisis, under the influence of substances, psychotic, very impulsive, and/or very angry/agitated. A contract does not take the place of suicide precautions.

- If suicidal ideation or threats are successfully ended, encourage the client to write a safety plan to follow if thoughts return. The plan might include someone to call if she is feeling hopeless.

Δ Specific Activities – Safety is the highest priority.

- Establish a trusting therapeutic relationship.

- Limit the amount of time an at-risk client spends alone.

- Assess risk factors, using the SAD PERSONS tool or other tools.

- If there is a history of attempt, assess intent and lethality.

- If the client suddenly goes from sad and depressed to happy and peaceful, there is a high risk for suicide. The client now has the energy to carry out the plan.

- Involve significant others in the care plan and the treatment plan.

- Carry out treatment plans for the client with comorbid disorders, such as a dual diagnosis of substance abuse.

- Suicide precautions include **milieu therapy** within the facility.

  ◊ Conduct frequent nursing observations and interactions at all times.

  ◊ Assign staff to observe the client closely or consider one-on-one constant supervision if necessary.

  ◊ Document the client's whereabouts and record mood, verbatim statements, and behavior every 15 min or per facility protocol.

  ◊ Remove all glass, metal silverware, electrical cords, vases, belts, shoe laces, metal nail files, tweezers, matches, razors, perfume, shampoo, and plastic bags from the client's room and vicinity.

  ◊ Remove glass and metal utensils from food trays.

  ◊ Check the environment for possible hazards (e.g., windows that open, open overhead pipes).

  ◊ During observation periods, always check the client's hands, especially if they are hidden from sight.

  ◊ Carefully observe that the client swallows all medications.

  ◊ Identify if the client's current medications can be lethal with overdose. If so, collaborate with the primary care provider to have less dangerous medications substituted if possible, such as selective serotonin reuptake inhibitors.

  ◊ Ensure that visitors are aware of suicide precautions and rules restricting bringing possibly harmful items to the client.

Δ   Create a support system list – specific names, agencies, and telephone numbers the client can call for support (especially important if the client is not in an acute care setting).

Δ   Strategies for assisting survivors of victims who committed suicide (e.g., family, friends, coworkers, health care staff) include:

- Encouraging survivors to talk about the suicide.

- Using therapeutic communication techniques (e.g., active listening, silence).

- Listening to feelings of guilt and self-persecution.

- Encouraging survivors to discuss individual relationships with the victim and discussing the positive and negative aspects of that relationship.

- Allowing survivors to grieve in their own way.

- Identifying resources in the community for support and education.

Primary Reference:

Varcarolis, E. M., Carson, V. B., & Shoemaker, N. C. (2006). *Foundations of psychiatric mental health nursing: A clinical approach* (5th ed.). St. Louis, MO: Saunders.

Additional Resources:

Basco, W. T. (2006). Teens at risk: A focus on adolescent suicide. *Medscape Today*, Article 540353. Retrieved November 30, 2006, from http://www.medscape.com/viewarticle/540353

Conwell, Y., Cholette, J., & Duberstein, P. R. (1998). Suicide and schizophrenia: Identifying risk factors and preventive strategies. *Medscape Today*, Article 430625. Retrieved November 30, 2006 from http://www.medscape.com/viewarticle/430625

Knesper, D. J. (2003). *Guide to suicide assessment*. Retrieved December 1, 2006, from University of Michigan Depression Center Web site: http://www.med.umich.edu/depression/suicide_assessment/suicide_info.htm

NANDA International (2004). *NANDA nursing diagnoses: Definitions and classification 2005-2006*. Philadelphia: NANDA.

Stuart, G. W., & Laraia, M. T. (2005). *Principles and practice of psychiatric nursing* (8th ed.). St. Louis, MO: Mosby.

Townsend, M. C. (2006). *Psychiatric mental health nursing: Concepts of care in evidence-based practice* (5th ed.). Philadelphia: F.A. Davis.

Videbeck, S. L. (2006). *Psychiatric mental health nursing* (3rd ed.). Philadelphia: Lippincott Williams & Wilkins.

Chapter 31: Suicide

Application Exercises

Scenario: A nurse is working with a 22-year-old single male client, committed involuntarily 1 week ago to an acute care mental health facility. He has been diagnosed with bipolar disorder and a history of alcohol abuse. The client ran away from home as a teenager and has been living on city streets ever since. He states he was raised Roman Catholic and is still very religious. At the time of admission, he had been found intoxicated and ranting about being kidnapped by space creatures. He has a history of one previous suicide attempt by hanging.

1. Describe the client's risk factors, as well as any protective factors.

2. The nurse and the client are standing near a window on the sixth floor of the mental health facility. The client is quite lucid with no sign of psychosis today. He remarks, "I wonder if anyone has ever jumped from up here." How should the nurse reply?

3. The client replies that he would like to talk to the nurse about what he's been thinking and planning, but he says, "I'll talk to you, but please, please don't tell anyone else what I am going to tell you now! Will you promise me?" What should the nurse say and do now?

4. The client describes a suicide plan that he wanted to carry out while in the mental health facility so that he would be found by people who cared about him. He is immediately placed on suicide precautions. What should suicide precautions involve for this client?

5. A nurse assesses a client at a community mental health facility using the SAD PERSONS tool. This tool provides data related to a client's

    A. current anxiety level.

    B. problem-solving ability.

    C. suicide potential.

    D. mood disturbance.

6. A client who previously made a suicide plan develops a no-suicide contract with the nurse. The most appropriate wording for this written contract is,

    A. "I will not make a suicide attempt for the next week."

    B. "I will not kill myself until I call you."

    C. "I will not harm myself during the next 24 hr."

    D. "During the next 24 hr I will not, for any reason, accidentally or on purpose, try to kill myself."

7. A client states she has a plan to commit suicide. The priority assessment at this time is the

    A. client's educational and economic background.

    B. lethality of method and availability of means.

    C. quality of the client's social support.

    D. client's insight into the reasons for her decision.

Chapter 31: Suicide

Application Exercises Answer Key

Scenario: A nurse is working with a 22-year-old single male client, committed involuntarily 1 week ago to an acute care mental health facility. He has been diagnosed with bipolar disorder and a history of alcohol abuse. The client ran away from home as a teenager and has been living on city streets ever since. He states he was raised Roman Catholic and is still very religious. At the time of admission, he had been found intoxicated and ranting about being kidnapped by space creatures. He has a history of one previous suicide attempt by hanging.

1. Describe the client's risk factors, as well as any protective factors.

   Risk factors:

   > **Single, young adult male**
   > **History of bipolar disorder and recent substance abuse**
   > **Disturbed thought processes on admission**
   > **Previous suicide attempts using a lethal method**
   > **No family support system**

   Protective factors:

   > **Religious background**

2. The nurse and the client are standing near a window on the sixth floor of the mental health facility. The client is quite lucid with no sign of psychosis today. He remarks, "I wonder if anyone has ever jumped from up here." How should the nurse reply?

   The nurse should assess the client's suicidal ideation with a question such as, "Why do you ask? Are you thinking about suicide yourself?" If the answer is negative, the nurse should rephrase the question and ask it again.

3. The client replies that he would like to talk to the nurse about what he's been thinking and planning, but he says, "I'll talk to you, but please, please don't tell anyone else what I am going to tell you now! Will you promise me?" What should the nurse say and do now?

   The nurse should tell the client that she cannot keep a secret that is related to his safety and welfare. She is required to talk to the health care team about something so important. She should make it clear that she cares what happens to him and invite him to sit down and talk with her anyway.

4. The client describes a suicide plan that he wanted to carry out while in the mental health facility so that he would be found by people who cared about him. He is immediately placed on suicide precautions. What should suicide precautions involve for this client?

The client not only has suicidal ideation, but he also has a plan for carrying out the suicide. The client should be on one-to-one supervision by a staff member at all times. The milieu of the acute care mental health facility should already be free of most potentially harmful objects, but the nurse should make sure that this client's immediate environment is checked for possible harmful objects (e.g., shoe laces, belt, plastic bags). Collaboration with the client's treatment team is vital to make sure a specific plan is in place to keep this client safe.

5. A nurse assesses a client at a community mental health facility using the SAD PERSONS tool. This tool provides data related to a client's

        A. current anxiety level.

        B. problem-solving ability.

        C. suicide potential.

        D. mood disturbance.

The SAD PERSONS tool is used specifically to assess the client's potential for committing suicide. Information on the other options is not provided by this tool.

6. A client who previously made a suicide plan develops a no-suicide contract with the nurse. The most appropriate wording for this written contract is,

        A. "I will not make a suicide attempt for the next week."

        B. "I will not kill myself until I call you."

        C. "I will not harm myself during the next 24 hr."

        D. "During the next 24 hr I will not, for any reason, accidentally or on purpose, try to kill myself."

The correct option (D) is complete and leaves no loopholes. In option A, the client might be able to say, "I am not going to attempt suicide, I am actually going to kill myself." Option B leaves the loophole that the client could call the nurse and then commit suicide. Option C is too vague.

7. A client states she has a plan to commit suicide. The priority assessment at this time is the

    A. client's educational and economic background.

    B. lethality of method and availability of means.

    C. quality of the client's social support.

    D. client's insight into the reasons for her decision.

It is important to assess more about the plan: Will the method allow the client to die with little chance of intervention, and how available is that method to the client? The other areas of assessment are less important, especially after a plan has been made and the client's imminent safety is at stake.

Unit 4   Psychobiologic Disorders, Psychiatric Emergencies, and Mental Health Nursing Care of Special Populations

Section: Psychiatric Emergencies

Chapter 32:   Anger Management
Contributor: Susan Dawson, EdD, RN, APRN-BC

 NCLEX-RN® Connections:

Learning Objective: Review and apply knowledge within "**Anger Management**" in readiness for performance of the following nursing activities as outlined by the NCLEX-RN® test plan:

Δ   Assess the client's potential for causing injury to self and others.

Δ   Plan and provide care to protect the client and others from injury.

Δ   Assist the client to cope by using crisis intervention techniques.

Δ   Place limits on the client's inappropriate behavior and support the client's efforts to explore options to cope with anger.

Δ   Teach the client management strategies to cope with anger.

Δ   Evaluate and document the client's response to anger management techniques.

 Key Points

Δ   **Anger**, a normal feeling, is an emotional response to frustration of desires or needs as perceived by the individual. It can be positive if there is truly an unfair or wrong situation that needs to be righted.

Δ   Anger becomes negative when it is denied, suppressed, or expressed inappropriately, such as by using aggressive behavior.

• Denied or suppressed anger can manifest as physical or psychologic symptoms, such as headaches, coronary artery disease, hypertension, gastric ulcers, depression, or low self-esteem.

• Inappropriately expressed anger can become hostility or aggression.

Δ **Aggression**

- Aggression includes physical or verbal responses that indicate rage and potential harm to self, others, or property.

- Aimed at things like a punching bag, aggression can be cathartic and release the anger. But it also can increase anger.

- Aimed at people (e.g., yelling, hitting), aggression can be sudden and can escalate.

Δ A client who is often angry and aggressive may have underlying feelings of inadequacy, insecurity, guilt, fear, and rejection.

Key Factors

Δ Factors Influencing the Expression of Anger and Aggression

- **Impulsivity** (i.e., actions carried out with little or no consideration for consequences) can cause a client to move from anger to aggressive or violent behavior without warning.

- The client with paranoid delusions may imagine that he is being stalked or attacked and react with hostility or aggression.

- Auditory hallucinations can command the client to commit acts of hostility or aggression.

- Dementia, delirium, head injury, drugs and alcohol, and antisocial and borderline personality disorders all can cause violent anger reactions.

- Depression can trigger anger attacks that are very intense.

- Intermittent explosive disorder is a rare disorder that causes aggressive behavior without any cause or trigger, and clients having this disorder may feel useless or ineffective.

- Acting out is an aggressive behavior that is an immature defense mechanism characterized by an inability to handle feelings and emotions.

Δ The client who is aggressive is often impulsive and unable to control those impulses. Criteria characterizing impulse-control disorders include:

- An inability to control an impulse that could be harmful, such as the impulse to throw a lunch tray at another client.

- A buildup of feelings of tension or pressure before acting on the impulse.

- Some sense of excitement and release of tension when actually acting on the impulse.

- Clients who frequently act on impulses may have a degree of remorse about their behavior, but they are quickly able to rationalize it. For example, the client who threw her lunch tray may say, "I'm sorry I hurt him, but he actually deserved it!"

Δ The stages of anger and aggressive behavior on a mental health unit are:

- Preassaultive – The client begins to become angry.

- Assaultive – Seclusion and physical restraints may be required for the client.

- Postassaultive – Staff reviews the incident with the client during this stage.

Δ Intervention during the preassaultive stage is important to prevent more aggressive behaviors and possible harm to clients and/or staff.

Δ The interaction style of staff members can affect the number and intensity of outbursts by the client. Staff behaviors that increase client frustration, such as disputes over food or privileges, can lead to escalating behaviors in some clients.

Δ Despite the potential for anger and aggression among individuals with mental illness, it is important to know that individuals who are mentally ill are more likely to hurt themselves than to express aggression against others.

Δ Due to cultural preoccupations with violence and representations of violence among individuals with mental illness (e.g., in the media), many people have exaggerated fears of people with mental illness.

Assessment

Δ Assess the client for the likelihood of **aggressive** and **violent** behavior.

- Males in their late teens to early 20s with limited education (more likely to be violent)

- Clients with a history of aggressiveness, violence, and poor impulse control

- Clients with a DSM-IV-TR diagnosis of antisocial personality disorder, psychotic illness (e.g., paranoid schizophrenia), schizoaffective disorder, and/or substance abuse

- Clients with a history of traumatic brain injury or other CNS dysfunction

- Clients who live in a violent environment (or with other social or environmental factors)

Δ Assess the client population or milieu frequently to identify escalating behaviors in the earliest possible stage. Clues to beginning of aggressive behavior include:

- Facial expression, such as frowning or grimacing.

- Body language, such as clenching fists, waving arms.

- Rapid breathing.

- Aggressive postures, such as leaning forward, appearing tense.

- Verbal clues, such as loud, rapid talking.

Δ Self-assessment of feelings is important for staff members who deal frequently with clients who are angry and aggressive.

NANDA Nursing Diagnoses

Δ   Decisional conflict

Δ   Ineffective coping

Δ   Readiness for enhanced family processes

Δ   Risk for other- or self-directed violence

Nursing Interventions

Δ   Steps to handle aggressive and/or escalating behavior in a mental health setting include:

- **Remain calm and in control**.

- Encourage the client to express feelings verbally, using therapeutic communication techniques (e.g., reflective techniques, silence, active listening).

- Attempt to move the client to a quiet area or move others away from the client.

- **Set limits** for the client by:

  ◊   Telling the client calmly and matter-of-factly what he must do in the situation, such as, "I need you to stop yelling and walk with me to the day room where we can talk."

  ◊   Using physical activity, such as walking, to de-escalate anger and behaviors.

  ◊   Informing the client of the consequences of his behavior, such as loss of privileges.

- If the client does not respond to calm limit setting, medications should be offered.

- Four to six staff members should remain in sight of the client as a "show of force."

- If the client cannot control himself, tell the client that the staff will have to control him.

Δ   For the safety of those present, physical aggression must be handled according to the policies of the mental health setting.

Δ   **Seclusion** and **restraint** must be used only according to legal guidelines and should be the interventions of last resort after other less restrictive options have been tried.

- Seclusion and restraint do not usually lead to positive behavior change. Seclusion and restraint may keep individuals safe during a violet outburst, but use of restraint, itself, can be dangerous and has, on rare occasions, led to death of clients due to suffocation, strangulation, and other problems.

- Intramuscular medication may need to be given if aggression is threatening and if no medications were previously given.

- Remove the client from seclusion or restraint as soon as the crisis ends and when the client attempts reconciliation and is no longer aggressive.

Δ   Pharmacologic Interventions

- Sedative and hypnotic medications, such as benzodiazepines

- Antidepressants, such as SSRIs

- Antipsychotics, such as the typical antipsychotic medication haloperidol (Haldol)

- Mood stabilizers, such as lithium

- Anticonvulsants, such as carbamazepine (Tegretol)

- Beta blockers, such as propanolol (Inderal)

Δ   Following an aggressive/violent episode:

- Discuss ways for the client to keep control during the aggression cycle.

- Encourage the client to talk about the incident and what triggered and escalated the aggression from the client's perspective.

- Debrief the staff to evaluate the effectiveness of actions.

- Document the entire incident completely by including:

    ◊   Behaviors leading up to and those seen throughout the critical incident.

    ◊   Nursing interventions used and the client's response.

    ◊   Evaluation of the interventions used.

Δ   Preventive Measures

- Behavior therapy includes use of tokens for acceptable behaviors and the loss of tokens or privileges for unacceptable behaviors.

- Cognitive-behavioral therapy – Anger management classes are one type of cognitive training where the client learns to identify triggers for his own anger and new ways to cope with that anger.

- Group therapy can be helpful so that the client can receive feedback from his peers.

- Family therapy may be useful when violent behavior occurs within the family structure.

Primary Reference:

Varcarolis, E. M., Carson, V. B., & Shoemaker, N. C. (2006). *Foundations of psychiatric mental health nursing: A clinical approach* (5th ed.). St. Louis, MO: Saunders.

Additional Resources:

Masand, P. S., & Nemec, C. (2002, September 11). Aggression management: Childhood to old age. *Medscape Today*, Program 2013. Retrieved December 2, 2006, from http://www.medscape.com/viewprogram/2013

Mohr, W. K. (2002). *Johnson's psychiatric-mental health nursing: Adaptation and growth* (5th ed.). Newark, NJ: Lippincott Williams and Wilkins.

NANDA International (2004). *NANDA nursing diagnoses: Definitions and classification 2005-2006*. Philadelphia: NANDA.

Videbeck, S. L. (2006). *Psychiatric mental health nursing* (3rd ed.). Philadelphia: Lippincott Williams & Wilkins.

Chapter 32: Anger Management

Application Exercises

1. Which of the following statements made by a client is an example of aggressive communication?

        A. "I wish you would not make me angry."

        B. "I feel angry when you leave me."

        C. "It makes me angry when you interrupt me."

        D. "You'd better listen to me."

2. Which of the following is true about anger?

        A. Suppressing anger is a sign of maturity.

        B. Anger is a negative feeling.

        C. Anger can result from hurt feelings or frustration.

        D. Anger always leads to arguments.

3. In approaching a client who is speaking in a loud voice with clenched fists, the nurse should remember that

        A. clients who verbalize their anger will not act on it.

        B. the staff should be made aware of the situation as the nurse intervenes.

        C. there needs to be six staff members present if the client is delusional.

        D. verbally aggressive clients will calm down on their own if they are left alone.

4. Providing safe care for a client who is acting out includes

        A. moving others away from the client.

        B. getting medication ready to inject.

        C. avoiding talking to the client.

        D. keeping the client in a seclusion room.

5. Which of the following nursing actions is most appropriate after an episode of explosive anger during which a client throws a chair and is moved to a quiet room with a staff member for an hour?

        A. Move the client to another unit.

        B. Increase the dose of sedative medication for the client.

        C. Determine a punishment for the client.

        D. Evaluate the incident with both the client and staff.

6. True or False: Anger management training is an example of using cognitive techniques to change unacceptable behavior.

7. True or False: The most effective nursing intervention for a client who is pacing, shaking her fists, and looking angry is to administer a prescribed sedative medication.

Chapter 32: Anger Management

Application Exercises Answer Key

1. Which of the following statements made by a client is an example of aggressive communication?

> A. "I wish you would not make me angry."
>
> B. "I feel angry when you leave me."
>
> C. "It makes me angry when you interrupt me."
>
> **D. "You'd better listen to me."**

Using the words, "You'd better...," implies a threat (that something bad will happen if the person does not listen) and a lack of respect for the other individual. The other options do not imply a threat to another individual.

2. Which of the following is true about anger?

> A. Suppressing anger is a sign of maturity.
>
> B. Anger is a negative feeling.
>
> **C. Anger can result from hurt feelings or frustration.**
>
> D. Anger always leads to arguments.

Anger can result from hurt feelings or can be caused by frustration in the nondelusional client. Anger becomes negative and can cause somatic symptoms, such as headache, when it is suppressed. A mature individual will discuss his anger or work it out in some way. Anger, itself, is a normal emotion and is not negative. Anger does not always lead to arguments if it is used in a mature way to change a frustrating situation.

3. In approaching a client who is speaking in a loud voice with clenched fists, the nurse should remember that

> A. clients who verbalize their anger will not act on it.
>
> **B. the staff should be made aware of the situation as the nurse intervenes.**
>
> C. there needs to be six staff members present if the client is delusional.
>
> D. verbally aggressive clients will calm down on their own if they are left alone.

Before the nurse intervenes, he should alert staff that there is the possibility of a safety issue. Verbalizing anger is no guarantee that the individual will not act on his anger, especially if he has a history of or is at risk for anger and aggressive behavior. A "show of force" with several staff members can be helpful to defuse anger, but there is no need to assemble a group until the nurse assesses that a threat exists. Aggressive clients with mental illness may continue escalating behaviors if left alone.

4. Providing safe care for a client who is acting out includes

    A. moving others away from the client.

    B. getting medication ready to inject.

    C. avoiding talking to the client.

    D. keeping the client in a seclusion room.

Other clients should be moved to a safe place when one client is angry and aggressive. Preparing medication to inject is very premature and may not be needed. It is vital to talk to the client and try to defuse the situation. Keeping the client in a seclusion room may be seen as punitive and should only be used if less restrictive means do not work.

5. Which of the following nursing actions is most appropriate after an episode of explosive anger during which a client throws a chair and is moved to a quiet room with a staff member for an hour?

    A. Move the client to another unit.

    B. Increase the dose of sedative medication for the client.

    C. Determine a punishment for the client.

    D. Evaluate the incident with both the client and staff.

An evaluation of the critical incident is important for both the staff and the client in order to discuss how interventions worked and how such an incident can be avoided in the future. Moving the client to another unit could be indicated in some situations but would generally not resolve the underlying problem. Increasing medication dosages is also not a good solution for dealing with the problem. The client may have to deal with consequences for his behavior, but punishment is inappropriate.

6. True or False: Anger management training is an example of using cognitive techniques to change unacceptable behavior.

True: Cognitive-behavioral therapy helps clients identify unacceptable behavior (anger and aggression) and learn acceptable ways to cope with anger and frustration.

7. True or False: The most effective nursing intervention for a client who is pacing, shaking her fists, and looking angry is to administer a prescribed sedative medication.

False: The best intervention, especially at the early stage of anger and aggression, is to talk with the client, discover what is bothering her, and help her to cope with the problem.

Unit 4   Psychobiologic Disorders, Psychiatric Emergencies, and Mental Health Nursing Care of
                Special Populations
Section: Psychiatric Emergencies

Chapter 33:   Family and Community Violence
                Contributors: Susan Dawson, EdD, RN, APRN-BC
                              Anne W. Ryan, MSN, MPH, RN-BC

 NCLEX-RN® Connections:

> **Learning Objective**: Review and apply knowledge within **"Family and Community
> Violence"** in readiness for performance of the following nursing activities as outlined by
> the NCLEX-RN® test plan:
>
> Δ Assess the client's risk for injury from violence, including violence within the
>   family and community violence, and intervene appropriately.
>
> Δ Plan and provide care to protect the client and others from injury due to
>   violence.
>
> Δ Assist the client to cope by using crisis intervention techniques.
>
> Δ Support the client's efforts to explore options to cope with violence.
>
> Δ Support victims/suspected victims of abuse and their families with coping
>   strategies to prevent abuse or neglect.
>
> Δ Teach the client management strategies to cope with violence, including abuse
>   and neglect.
>
> Δ Evaluate and document the client's response to interventions to control violence.
>
> Δ Follow facility policy for reporting client abuse, neglect, and injury.
>
> Δ Identify the client's risk of being abused or neglected and intervene
>   appropriately.
>
> Δ Plan and provide a safe environment, physical care, and emotional care for
>   clients who have been victims of violence.

Key Points

Δ   **Violence** from one person toward another is a social act involving a serious abuse of power. Usually, a relatively stronger person controls or injures another, typically the least powerful person accessible to the abuser.

Δ   The nurse must be prepared to deal with various types of violence and the mental health consequences.

 •   Violence may be caused by a family member, a stranger, or an acquaintance, or it can come from a human-made mass-casualty incident, such as a terrorist attack.

 •   Natural disasters, such as hurricanes and earthquakes, can cause mental health effects comparable to those caused by human-made violence.

Δ   Current research shows that individuals with a major mental illness are 2.5 times more likely to be victims of violence than those who have no mental illness.

 •   Violence against a person with mental illness is more likely to occur when factors such as poverty, transient lifestyle, and substance abuse are present.

 •   Despite the fears of the public, a person with mental illness is no more likely to harm strangers than is anyone else.

 •   The factor most likely to cause violence between strangers is a past history of violence and criminal activity.

Δ   **Violence is most common within family groups**, and most violence is aimed at family and friends rather than strangers.

 •   Family violence occurs across all economic and educational backgrounds and racial/ethic groups in the United States and is often termed "maltreatment."

 •   Family violence/maltreatment can occur against children, domestic partners, or older adult family members.

Δ   Violence is made up of several specific types of behaviors:

 •   **Physical violence**, which causes pain or harm.

   ◊   Toward an infant or child, as is the case with shaken baby syndrome (caused by violent shaking of young infants)

   ◊   Toward a domestic partner, such as striking or strangling the partner

   ◊   Toward an older adult in the home (elder abuse), such as pushing an older adult parent and causing her to fall

 •   **Sexual violence**, which is any situation in which the victim does not give consent or is incapable of giving consent. (*Refer to chapter 34, Sexual Assault.*)

- **Emotional violence**, which includes behavior that minimizes an individual's feelings of self-worth or humiliates, threatens, or intimidates a family member, such as repeated angry and belittling verbal comments.

- **Neglect**, which includes the failure to provide:

  ◊ Physical care, such as feeding.

  ◊ The emotional care and/or stimulation necessary for a child to develop normally, such as speaking and interacting with a child.

  ◊ An education for a child, such as enrolling a young child in school.

- **Economic violence**, which includes depriving family members of resources or support.

Δ All states have mandatory reporting laws that require nurses to report suspected abuse; there are civil and criminal penalties for NOT reporting suspicions of abuse.

Key Factors

Δ Family violence creates a crisis situation within the home.

Δ While the victim in the majority of family violence is the female partner, surveys have indicated that the male partner may be the victim 30 to 40% of the time.

Δ Within the family, a cycle of violence can occur between domestic (intimate) partners:

- Tension-building phase – The abuser has minor episodes of anger and may be verbally abusive and responsible for some minor physical violence. The victim is tense during this stage and tends to accept the blame for what is happening.

- Serious battering phase – The tension becomes too much to bear and a serious incident takes place. The victim may try to cover up the injury or may get help.

- Honeymoon phase – The situation is defused for awhile after the violent episode. The abuser becomes loving, promises to change, and is sorry for the behavior. The victim wants to believe this and hopes for a change. Eventually, the cycle begins again.

Δ Victims are at the greatest risk for violence when they try to leave the relationship.

Δ Pregnancy tends to increase the likelihood of violence toward the domestic partner. Up to 20% of pregnant women may have been abused by their partner. The reason for this is unclear.

Δ Factors that make **abuse against children** more likely include:

- The child is under 3 years of age.

- The child is perceived by the perpetrator as being different (e.g., the child is the result of an unwanted pregnancy, is physically disabled, or has some other trait that makes him particularly vulnerable).

Δ Older adults within the home may be abused because they are in poor health or because they have disruptive behavior (e.g., dementia) and because they are dependent on a caregiver. The potential for violence against an older adult is highest in families where violence has already occurred.

Δ **Victim Characteristics**

- Demonstrates low self-esteem and feelings of helplessness, hopelessness, powerlessness, guilt, and shame

- May attempt to protect the perpetrator and accept responsibility for the abuse

- May deny the severity of the situation and feelings of anger and terror

Δ **Perpetrator Characteristics**

- May use threats and intimidation to control the victim

- Is usually an extreme disciplinarian who believes in physical punishment

- May have a history of substance abuse problems

- Is likely to have experienced family violence as a child

Assessment

Δ Cultural differences can influence whether or not the nursing assessment data is valid, how the client responds to interventions, and the appropriateness of nursing interactions with the client.

Δ Screening Assessment Tools – Multiple tools are available for health professionals, such as the Woman Abuse Screening Tool (WAST) developed in England. This tool consists of seven questions that begin generally and end with questions regarding whether or not the woman has ever been abused physically or emotionally by her partner.

Δ Many professional groups believe that all women who come into contact with the health care system should be screened for domestic partner abuse.

Δ **Nursing History**

- Conduct interviews about family abuse in private.

- Be direct, honest, and professional.

- Use language the client understands.

- Be understanding and attentive.

- Inform the client if a referral must be made to children's or adult protective services and explain the process.

- Assess safety and help reduce danger for the victim.

- Questions that are open-ended and require descriptive responses can be less threatening and elicit more relevant information.

Δ **Physical Assessment**

- **Infants**

  ◊ Shaken baby syndrome – Shaking may cause intracranial hemorrhage. Assess for respiratory distress, bulging fontanelles, and increased head circumference. Retinal hemorrhage may be present.

  ◊ Any bruising on an infant before age 6 months is suspicious.

- **Preschoolers to adolescents**

  ◊ Assess for unusual bruising, such as on abdomen, back, or buttocks. Bruising is common on arms and legs in these age groups.

  ◊ Assess the mechanism of injury, which may not be congruent with the physical appearance of the injury. Numerous bruises at different stages of healing may indicate continued beatings. Be suspicious of bruises or welts that have taken on the shape of a belt buckle or other object.

  ◊ Assess for burns. Burns covering "glove" or "stocking" areas of the hands or feet may indicate forced immersion into boiling water. Small, round burns may be caused by lit cigarettes.

  ◊ Assess for fractures with unusual features, such as forearm spiral fractures, which could be caused by twisting the extremity forcefully. The presence of multiple fractures is suspicious.

  ◊ Assess for human bite marks.

  ◊ Assess for head injuries – level of consciousness, equal and reactive pupils, nausea/vomiting.

- **Older adults**

  ◊ Assess for any bruises, lacerations, abrasions, or fractures in which the physical appearance does not match the history or mechanism of injury.

NANDA Nursing Diagnoses

Δ Ineffective coping

Δ Dysfunctional family processes: Alcoholism

Δ Interrupted family processes

Δ Helplessness

Δ   Impaired parenting

Δ   Powerlessness

Δ   Situational low self-esteem

Δ   Risk for self- or other-directed violence

Δ   Risk for suicide

Nursing Interventions

Δ   Nursing care for those experiencing violence must be culturally sensitive. Even the most acculturated people have a tendency to revert to their cultural past in organizing coping strategies after a stressful event.

Δ   Counseling is an important nursing intervention for all types of violent incidents. It should emphasize that persons have a right to live without fear of violence or physical harm.

Δ   Case management is needed to coordinate community, medical, criminal justice, and social services to provide comprehensive assistance to families experiencing violence.

Δ   Crisis intervention techniques may be useful in resolving family or community situations where violence has been devastating. (*Refer to chapter 30, Crisis Management.*)

Δ   Mental health therapies include:

Individual psychotherapy	• Use for family violence, stranger violence situations, or for mass casualty community violence. • Use for depression, posttraumatic stress, anxiety, and feelings of guilt.
Family therapy	• This may be useful if the violent episode was recent and if both partners agree to take part. • The perpetrator must first take steps to control violence, such as learning anger management strategies.
Group therapy	• Therapy groups or self-help groups (e.g., survivor support groups, empowerment groups, Al-Anon, Alcoholics Anonymous)

Δ   Nursing interventions for **child** or **elder abuse** include:

•   **Nurses have a legal responsibility and are mandated to report suspected or actual cases of child or elder abuse.**

•   Complete, objective documentation of what the nurse saw and information obtained in the interview must be made.

Δ   Nursing interventions for **domestic partner violence** include:

- Making a safety plan for fast escape when violence occurs; this is important for victims who are not yet ready to leave the perpetrator.

- Teaching empowerment skills to the client.

- Teaching the client to recognize behaviors and situations that might trigger violence.

Δ   Nursing interventions for **family violence** include:

- Stabilizing the home situation.

- Maintaining an environment without violence and a higher quality of life for all family members.

- Empowering the vulnerable members and promoting the growth and development of all family members.

- Teaching and promoting normal growth and development.

- Teaching strategies to manage stress.

Δ   Nursing interventions for **community-wide** or **mass casualty incidents** include:

- **Early intervention**.

  ◊   Provide psychological first aid, which includes:

    °   Making sure the clients are physically and psychologically safe from harm.

    °   Reducing stress-related symptoms (e.g., using techniques to alleviate a panic attack).

    °   Providing interventions to restore rest/sleep and provide links to social supports and information about critical resources.

  ◊   Depending on their level of expertise and training, mental health nurses may provide assessment, consultation, therapeutic communication and support, triage, and psychological/physical care.

- **Critical incident stress debriefing**

  ◊   This is a strategy of crisis intervention used to assist individuals who have experienced a traumatic event, usually involving violence (e.g., staff experiencing client violence, school children and personnel experiencing the violent death of a student, rescue workers after an earthquake), to express thoughts and feelings in a safe environment.

  ◊   Debriefing may take place in group meetings with a facilitator.

  ◊   The facilitator provides the guidelines for the process, assures confidentiality, and answers any questions from the participants.

◊ The participants will then have the opportunity to share facts, perceptions, thoughts, feelings, and symptoms experienced during the event.

◊ Work of the facilitator then includes: acknowledging reactions, providing anticipatory guidance for symptoms that may still occur, giving instruction in stress management, and providing referrals.

◊ The group may choose to meet on an ongoing basis or disband after resolution of the crisis.

Primary Reference:

Varcarolis, E. M., Carson, V. B., & Shoemaker, N. C. (2006). *Foundations of psychiatric mental health nursing: A clinical approach* (5th ed.). St. Louis, MO: Saunders.

Additional Resources:

American Academy of Pediatrics. (2006, October). Pediatric mental health emergencies in the emergency medical services system. *PEDIATRICS, 118* (4), 1764-1767. Retrieved December 8, 2006, from http://aappolicy.aappublications.org/cgi/reprint/pediatrics;118/4/1764?eaf

Canadian Mental Health Association. (n.d.). *Violence and mental health.* Retrieved December 7, 2006, from http://www.cmha.ca/bins/content_page.asp?cid=3-108

Kimberg, L. (2001, February 12). Addressing intimate partner violence in primary care practice. *Medscape Today*, Article 408937. Retrieved December 2, 2006, from http://www.medscape.com/viewarticle/408937

NANDA International (2004). *NANDA nursing diagnoses: Definitions and classification 2005-2006.* Philadelphia: NANDA.

National Institute of Mental Health. (2002). *Mental health and mass violence: Evidence-based early psychological intervention for victims/survivors of mass violence. A workshop to reach consensus on best practices* (NIH Publication No. 02-5138). Washington, DC: U.S. Government Printing Office. Retrieved December 27, 2006, from http://www.nimh.nih.gov/publicat/massviolence.pdf

Ristock, J. L. (1995). *The impact of violence on mental health: A guide to the literature.* Public Health Agency of Canada. Retrieved December 7, 2006, from http://www.phac-aspc.gc.ca/ncfv-cnivf/familyviolence/html/fvdiscussion_e.html

The Society of Obstetricians and Gynaecologists of Canada. (2006). *Domestic violence: Screening.* Retrieved December 14, 2006, from http://masexualite.ca/professionals/domestic-violence-4.aspx

Chapter 33: Family and Community Violence

Application Exercises

Scenario: A nurse is visiting the home of a female client who is in the intermediate stage of Alzheimer's disease. The caregiver is the client's 35-year-old daughter, who also has three school-age children and a husband who travels most of each week. During the assessment, the nurse finds bruising in the shape and size of handprints scattered throughout the client's torso. When questioned, the caregiver states that the client was striking out at her and needed to be "quieted." The client is sleeping quietly, and the daughter states that she frequently needs to give her mother the anxiolytic medication diazepam (Valium) to keep her calm.

1. What factors regarding the client and the home situation should alert the nurse to the possibility of abuse?

2. If the nurse is not sure that abuse has taken place, should she wait until another visit to gather more evidence before reporting her suspicions to adult protective services?

3. What is the nurse's responsibility in this situation and how should it be handled?

4. The nurse interviews the client's caregiver with the goal of gathering assessment data. Which of the following would most likely create a block between the nurse and the caregiver?

    A. "Caring for your mother and three children must be difficult."

    B. "Did you actually hit your mother with your hands?"

    C. "Tell me how your mother got bruised."

    D. "What is your mother's behavior like most of the time?"

5. An 8-year-old child has not been attending school, and a community nurse makes a home visit to find out why. The child has been staying home to care for a preschool sibling while the parents, ages 25 and 26, work outside the home. The mother tells the nurse that she got married 7 years ago when she became unexpectedly pregnant with her oldest child. Which of the following factors in the child's life makes her vulnerable to abuse?

    A. She is the oldest sibling.

    B. She is female.

    C. Both parents work outside the home.

    D. Her birth was unplanned.

6. True or False: Having a major mental illness is one of the most common factors that makes an individual likely to behave violently toward a stranger.

7. True or False: A nurse who feels empathy toward a family where violence has occurred is more likely to be objective and therapeutic than a nurse who feels shock and anger about the situation.

Chapter 33: Family and Community Violence

Application Exercises Answer Key

Scenario: A nurse is visiting the home of a female client who is in the intermediate stage of Alzheimer's disease. The caregiver is the client's 35-year-old daughter, who also has three school-age children and a husband who travels most of each week. During the assessment, the nurse finds bruising in the shape and size of handprints scattered throughout the client's torso. When questioned, the caregiver states that the client was striking out at her and needed to be "quieted." The client is sleeping quietly, and the daughter states that she frequently needs to give her mother the anxiolytic medication diazepam (Valium) to keep her calm.

1. What factors regarding the client and the home situation should alert the nurse to the possibility of abuse?

   Client factors: There are bruises in the shape of hand prints and the possibility that diazepam (Valium) may be used "to keep her calm" more often than necessary. The client has Alzheimer's disease and is in the intermediate stage, which means she is quite confused and vulnerable.

   Caregiver factors: Caregiver role strain may be present, since the caregiver is also caring for three school-age children. She may lack support systems, since the husband is away during the week and she seems to be the only caregiver. More information is needed to assess both client and caregiver factors thoroughly.

2. If the nurse is not sure that abuse has taken place, should she wait until another visit to gather more evidence before reporting her suspicions to adult protective services?

   No. As a professional, the nurse is liable and must report any suspicion of child or elder abuse.

3. What is the nurse's responsibility in this situation and how should it be handled?

   The nurse has the responsibility to contact adult protective services if she suspects any abuse has taken place. She must also make a decision about the client's safety regarding whether or not it is safe to keep the client in the home on the day of the visit. The nurse should thoroughly interview the caregiver, remaining calm, objective, understanding, and professional. Questions should be used that are open-ended and require a descriptive response so that they are less threatening and elicit more relevant information. The nurse should inform the daughter that a referral to adult protective services is necessary and explain the process. Documentation of the visit must be detailed, objective, and thorough.

4. The nurse interviews the client's caregiver with the goal of gathering assessment data. Which of the following would most likely create a block between the nurse and the caregiver?

    A. "Caring for your mother and three children must be difficult."

    B. "Did you actually hit your mother with your hands?"

    C. "Tell me how your mother got bruised."

    D. "What is your mother's behavior like most of the time?"

An interview with an individual who is possibly abusing an adult or a child should be based on concern and carried out in a nonthreatening, nonjudgmental way. Option B is judgmental, and it is likely the caregiver would refuse to answer it or other questions. The other options are open-ended, nonjudgmental questions that could be used to elicit important assessment information.

5. An 8-year-old child has not been attending school, and a community nurse makes a home visit to find out why. The child has been staying home to care for a preschool sibling while the parents, ages 25 and 26, work outside the home. The mother tells the nurse that she got married 7 years ago when she became unexpectedly pregnant with her oldest child. Which of the following factors in the child's life makes her vulnerable to abuse?

    A. She is the oldest sibling.

    B. She is female.

    C. Both parents work outside the home.

    D. Her birth was unplanned.

An unplanned pregnancy puts the child at risk for abuse. The other factors mentioned do not put her at risk for abuse.

6. True or False: Having a major mental illness is one of the most common factors that makes an individual likely to behave violently toward a stranger.

False: Mental illness plays no part in most of the violent crimes in society, and people with mental illness are no more likely than anyone else to harm strangers. Factors that favor violence toward strangers include a past history of violence and criminal intent.

7. True or False: A nurse who feels empathy toward a family where violence has occurred is more likely to be objective and therapeutic than a nurse who feels shock and anger about the situation.

True: The nurse who has strong negative feelings toward a situation where family violence is occurring may have great difficulty being objective and therapeutic.

Unit 4   Psychobiologic Disorders, Psychiatric Emergencies, and Mental Health Nursing Care of Special Populations

Section: Psychiatric Emergencies

Chapter 34:   Sexual Assault

Contributor: Anne W. Ryan, MSN, MPH, RN-BC

 NCLEX-RN® Connections:

> **Learning Objective**: Review and apply knowledge within "**Sexual Assault**" in readiness for performance of the following nursing activities as outlined by the NCLEX-RN® test plan:
>
> Δ   Assess the client's risk for injury from sexual assault.
>
> Δ   Plan and provide care to protect the client from injury caused by sexual assault.
>
> Δ   Assist the client to cope by using crisis intervention techniques.
>
> Δ   Teach the client management strategies to cope with sexual assault.
>
> Δ   Evaluate and document the client's response to interventions following sexual assault.

 Key Points

Δ   Sexual assault is defined as pressured or forced sexual contact, including sexually stimulated talk or actions, inappropriate touching or intercourse, incest, and rape (forced sexual intercourse).

Δ   Rape is a crime of violence, aggression, anger, and power.

Δ   There is no "typical" rape survivor. Victims include individuals of all ages (e.g., small children, adolescents, older adults) and can be either male or female.

Δ   The majority of rapists are known to the person who is raped.

Δ   Reports of "date" or "acquaintance" rape have increased in recent years, often with drugs and alcohol used to facilitate the sexual assault.

Δ   Most people who are raped suffer long-term and severe emotional trauma.

Δ   Rape-trauma syndrome, which is similar to posttraumatic stress disorder (*Refer to chapter 19, Anxiety Disorders.*), may occur after a rape.

Key Factors

Δ   **Rape-Trauma Syndrome**

- **Acute phase** – occurs immediately following the rape and lasts for about 2 weeks. It consists of:

  ◊   An initial emotional reaction – either expressed or controlled.

     °   An expressed reaction is overt and consists of emotional outbursts, including crying, laughing, hysteria, anger, and incoherence.

     °   A controlled reaction is ambiguous; the survivor may appear calm but may also be confused, have difficulty making decisions, and feel numb.

  ◊   A somatic reaction occurs later and lasts about 2 weeks. The client may have a variety of symptoms, including:

     °   Bruising and soreness from the attack.

     °   Muscle tension, headaches, and sleep disturbances.

     °   Gastrointestinal symptoms (e.g., nausea, anorexia, diarrhea, abdominal pain).

     °   Genitourinary symptoms (e.g., vaginal pain or discomfort).

     °   A variety of emotional reactions, including embarrassment, a desire for revenge, guilt, anger, fear, anxiety, and denial.

- **Long-term reorganization phase** – occurs 2 weeks or more after the attack. Long-term psychological effects of sexual assault include:

  ◊   Flashbacks and other intrusive thoughts about the assault.

  ◊   Increased activity – The survivor may perform activities, such as visiting friends frequently or moving her residence, due to a fear that the assault will recur.

  ◊   Increased emotional responses (e.g., crying, anxiety, rapid mood swings).

  ◊   Fears and phobias (e.g., fear of being alone, fear of sexual encounters).

  ◊   Difficulties with daily functioning, low self-esteem, depression, sexual dysfunction, and somatic reports, such as headache or fatigue.

- Other reactions to rape-trauma syndrome may include a reliance on alcohol or drugs or an inability to communicate any information about the rape experience.

Assessment

Δ   Perform a self-assessment. It is vital that the nurse who works with the client who has been sexually assaulted be empathetic, objective, and nonjudgmental. If the nurse feels emotional about the assault due to some event or person in her own past, it may be better to allow another nurse to work with the client.

Δ   Provide a private environment for an examination with a specially trained nurse-advocate, if available. A sexual assault nurse examiner (SANE) is a specially trained nurse who performs such examinations.

Δ   Assess for signs and symptoms of psychological trauma (e.g., blunt affect, suicidal thoughts).

Δ   Assess for signs and symptoms of physical trauma (e.g., injuries to the face, neck, head, arms, and legs).

Δ   Assess the client's:

   •   Level of anxiety.

   •   Coping mechanisms.

   •   Support systems, including both personal and community supports, such as an attorney.

Δ   Obtain blood for laboratory tests (HIV, hepatitis B and C).

Δ   Collect samples for legal evidence (e.g., samples of hair, skin, semen).

NANDA Nursing Diagnoses

Δ   Anxiety

Δ   Acute confusion

Δ   Ineffective coping

Δ   Fear

Δ   Powerlessness

Δ   Rape-trauma syndrome

Δ   Risk for self-directed violence

Δ   Disturbed sleep pattern

Nursing Interventions

Δ   Provide nonjudgmental and empathetic care.

Δ   Obtain informed consent to collect data that can be used as legal evidence (e.g., photos, pelvic exam). The rape victim has the right to refuse either a medical examination or a legal exam, which provides forensic evidence for the police.

Δ   Perform a rapid physical assessment of injuries.

Δ   Treat any injuries and document care given.

Δ   Assist the specialist with the physical examination and the collection, documentation, and preservation of forensic evidence.

Δ   Support the client while legal evidence is being collected (e.g., samples of hair, skin, semen).

Δ   Evaluate for and treat sexually transmitted diseases by following the Centers for Disease Control and Prevention guidelines for prophylactic treatment of syphilis, chlamydiosis, and gonorrhea.

Δ   Evaluate for pregnancy risk and provide for prevention.

Δ   Call the client's available personal support system, such as a partner or parents, if the client gives permission.

Δ   Assist the client during the acute phase of rape-trauma syndrome to prepare for thoughts, symptoms, and emotions that may occur during the long-term phase of the syndrome.

  •   Encourage the client to verbalize her story and her emotions.

  •   Listen and let the survivor talk; use therapeutic techniques of reflection, open-ended questions, and active listening.

Δ   Counseling begins in the emergency department and may continue with a referral from the primary care provider.

Δ   Ongoing care includes:

  •   Providing phone numbers for 24-hr hotlines for rape survivors.

  •   Promotion of self-care activities – Give follow-up instructions in writing, since the client may be unable to comprehend or remember verbal instructions.

  •   Referrals for needed resources and support services – Individual psychotherapy and group therapy may be helpful to increase coping skills and prevent long-term disability, such as depression, or suicidal ideation.

  •   Nursing case management – Schedule follow-up calls or visits at intervals after the assault.

Primary Reference:

Varcarolis, E. M., Carson, V. B., & Shoemaker, N. C. (2006). *Foundations of psychiatric mental health nursing: A clinical approach* (5th ed.). St. Louis, MO: Saunders.

Additional Resources:

NANDA International (2004). *NANDA nursing diagnoses: Definitions and classification 2005-2006*. Philadelphia: NANDA.

Townsend, M. C. (2006). *Psychiatric mental health nursing: Concepts of care in evidence-based practice* (5th ed.). Philadelphia: F.A. Davis.

Chapter 34: Sexual Assault

Application Exercises

1. A woman is brought to the emergency department by her roommate. The roommate says that she came home and found the client lying on the floor beaten and sexually assaulted. How should the nurse intervene with the client until the sexual assault nurse specialist arrives?

2. A rape victim states, "I never should have been out on the street alone at night." The most therapeutic response by the nurse is,

    A. "Your actions had nothing to do with what happened."

    B. "Blaming yourself only increases your anxiety and discomfort."

    C. "You believe this wouldn't have happened if you hadn't been out alone?"

    D. "You're right. You should not have been alone on the street at night."

3. A rape victim reports to the nurse that his family is not very supportive. Which of the following is a myth or belief about rape that might contribute to the family's response to the client?

    A. Rape is an act of aggression.

    B. No one asks to be raped.

    C. Men do not get raped.

    D. The majority of rapists are known to the victims.

4. A rape victim tells the emergency department nurse, "I feel so dirty. Please let me take a shower before anyone examines me. I just can't stand being so filthy!" The nurse should

    A. arrange for the client to shower.

    B. give the client a basin of hot water and towels.

    C. explain that washing would destroy evidence.

    D. explain that bathing facilities are not available in the emergency department.

5. Rape-trauma syndrome is comparable to

    A. a panic attack.

    B. disorganized schizophrenia.

    C. posttraumatic stress disorder.

    D. somatization disorder.

Chapter 34: Sexual Assault

Application Exercises Answer Key

1. A woman is brought to the emergency department by her roommate. The roommate says that she came home and found the client lying on the floor beaten and sexually assaulted. How should the nurse intervene with the client until the sexual assault nurse specialist arrives?

> **Be nonjudgmental.**
> **Assure the client that she is safe and that she did the right thing by coming to the emergency department.**
> **Provide privacy, but do not leave the client alone.**
> **Allow the roommate to stay, if the client wishes.**
> **Offer to call support persons.**
> **Do NOT allow her to shower or otherwise clean up, so that evidence is preserved.**
> **Follow department/facility protocol.**

2. A rape victim states, "I never should have been out on the street alone at night." The most therapeutic response by the nurse is,

> A. "Your actions had nothing to do with what happened."
>
> B. "Blaming yourself only increases your anxiety and discomfort."
>
> C. **"You believe this wouldn't have happened if you hadn't been out alone?"**
>
> D. "You're right. You should not have been alone on the street at night."

> **The nurse is using the therapeutic technique of reflection to help the client verbalize her feelings in option C. The other options give the nurse's opinion, and the nurse should remain nonjudgmental.**

3. A rape victim reports to the nurse that his family is not very supportive. Which of the following is a myth or belief about rape that might contribute to the family's response to the client?

> A. Rape is an act of aggression.
>
> B. No one asks to be raped.
>
> C. **Men do not get raped.**
>
> D. The majority of rapists are known to the victims.

> **A fairly common myth is the notion that men do not experience sexual assault. The other options are true statements about sexual assault.**

4. A rape victim tells the emergency department nurse, "I feel so dirty. Please let me take a shower before anyone examines me. I just can't stand being so filthy!" The nurse should

    A. arrange for the client to shower.

    B. give the client a basin of hot water and towels.

    C. explain that washing would destroy evidence.

    D. explain that bathing facilities are not available in the emergency department.

Until evidence is collected and a physical examination is completed, the sexual assault survivor should not bathe or change clothes.

5. Rape-trauma syndrome is comparable to

    A. a panic attack.

    B. disorganized schizophrenia.

    C. posttraumatic stress disorder.

    D. somatization disorder.

Rape-trauma syndrome is comparable to posttraumatic stress disorder (PTSD), in which a person experiences or witnesses a threatening, horrific event. In PTSD, the person experiences stages of signs/symptoms including flashbacks, insomnia, anxiety, and many others. The other options are unlike rape-trauma syndrome in that they are either short-lived (panic attack) or are not precipitated by a traumatic event and do not occur in stages (schizophrenia and somatization disorder).

Unit 4   Psychobiologic Disorders, Psychiatric Emergencies, and Mental Health Nursing Care of Special Populations

Section: Mental Health Nursing Care of Special Populations

Chapter 35:   Care of Those Who are Dying and/or Grieving

Contributors: Ann Schide, MSN, MS, RN, LCCE, BSC
Patti Simmons, MN, RN, CHPN

 NCLEX-RN® Connections:

> **Learning Objective**: Review and apply knowledge within "**Care of Those Who are Dying and/or Grieving**" in readiness for performance of the following nursing activities as outlined by the NCLEX-RN® test plan:
>
> Δ   Assess the client and family for their ability to cope with grief, loss, and end-of-life issues.
>
> Δ   Identify and provide for end-of-life needs of the client/family.
>
> Δ   Identify the need for and offer support to the family/caregiver.
>
> Δ   Plan and provide for the client/family to have resources, such as support groups, related to the loss or end of life.
>
> Δ   Instruct the client/family regarding normal feelings, sensations, and thoughts experienced by those experiencing grief and loss.
>
> Δ   Be responsive to the cultural practices of the client/family surrounding death and dying.
>
> Δ   Evaluate and document the effectiveness of end-of-life or grief interventions.

 Key Points

Δ   The nurse serves as an advocate for the client's sense of dignity and self-esteem.

Δ   **Palliative care** is a management approach for end-of-life issues that prevents, relieves, reduces, and/or eases the symptoms of the disease without compromising medical interventions.

•   Palliative care is provided not only for the dying client but also for the family and support network who are intimately involved with the client's life.

•   Palliative care provides for a "good death" that liberates the client from needless suffering, allows for preparation for life closure, and grants the client and family's wishes for end-of-life care.

Δ **Hospice** care is a comprehensive care delivery system for the terminally ill.

- Care is provided for the client as well as the client's family.

- Hospice care uses an interdisciplinary approach.

- Controlling symptoms is a priority.

- Hospice care services are directed by the primary care provider and managed by the nurse.

- Volunteers are used for nonmedical care.

- Hospice services may be provided in a facility or at home.

- Hospice care can be given within 6 months of the expected death.

- Bereavement services postmortem are offered for the family.

Δ **Types of Loss**

Necessary loss	Part of the cycle of life; anticipated but still may be intensely felt
Actual loss	Any loss of a valued person or item that can no longer be experienced
Perceived loss	Any loss defined by the client but not obvious to others
Maturational loss	Losses normally expected due to the developmental processes of life
Situational loss	Unanticipated loss caused by an external event

Δ **Grief** is the inner emotional response to loss and is exhibited in as many ways as there are individuals. In grief, the emotional ties of an important relationship are disengaged and finally reinvested in a new direction.

Δ **Dysfunctional grieving** is when the work of grieving is not resolved. Usually the work of grief is prolonged, resulting in stress-related disorders such as depression. Unresolved grief can exacerbate symptoms of any existing disorders, such as panic disorder, depression, or psychosis.

Δ **Bereavement** includes both grief and mourning (the outward display of loss) as the individual deals with the death of a significant individual in his life.

Δ Theories of Grief

- **Kübler-Ross**: Five stages of dying

  ◊ Denial – The client has difficulty believing a terminal diagnosis or loss.

  ◊ Anger – The client lashes out at other people or things.

  ◊ Bargaining – The client negotiates for more time or a cure.

  ◊ Depression – The client is saddened over the inability to change the situation.

  ◊ Acceptance – The client recognizes what is happening and plans for the future.

- **Bowlby**: Four stages of mourning

  ◊ Numbing – This includes a lack of understanding and feelings of unreality and disbelief over the loss.

  ◊ Yearning and searching – The bereaved person emotionally and physically "pines" for the loved one. She may also search for the deceased in familiar places and even feel that she can hear the deceased person's voice at times.

  ◊ Disorganization and despair – This stage includes the pain of loss and the feelings and behaviors that the grieving individual goes through, knowing that the loved individual will never return.

  ◊ Reorganization – The bereaved person begins to heal and reorganize her life. For some, this stage may never occur and the bereaved person will remain in earlier stages of mourning.

- **Worden**: Four tasks of mourning

  ◊ Accept reality of loss.

  ◊ Work through the pain of grief.

  ◊ Adjust the environment to accommodate for the missing deceased.

  ◊ Emotionally relocate the deceased and move forward in life.

Δ Working through the acute early stage of mourning typically takes at least 4 to 8 weeks. The entire task of mourning may take 1 to 2 years to complete.

Key Factors

Δ An individual's stage of growth and development (e.g., adolescence, middle adulthood) may impact how that individual will grieve.

Δ Psychosocial perspectives include:

- Valuation of individuals – a learned response per culture and society.

- The grief response develops as an individual's coping mechanisms mature.

Δ Socioeconomic status influences the options the individual has to express grief and mourning.

Δ Personal relationships prescribe what type of grief will be experienced, as well as the element of support for the grief process.

Δ Nature of loss associates the meaning of and the situation surrounding the loss to the type of grief process anticipated.

Δ Culture and ethnicity influence the interpretation of a loss and expression of grief.

Δ Spiritual beliefs affect the individual's ability to cope.

Δ   Factors that can increase the potential for dysfunctional grieving for the client who is bereaved include:

- Having a high degree of dependence on the deceased.

- The age of the deceased and the relationship of the bereaved to the deceased. For example, the death of one's child is more likely to cause dysfunctional grieving.

- The presence of conflicts between the deceased and the client.

- A lack of a support system.

- Poor coping skills.

- A history of difficulty resolving past losses.

- Social stigma, such as suicide, associated with the deceased's death.

- A violent death.

- A sudden and unexpected death.

- A history of substance abuse/dependence or other mental health disorder.

Δ   Nurses experience personal grief when caring for clients with whom they have developed rapport and intimacy. Such times require self-reflection and perhaps debriefing for the entire staff by professional grief/mental health counselors.

Δ   End-of-life issues include decision making in a highly stressful time during which the nurse must consider the desires of the client and the family. Any decisions must be shared with other health care personnel for smooth transition during this time of stress, grief, and bereavement.

Δ   **Advance directives** are legal documents that direct end-of-life issues. Advance directives include:

- **Living wills** – directive documents for medical treatment per the client's wishes.

- **Durable power of attorney** for health care – an agent appointed by the client or the courts to make medical decisions when the client is no longer able to do so.

Assessments

Δ   Assess for symptoms of normal grief, including:

- Feelings ranging from sadness to anxiety to yearning.

- Feelings of guilt and/or anger toward the deceased.

- Thoughts that are confused, hopeless, and preoccupied with the deceased.

- Difficulties sleeping and eating, restlessness, depression, and crying.

- Fatigue, muscle tension, weakness, and oversensitivity to stimuli.

- Depersonalization (feeling unreal, as if observing oneself from the outside) and derealization (experiencing familiar persons and surroundings as if they were unfamiliar and strange or unreal).

Δ Determine the stage of grief the client and family are experiencing.

Δ Assess for the possibility of suicide in clients who are grieving.

Δ Use appropriate assessment tools to determine the presence of depression or anxiety in grieving clients, such as the Geriatric Depression Scale for an older adult.

NANDA Nursing Diagnoses

Δ Anxiety

Δ Ineffective coping

Δ Dysfunctional grieving

Δ Hopelessness

Δ Spiritual distress

Δ Risk for self-directed violence

Nursing Interventions

Δ Provide symptom control for the dying client, including:

- Comfort from the distress and anxiety that accompanies disease systems.

- Information about treatment choices.

- Granting choices to clients to minimize anxiety and discomfort.

- Administration of medications that manage pain and air hunger.

- Encouraging the client to participate in religious practices that bring comfort and strength, if appropriate.

Δ Maintain the dignity and self-esteem for the dying client.

- The concept of dignity varies from individual to individual; therefore, listen to the client's concerns.

- Environmental considerations include:

  ◊ Cleanliness.

  ◊ Odor control – Remove products of elimination as soon as possible.

◊   Attractive clothing – Comfort prevails.

◊   Meticulous grooming (e.g., hair, nails, skin).

- Allow the client to make decisions in food selection, activities, and health care to permit the client as much control as possible.

- Allow the client to perform self-care as he is able and desires.

- There should be a continuous flow of information from the primary care provider to the client's family.

- Be sensitive to comments made in the presence of the unconscious client, as hearing is the last sensation lost as a person dies.

Δ   Prevent feelings of abandonment and isolation for the dying client.

- Prevent the fear of dying alone.

- Provide a peaceful environment with family mementos, cards, fresh flowers, back massages, and relaxation techniques.

Δ   Facilitate mourning for bereaved individuals.

- Grant time for the grieving process.

- Use therapeutic communication. The nurse should name the emotion he believes the person is feeling. For example, the nurse may say, "You sound as though you are angry. Anger is a normal feeling for people who have lost a loved one. Tell me about how you are feeling."

- Assist the grieving individual to accept the reality of the loss.

- Support efforts to "move on" in the face of the loss.

- Encourage the building of new relationships.

- Provide continuing support; encourage the support of family and friends.

- Assess for signs of ineffective coping, such as an individual who refuses to leave her home months after her spouse has died.

- Be mindful of "normal" grieving behaviors (e.g., crying, somatic reports, anxiety).

- Share information about normal mourning and grieving behaviors with the client, who may not realize that her feelings, such as anger toward the deceased, are normal and expected.

- Bereavement or grief groups are helpful for some individuals.

- In addition to grief/bereavement groups, individual psychotherapy may be helpful for individuals who are having difficulty resolving grief.

- Encourage advice and counseling from the client's spiritual advisor, as appropriate.

Primary Reference:

Varcarolis, E. M., Carson, V. B., & Shoemaker, N. C. (2006). *Foundations of psychiatric mental health nursing: A clinical approach* (5th ed.). St. Louis, MO: Saunders.

Additional Resources:

Potter, P. A., & Perry, A. G. (2005). *Fundamentals of nursing* (6th ed.). St. Louis, MO: Mosby.

NANDA International (2004). *NANDA nursing diagnoses: Definitions and classification 2005-2006.* Philadelphia: NANDA.

Wilkinson, J. M. (2005). *Prentice Hall nursing diagnosis handbook: With NIC interventions and NOC outcomes* (8th ed.). Upper Saddle River, NJ: Prentice Hall.

Chapter 35: Care of Those Who are Dying and/or Grieving

Application Exercises

Scenario: A 68-year-old client, accompanied by her grown daughter, comes to the community mental health facility. She tells the nurse that her husband of 45 years died suddenly in a motor vehicle crash over 1 year ago. He ran into another car while drunk, killing both himself and a child passenger in the other car. Since that time, the client has been unable to continue any of her normal activities. She states she has been too tired even to keep the house clean and has experienced long bouts of crying every day. She relates that she feels angry at her husband for drinking and for leaving her alone, since he was "supposed to be the one to take care of me!" The client relates that she only came to the mental health agency because her daughter was visiting from across the country and "made me come." The daughter says that the client seldom leaves the house and will not see her old friends.

1. Identify factors that put the client at risk for dysfunctional grieving.

2. What signs are present to indicate that this client's grief is becoming prolonged?

3. What further assessments should be made at this time?

4. Which of the following stages of mourning describes this client's situation?

    A. Numbing

    B. Yearning and searching

    C. Disorganization and despair

    D. Reorganization

5. Grief is best defined as

    A. a mild to severe depressive mood.

    B. an individual's response to a significant loss.

    C. emotional trauma, such as denial or anger as a result of a loss.

    D. the display of abnormal feelings following a loss.

6. A client is grieving after the death of his 6-year-old daughter following a fall. He has been completely distraught, lying in bed, and crying for the past week. Today, the client says, "I feel better because I'll soon be with my daughter." The priority nursing diagnosis for this client is

    A. self-care deficit.

    B. risk for self-directed violence.

    C. ineffective coping.

    D. disturbed sensory perception.

Chapter 35: Care of Those Who are Dying and/or Grieving

Application Exercises Answer Key

Scenario: A 68-year-old client, accompanied by her grown daughter, comes to the community mental health facility. She tells the nurse that her husband of 45 years died suddenly in a motor vehicle crash over 1 year ago. He ran into another car while drunk, killing both himself and a child passenger in the other car. Since that time, the client has been unable to continue any of her normal activities. She states she has been too tired even to keep the house clean and has experienced long bouts of crying every day. She relates that she feels angry at her husband for drinking and for leaving her alone, since he was "supposed to be the one to take care of me!" The client relates that she only came to the mental health agency because her daughter was visiting from across the country and "made me come." The daughter says that the client seldom leaves the house and will not see her old friends.

---

1. Identify factors that put the client at risk for dysfunctional grieving.

   The client seemed to be very dependent on her deceased husband.
   The husband died suddenly in a violent accident, which included the stigma of the husband being under the influence of alcohol and responsible for the death of a child.
   There is a lack of social support, and her daughter lives far away.

2. What signs are present to indicate that this client's grief is becoming prolonged?

   The client has bouts of crying every day and remains angry at her husband.
   Behavior changes include being too tired to keep house and seldom leaving home.
   The client no longer sees her old friends.

3. What further assessments should be made at this time?

   Assessment for suicidal ideation
   Use of an assessment tool for depression and possibly for anxiety

4. Which of the following stages of mourning describes this client's situation?

    A. Numbing

    B. Yearning and searching

    C. Disorganization and despair

    D. Reorganization

This client has withdrawn from the activities and friends she had before her spouse died. She appears depressed and she is actively mourning her loss, putting her in the stage of disorganization and despair. In the numbing stage, she would feel disbelief at her loss. In yearning and searching, she would begin to come to terms with the fact that her spouse was gone. In reorganization, she would be able to enjoy activities and start a new life without her spouse.

5. Grief is best defined as

    A. a mild to severe depressive mood.

    B. an individual's response to a significant loss.

    C. emotional trauma, such as denial or anger as a result of a loss.

    D. the display of abnormal feelings following a loss.

Grief is a normal response by an individual to a significant loss. Depression may be one aspect of the work of grief, but it is not the whole picture of grief and mourning. That is also true for denial and anger, which may occur after a loss, but are only part of the whole process. Feelings displayed after a loss, such as anger and guilt, are not abnormal; they are part of normal grieving.

6. A client is grieving after the death of his 6-year-old daughter following a fall. He has been completely distraught, lying in bed, and crying for the past week. Today, the client says, "I feel better because I'll soon be with my daughter." The priority nursing diagnosis for this client is

    A. self-care deficit.

    B. risk for self-directed violence.

    C. ineffective coping.

    D. disturbed sensory perception.

A client who is devastated by grief may be at risk for suicide. This client's verbal communication may be a covert message that he has decided on a plan to kill himself in order to "be with" his daughter. This safety risk is the greatest priority for the client. The other nursing diagnoses, if present, would be lower priority.

Unit 4   Psychobiologic Disorders, Psychiatric Emergencies, and Mental Health Nursing Care of
                Special Populations

Section: Mental Health Nursing Care of Special Populations

Chapter 36:   **Mental Health Issues of the Adolescent**
                Contributor: Jené M. Hurlbut, MSN, RN, APRN-BC

 NCLEX-RN® Connections:

> **Learning Objective**: Review and apply knowledge within "**Mental Health Issues
> of the Adolescent**" in readiness for performance of the following nursing activities as
> outlined by the NCLEX-RN® test plan:
>
> Δ   Apply knowledge of psychobiologic disorders to the nursing process when caring
>   for adolescents with acute or chronic mental health disorders.
>
> Δ   Identify the adolescent/family's responses to the diagnosis of a mental health
>   disorder.
>
> Δ   Plan/provide care for the adolescent with a mental health disorder.
>
> Δ   Support the adolescent's efforts in the use of strategies to decrease anxiety and
>   manage stress.
>
> Δ   Identify the adolescent's risk for injury from high-risk behaviors.
>
> Δ   Evaluate and document the adolescent's response to treatment of a mental
>   health disorder.
>
> Δ   Evaluate the adolescent's ability to follow the treatment plan for a mental health
>   disorder.
>
> Δ   Teach the adolescent/family signs and symptoms of relapse of a mental health
>   disorder.

 Key Points

Δ   In the adolescent who is mentally healthy, previous and current developmental
    tasks are mastered, and the young person is generally satisfied with life. The
    characteristics of good mental health for an adolescent include:

    •   Ability to trust others and to view the world as generally safe and supportive.

    •   Ability to interpret reality correctly and perceive the surrounding
        environment correctly.

- Positive self-concept.

- Ability to cope with stress and anxiety in an age-appropriate way.

- Mastery of developmental tasks.

- Ability to express himself spontaneously and creatively.

- Ability to develop satisfying relationships.

Δ   According to Erikson's stages of development, the task of an adolescent from age **12 to 20** is to successfully make the transition from childhood to adulthood and to develop a sense of identity as an individual. In order to make this transition, the adolescent must have successfully mastered the developmental tasks of childhood.

Δ   Adolescence is a stressful time for both teens and family members as teens strive to become more independent.

Δ   Increased stress and anxiety are related to developmental changes and self-esteem issues.

Δ   Unrealistic body-image expectations may be related to media portrayal.

Δ   It is a time of intense peer pressure related to wanting to "fit in" to a group norm.

Δ   Mental health disorders prevalent among adolescents include:

- **Eating disorders**, particularly among girls (*Refer to chapter 23, Eating Disorders.*).

- **Mood disorders** (e.g., major depressive disorder, dysthymic disorder, bipolar disorder). These may also occur in younger children. It has been estimated that 1 in 20 adolescents experience some form of depression. (*Refer to chapter 24, Mood Disorders: Depression.*)

- **Anxiety disorders**, which affect as many as 10% of children and adolescents and are most common to young people whose parents also have anxiety disorders. (*Refer to chapter 19, Anxiety Disorders.*)

- **Developmental disorders**, such as autism and Asperger's disorder. (*Refer to chapter 28, Developmental and Behavioral Disorders.*)

- **Behavioral disorders**, such as attention deficit hyperactivity disorder, oppositional defiant disorder, and conduct disorder. (*Refer to chapter 28, Developmental and Behavioral Disorders.*)

  ◊   Adolescent males diagnosed with conduct disorder are more likely than peers without conduct disorder to be diagnosed with antisocial personality disorder as adults and to have substance abuse problems.

  ◊   Adolescent females with conduct disorder are more likely to have a mental health disorder (e.g., depression, anxiety disorder) in adulthood.

Δ   **Suicide** rates are increasing in both children and adolescents, with suicide being the third-leading cause of death in adolescents.

Key Factors

Δ   Studies have found that 75% of adolescents who engage in one risk behavior are also involved in a second risk behavior. High-risk behaviors of adolescents that result in high rates of trauma/injury for this age group include:

   • Engaging in sexual activity and unprotected sex.

   • Carrying a handgun or other potentially lethal weapon.

   • Fighting with other adolescents.

   • Use of tobacco, alcohol, or other drugs.

   • Having suicidal thoughts.

Δ   **Depression**

   • Factors associated with adolescent depression include:

      ◊ Physical or sexual abuse or neglect.

      ◊ Homelessness.

      ◊ Disputes among parents, conflicts with peers or family, and rejection by peers or family.

      ◊ Engaging in high-risk behavior.

      ◊ Learning disabilities.

      ◊ Having a chronic illness.

   • Depression in adolescents may be manifested by feelings of sadness, loss of appetite, anhedonia, irritability, aggressiveness, engaging in high-risk behavior, dropping out of school, psychomotor retardation, increased time spent sleeping (hypersomnia), and feelings of hopelessness about the future.

   • Depression in adolescents is treated with antidepressants and psychotherapy, similar to how depression in adults is treated.

   • Both male and female adolescents who engage in a risk behavior (e.g., cigarette smoking, drinking alcohol, unprotected sex) – no matter what degree – are more likely to develop symptoms of depression.

Δ   **Anxiety Disorders**

   • **Separation anxiety disorder**

      ◊ Characteristics include distress when separated from home or parental figures, refusing to attend school, and refusing to be home alone. Depression is also common.

      ◊ Untreated separation anxiety may progress to panic disorder with agoraphobia as an adult.

- **Posttraumatic stress disorder (PTSD)**

    ◊ PTSD is brought on by experiencing or seeing a traumatic event.

    ◊ The anxiety is displayed externally with symptoms such as irritability and aggression with family and friends, poor academic performance, somatic reports, belief that life will be short, and difficulty sleeping. The client may also display "omen formation," in which she believes she can foresee the future.

Assessment

Δ   Perform a nursing history, including assessing:

- For the presence of depression and suicidal ideation, including a plan, the lethality of the plan, and the means to carry out the plan.

- For substance abuse, even in young teens and school-age children.

    ◊ Use of tobacco products (e.g., cigarettes, cigars, snuff, chewing tobacco) and frequency of use

    ◊ Use of alcohol, frequency of use, driving under the influence, and family history of abuse

    ◊ Use of drugs (illegal or nonprescription) to get high, stay calm, lose weight, or stay awake

- For eating disorders.

    ◊ Recent weight loss

    ◊ History of obesity and weight gain

    ◊ Ideation regarding food and eating

    ◊ Pattern of physical activity, such as constant exercising

- Friendships among peers.

- Relationships with parents and significant others.

- Feelings of safety in the home and school environment.

- For mutilation behavior, such as "cutting" self.

- Sexual activity (including oral sex and intercourse) and use of contraceptives.

- Feelings of happiness and fulfillment or hopelessness and despair.

- History of emotional, physical, or sexual abuse.

- History of academic performance.

- Use of helmet and/or pads when performing such activities as rollerblading, bicycling, and riding a motorcycle or ATV.

- Use of a seatbelt when in a vehicle.

Δ The **HEADSSS psychosocial interview technique** is an interviewing tool useful with adolescents.

The HEADSSS Psychosocial Interview Technique
H Home environment (e.g., relations with parents and siblings)
E Education and employment (e.g., school performance)
A Activities (e.g., sports participation, after-school activities, peer relations)
D Drug, alcohol, or tobacco use
S Sexuality (e.g., whether the client is sexually active, whether he/she uses contraception)
S Suicide risk or symptoms of depression or other mental disorders
S "Savagery" (e.g., violence or abuse in the home environment or in the neighborhood)

NANDA Nursing Diagnoses

Δ Anxiety

Δ Ineffective coping

Δ Interrupted family processes

Δ Hopelessness

Δ Imbalanced nutrition: Less than body requirements

Δ Risk for other- or self-directed violence

Δ Risk for situational low self-esteem

Δ Impaired social interaction

Nursing Interventions

Δ Use **primary prevention** (e.g., education, peer group discussions, mentoring) to prevent risky behavior and promote healthy behavior and effective coping.

- Work with adolescents to adopt a realistic view of their bodies and to improve overall self-esteem.

- Identify and reinforce the use of positive coping skills.

- Provide education on contraceptives and other sexual information, such as transmission and prevention of HIV and other sexually transmitted diseases.

- Encourage abstinence but keep the lines of communication open to allow the adolescent to discuss sexual practices.

- Employ the use of gun and weapon control strategies.

- Emphasize the use of seat belts when in motor vehicles.

- Encourage the use of protective gear for high-impact sports.

- Inform parents regarding classes on parenting skills for adults.

Δ   Intervene for adolescents who have engaged in **risk behaviors**.

- Instruct the adolescent on factors that contribute to substance dependency and tobacco use. Make appropriate referrals when indicated.

- Inform the adolescent and family members about support groups in the community for eating disorders, substance abuse, and general teen support.

- Instruct the adolescent regarding individuals within the school environment and community to whom concerns can be voiced about personal safety (e.g., police officers, school nurses, counselors, teachers).

- Make referrals to social services when indicated.

- Discuss the use and availability of support hotlines.

- Determine the availability of weapons in the home.

- Perform depression and suicide assessment. Make an immediate referral for professional care when indicated.

- Provide parents with information on support groups and classes on parenting skills.

Δ   Interventions for **depression** in adolescents include:

- Administration of an antidepressant. Fluoxetine (Prozac) is the only FDA approved SSRI to date for children under the age of 18.

  ◊ Studies have shown an increase in suicidal behavior early in the treatment of depression in adolescents who are taking SSRI antidepressants.

  ◊ Although use of SSRIs is not prohibited, health providers are cautioned to assess for increased suicidal ideation in adolescents who are using medication therapy for depression.

- Cognitive-behavioral therapy is useful in adolescents to change negative thoughts to positive outcomes.

Δ   Interventions for **anxiety disorders** in adolescents include:

- Emotional support that is accepting of regression and other defense mechanisms.

- Protection from panic levels of anxiety by providing for needs.

- Increasing self-esteem and feelings of achievement.

- Assisting with working through traumatic events or losses and acceptance of what has happened.

Δ   **Group therapy** can be beneficial for adolescents.

- The focus in this age group is on peer relationships and working out specific problems.

- The difficulty with group therapy for adolescents is that disruptive behavior, once begun within the group, is often contagious.

- Among the many techniques for managing disruptive behaviors are:

    ◊   Changing the activity.

    ◊   Removal of the individual who is disruptive.

    ◊   Use of humor.

    ◊   Use of signals or gestures to remind the individual that self-control is needed.

    ◊   Use of limit setting and permission granting (a type of behavioral therapy).

    ◊   Giving additional affection to the individual who is acting out.

Δ   Educate the adolescent who has a mental illness (and family members) about therapies, such as medication therapy information, signs/symptoms of returning illness, and information to report to health providers.

Primary Reference:

Varcarolis, E. M., Carson, V. B., & Shoemaker, N. C. (2006). *Foundations of psychiatric mental health nursing: A clinical approach* (5th ed.). St. Louis, MO: Saunders.

Additional Resources:

Bauchner, H. (2004, December 31). Adolescent depression: Complications of treatment with SSRIs. *Journal Watch Psychiatry*. Retrieved on December 16, 2006, from http://psychiatry.jwatch.org/cgi/content/full/2004/1231/13

Carpenter, S. (2001, January). Teens' risky behavior is about more than race and family resources. *Monitor on Psychology, 32*(1). Retrieved on December 16, 2006, from http://www.apa.org/monitor/jan01/teenbehavior.html

NANDA International (2004). *NANDA nursing diagnoses: Definitions and classification 2005-2006*. Philadelphia: NANDA.

National Institutes of Health. (2006, May 15). *Behaviors may indicate risk of adolescent depression*. Retrieved December 16, 2006, from http://www.nih.gov/news/pr/may2006/nida-15.htm

Pergamit, M. R., Huang, L., & Lane, J. (2001, August). *The long term impact of adolescent risky behaviors and family environment*. United States Department of Health and Human Services. Retrieved December 16, 2006, from http://aspe.hhs.gov/hsp/riskybehav01

Stanhope, M., & Lancaster, J. (2004). *Community and public health nursing* (6th ed.). St. Louis, MO: Mosby.

Townsend, M. C. (2006). *Psychiatric mental health nursing: Concepts of care in evidence-based practice* (5th ed.). Philadelphia: F.A. Davis.

Trudeau, M. (2004, June 4). Treating depression in adolescents: Cognitive therapy shows positive results in teens. *National public radio: All things considered* [Radio broadcast]. Retrieved on December 16, 2006 from http://www.npr.org/templates/story/story.php?storyId=1923943

Chapter 36: Mental Health Issues of the Adolescent

Application Exercises

Scenario: A 15 year old comes into the school health clinic reporting a stomachache. The nurse notices that the teen makes little eye contact when answering questions and has superficial scratches on her right wrist. The student appears underweight and emotionally distant. She states that her parents have recently divorced and that she just moved to this school district. She says, "I miss my boyfriend and friends from my old school."

1. What key areas should the nurse assess with this student?

2. The student tells the nurse that, "Nothing is fun anymore; it just doesn't seem worth the effort." How should the nurse respond?

3. What are appropriate nursing diagnoses to consider for this student?

4. What referrals are appropriate for this student?

5. Which of the following signs and symptoms are common in an adolescent who is depressed? (Select all that apply.)

    _____ Insomnia

    _____ Feelings of sadness

    _____ Increased activity level

    _____ Excelling at school work

    _____ Irritability

    _____ Aggressiveness

6. True or False: A factor that increases an adolescent's chance of having an anxiety disorder is having a parent with an anxiety disorder.

7. True or False: An example of a risk behavior among adolescents is alcohol and drug use.

Chapter 36: Mental Health Issues of the Adolescent

Application Exercises Answer Key

Scenario: A 15 year old comes into the school health clinic reporting a stomachache. The nurse notices that the teen makes little eye contact when answering questions and has superficial scratches on her right wrist. The student appears underweight and emotionally distant. She states that her parents have recently divorced and that she just moved to this school district. She says, "I miss my boyfriend and friends from my old school."

1. What key areas should the nurse assess with this student?

> **Dietary intake**
> **History of weight loss**
> **Peer relationships at new school**
> **Current contact with boyfriend or friends at previous school**
> **Feelings of safety at home and school**
> **Actual or potential self-injury**
> **Feelings of depression**
> **History of sexual activity, including possibility of pregnancy**
> **Substance use (alcohol, drugs, tobacco products)**
> **History of abuse (physical, emotional, sexual)**
> **Current history of academic performance and school involvement**

2. The student tells the nurse that, "Nothing is fun anymore; it just doesn't seem worth the effort." How should the nurse respond?

> **The nurse should ask the student to clarify what she means by, "It just doesn't seem worth the effort." Specifically, the nurse should ask if the teen has thoughts of hurting herself. If the teen states that she is thinking of suicide, the nurse needs to determine if she has a plan, what the plan is, the lethality of the plan, and the availability of the means to carry out the plan (e.g., guns in the home). The nurse should make an immediate referral for professional care based on the student's response. The nurse should stay with the student at all times until placement and offer support through listening and acceptance.**

3. What are appropriate nursing diagnoses to consider for this student?

> **Interrupted family processes**
> **Hopelessness**
> **Imbalanced nutrition: Less than body requirements**
> **Risk for self-directed violence**
> **Impaired social interaction**

4. What referrals are appropriate for this student?

Referral for inpatient treatment if at high risk for suicide or eating disorder
Counseling services
Teen support groups
Family support groups
Medical services for pregnancy if the student is pregnant

---

5. Which of the following signs and symptoms are common in an adolescent who is depressed? (Select all that apply.)

_____ Insomnia

_X_ **Feelings of sadness**

_____ Increased activity level

_____ Excelling at school work

_X_ **Irritability**

_X_ **Aggressiveness**

Feelings of sadness, irritability, and aggressiveness may all indicate depression in an adolescent. The adolescent with depression usually spends increased time sleeping (hypersomnia), has psychomotor retardation, and does poorly in school.

6. True or False: A factor that increases an adolescent's chance of having an anxiety disorder is having a parent with an anxiety disorder.

True: Anxiety disorders are more common in an adolescent who has a parent with an anxiety disorder.

7. True or False: An example of a risk behavior among adolescents is alcohol and drug use.

True. Other risk behaviors include:

Engaging in sexual activity and unprotected sex.
Carrying a handgun or other potentially lethal weapon.
Fighting with other adolescents.
Having suicidal thoughts.

Unit 4   Psychobiologic Disorders, Psychiatric Emergencies, and Mental Health Nursing Care of
                 Special Populations

Section: Mental Health Nursing Care of Special Populations

Chapter 37:   **Mental Health Issues of the Older Adult**
                 Contributors: Susan Adcock, MS, RN
                         Meredith Flood, PhD, RN, APRN-BC

 NCLEX-RN® Connections:

> **Learning Objective**: Review and apply knowledge within "**Mental Health Issues of
> the Older Adult**" in readiness for performance of the following nursing activities as
> outlined by the NCLEX-RN® test plan:
>
> Δ   Apply knowledge of psychobiologic disorders to the nursing process when caring
>   for older adults with an acute or chronic mental health disorder.
>
> Δ   Identify the older adult/family's responses to the diagnosis of a mental health
>   disorder.
>
> Δ   Plan/provide care for the older adult with a mental health disorder.
>
> Δ   Support the older adult's efforts in the use of strategies to decrease anxiety and
>   stress.
>
> Δ   Evaluate and document the older adult's response to treatment of a mental
>   health disorder.
>
> Δ   Evaluate the older adult's ability to follow the treatment plan for a mental health
>   disorder.
>
> Δ   Teach the older adult/family signs and symptoms of relapse of the mental health
>   disorder.

 Key Points

Δ   The population of people age 65 and older continues to grow and has unique
    problems related to chronic illness, loss, and disability.

Δ   **Ageism** is the bias that many younger people and even older people have against
    the aging population. Nurses must be aware of bias, because it may influence their
    practice. For example, the nurse who is biased may not teach an older adult client
    about his medications if she believes he is too old to learn new things.

Δ   Three key mental health problems found in older adults are **depression, suicide,
    and substance abuse.**

Key Factors

Δ   Although sight, hearing, taste, touch, smell, and muscular strength diminish with age, dementia is not present in all individuals over age 65.

Δ   Older adults continue to be interested in sexual activity, and regular sexual expressions are important.

Δ   Older adults lose at least 50% of their restorative sleep due to consequences of the aging process.

Δ   There is a very high incidence of chronic disease in this age group, which means that older adult clients use more prescription medications than younger clients.

Δ   Retirement is a difficult time of transition and high stress for many older adult clients who have worked all their lives.

Δ   The older adult client may be vulnerable to abuse and neglect.

Δ   **Depression** (*Refer to chapter 24, Mood Disorders: Depression.*)

   •   It is important to differentiate between early dementia and depression. Some symptoms of depression that may look like dementia are memory loss, confusion, and behavioral problems, such as social isolation or agitation.

   •   Causes of depression include medications (e.g., steroids), physical disorders (e.g., thyroid insufficiency), or acute medical events (e.g., myocardial infarction). Changing the client's medication or treating the underlying problem may treat the depression.

   •   Antidepressant medications

      ◊   Use of antidepressants may actually increase the risk of suicide if the client regains energy to complete a suicide plan.

      ◊   Use of lower doses, such as half the adult dose of some antidepressants, may be needed for the older adult client.

      ◊   SSRI antidepressants are generally safer than tricyclic antidepressants (TCAs), because lethal overdose may occur after taking only a few TCA tablets.

      ◊   Sertraline (Zoloft) and the selective norepinephrine reuptake inhibitor reboxetine (Vestra) may be better tolerated by the older adult client and may be used for short- or long-term treatment of depression.

Δ   **Suicide** (*Refer to chapter 31, Suicide.*)

   •   Untreated depression increases the risk for suicide in the older adult client.

   •   Factors that may lead to suicide include:

      ◊   Feelings of hopelessness, uselessness, and despair.

      ◊   Changes in occupational status, such as retirement.

◊ History of suicide attempts.

◊ History of severe mental illness, such as major depression.

◊ Presence of acute or chronic physical illness.

◊ Functional disability (inability to perform self-care).

◊ Alcohol or substance abuse.

◊ Financial need.

◊ History of losses, such as loss of a spouse.

Δ **Alcoholism and Substance Abuse** (*Refer to chapter 29, Substance-Related and Non-Substance-Related Dependencies.*)

- More than 10% of older adults who live at home and 20% who are hospitalized have serious problems with alcohol use.

- The older adult client may have a history of alcohol abuse or may develop a pattern of alcohol/substance abuse later in life due to life stressors (e.g., losing a spouse or a friend).

- Alcohol use can lead to falls and other injuries, memory loss, somatic reports (e.g., headaches), and can cause changes in sleep patterns, which are already problematic for older adult clients.

- Older adults may show symptoms of alcohol abuse at lower doses than younger adults.

- Younger clients with alcohol dependence may experience blackouts, acute pancreatitis, or liver disease. The older adult client with alcohol dependence generally has vague reports, a decrease in ability for self-care (functional status), urinary incontinence, and signs of dementia.

Assessment

Δ A comprehensive assessment of the older adult client includes:

- Functional ability (e.g., ability to get up out of a chair).

- Economic and social status.

- Environmental factors (e.g., stairways at home) that may affect the client's well-being and lifestyle.

- Physical assessment.

Δ Nursing History

- Conduct the nursing interview using a private space.

- Make an introduction and ask what the client would like to be called.

- Stand or sit at the client's level to conduct the interview, rather than standing over a client who is bed-bound or sitting in a chair.

- Assure adequate lighting and a quiet environment to accommodate for impaired vision and hearing.

- Respect the client's personal space if he does not wish to be touched, but use touch to communicate caring as appropriate.

- Be sure to include questions relating to difficulty sleeping, incontinence, falls or other injuries, depression, dizziness, and loss of energy.

- Use screening tools specific to older adult clients, such as the geriatric version of the Michigan Alcohol Screening Test (MAST) and the Geriatric Depression Scale (short version). The Mini-Mental State Examination is also a useful tool.

- Following the interview, summarize and ask for feedback from the client.

NANDA Nursing Diagnoses

Δ   Activity intolerance

Δ   Anxiety

Δ   Risk for falls

Δ   Hopelessness

Δ   Powerlessness

Δ   Disturbed sleep pattern

Δ   Social isolation

Δ   Impaired verbal communication

Nursing Interventions

Δ   When intervening with older adult clients, the nurse should:

- Utilize empathetic understanding.

- Encourage the client to talk about her feelings.

- Help the client to stabilize emotions.

- Help to re-establish emotional balance (if the client has anxiety).

- Provide health education, explaining alternative solutions.

- Help the client to use problem-solving techniques.

Δ   Use **crisis intervention** techniques for the older adult client with increased stressors, anxiety, depression, suicidal ideation, alcohol or substance abuse, or lack of social supports. (*Refer to chapter 30, Crisis Management.*)

Δ **Inpatient acute care** may be needed for the older adult client with major depressive disorder, suicidal thoughts, or those at risk to harm others.

- Utilize individual or group counseling, including:

  ◊ Remotivation therapy – Used for groups of 10 to 15 older adult clients, the objective is to increase the sense of reality. During each session, the clients discuss a specific topic, and the discussion assists clients to express their thoughts and become less apathetic.

  ◊ Reminiscence therapy (life review) – A small group of clients (6 to 8) share their memories of the past, thus achieving a new sense of identity and a more positive self-concept.

  ◊ Psychotherapy – An experienced nurse therapist or other health professional facilitates discussion of problems and information about client symptoms and needs within a small therapeutic group environment.

- Milieu therapy within the facility is geared to keep the client safe from harm, orient the client to reality, stabilize functional capacity, and allow the client to practice communicating with others.

- Psychobiological interventions – The nurse administers and/or monitors the effectiveness of the client's medications, teaching about adverse effects and other necessary information.

- Health teaching – Employ symptom management, self-care strategies, and coping skills.

- Promotion of self-care – Assist the client to remain or become independent in providing self-care.

Δ **Day treatment programs** can assist both the older adult client and family, who may need respite or to work outside the home.

- Social day care – Provides social interaction with the opportunity for recreation during the day for older adult clients with mild dementia.

- Adult day health or medical treatment programs may provide social programs as well as medical intervention, such as physical therapy, for clients who have a referral from their primary care provider.

- Maintenance day care programs – Clients with moderate or severe mental illnesses who are at risk to be reinstitutionalized get help in maintaining functional status and increasing quality of life.

Δ **Home care programs** provide nursing care and other needed services, enabling the client to remain at home in the least restrictive environment possible.

Δ   The use of **physical or chemical restraints** on the older adult client is an ethical, legal, and safety concern.

- Recommendations for the use of physical restraints developed by the Joint Commission (formerly known as JCAHO) include:

  ◊   A primary care provider's order is necessary to use restraints.

  ◊   Use of restraints must be limited by time, such as a 24-hr limit after the order is obtained.

  ◊   Documentation must be provided regarding attempts at alternatives to restraint.

  ◊   Ongoing observation of the restraint and the client must occur.

  ◊   Interventions must provide regular toileting, feeding, and other care, and this must also be documented.

- **Chemical restraints**, such as antipsychotic or antianxiety medications, must be used in a medically appropriate way and should be used due to client need rather than for staff convenience. The risk for falls and other injuries increases when clients are receiving psychotropic medications.

Primary Reference:

Varcarolis, E. M., Carson, V. B., & Shoemaker, N. C. (2006). *Foundations of psychiatric mental health nursing: A clinical approach* (5th ed.). St. Louis, MO: Saunders.

Additional Resources:

The Joint Commission. (n.d.). *The Joint Commission.* Retrieved February 16, 2007, from http://www.jointcommission.org/

NANDA International (2004). *NANDA nursing diagnoses: Definitions and classification 2005-2006.* Philadelphia: NANDA.

Chapter 37: Mental Health Issues of the Older Adult

Application Exercises

Scenario: A community health nurse is visiting an older adult client who lives alone since the death of his wife 6 months ago. He has hypertension and coronary artery disease. His neighbors called his daughter, who lives out of state, to tell her that they had not seen her father in several weeks. The daughter spoke to her father on the phone but had concerns about his health, because he sounded somewhat disoriented and subdued. She called her father's primary care provider, who contacted the community health nurse. The client opens his door for the nurse and seems coherent but quiet and weak. He agrees to an interview and physical assessment.

1. How should the nurse conduct the interview for this client, whom she has never met before?

2. What assessment tools should the nurse use as she begins the interview process?

3. What risks for suicide does this client have?

4. True or False: When a nurse meets an 84-year-old client for the first time, he should introduce himself by his first name and then call the client by her first name.

5. True or False: The geriatric version of the MAST assessment is used to screen for alcohol abuse by the older adult client.

6. Which of the following statements are the results of ageism in the delivery of health care? (Select all that apply.)

_____ Staff shortages are frequent in facilities for older adult clients because health care workers would rather work with younger clients.

_____ Older adult clients receive less health education and information from health care workers than do younger clients.

_____ Health care workers are less likely to ask permission from older adult clients before beginning a treatment or administering medication.

_____ The government has developed more programs to deal with needs of older adult clients.

Chapter 37: Mental Health Issues of the Older Adult

Application Exercises Answer Key

Scenario: A community health nurse is visiting an older adult client who lives alone since the death of his wife 6 months ago. He has hypertension and coronary artery disease. His neighbors called his daughter, who lives out of state, to tell her that they had not seen her father in several weeks. The daughter spoke to her father on the phone but had concerns about his health, because he sounded somewhat disoriented and subdued. She called her father's primary care provider, who contacted the community health nurse. The client opens his door for the nurse and seems coherent but quiet and weak. He agrees to an interview and physical assessment.

1. How should the nurse conduct the interview for this client, whom she has never met before?

   Introduce herself and ask the client what he would like to be called.
   Explain the purpose of the interview and tell him what she will be doing.
   Sit at the client's level during the interview.
   Since vision and hearing may be impaired, the nurse should assure adequate lighting and a quiet environment.
   Respect the client's comfort with touching, but use touch to communicate caring as appropriate.
   Be objective and do not assume that the client has dementia or any other problem until the assessment is complete.
   Following the interview, summarize and ask for feedback from the client.

2. What assessment tools should the nurse use as she begins the interview process?

   Geriatric Depression Scale
   Mini-Mental State Examination
   A screening tool for alcohol and drug use
   Other tools, depending on agency protocol, such as a geriatric functional assessment form

3. What risks for suicide does this client have?

   The client is an older adult male, which is a risk group for suicide. His wife died 6 months ago, his daughter lives out of state (lack of social support), and he has some chronic health problems, all of which are risk factors.

4. True or False: When a nurse meets an 84-year-old client for the first time, he should introduce himself by his first name and then call the client by her first name.

False: The nurse should introduce himself and tell the client what his job is. He should also ask the client what she wants to be called. This is an act of respect toward the client.

5. True or False: The geriatric version of the MAST assessment is used to screen for alcohol abuse by the older adult client.

True: The MAST is the Michigan Alcohol Screening Test, and there is a geriatric version specifically for older adult clients.

6. Which of the following statements are the results of ageism in the delivery of health care? (Select all that apply.)

  X   **Staff shortages are frequent in facilities for older adult clients because health care workers would rather work with younger clients.**

  X   **Older adult clients receive less health education and information from health care workers than do younger clients.**

  X   **Health care workers are less likely to ask permission from older adult clients before beginning a treatment or administering medication.**

       The government has developed more programs to deal with needs of older adult clients.

The correct statements describe actual problems in the health care industry resulting from ageism in the delivery of health care. The development of government programs aimed at the needs of older adults is based on public policy, not ageism.